Praise for *Building Intelligent .N...*

"In this important and timely book, Sara Rea demystifies key technologies for intelligent applications and clearly demonstrates how they can be applied in Microsoft's .NET generation of tools."

—**Peter O'Kelly, Senior Analyst,**
  Application and Platform Strategies, Burton Group

"Outstanding! Finally, a book exists for .NET programmers who want to get at a wealth of practical AI code and algorithms for use in everyday business applications."

—**Greg Binning, IS Analyst III \ Application Architect**
  for the ACESS Project, LA Dept. of Social Services—IS Division

"Sara provides an excellent introduction to Microsoft Data Mining and other AI technologies by giving instructive examples and code to get you started."

—**Jamie MacLennan, Development Lead,**
  SQL Server Data Mining, Microsoft

"Tying AI to .NET is a great idea for putting a fresh new face on the subject. And it's a friendly face too: Sara Rea's book shows how .NET technologies can help drag core AI techniques out of the research labs and into real applications, where they belong."

—**Steve Grand, Roboticist and Creator of *Creatures*,**
  Director, Cyberlife Research Ltd.

"If you have ever wondered how to use the latest .NET development tools to make the most of advanced technology, this book is for you. Using the .NET tools you depend on, Sara explains concepts normally reserved for scientists in a clear and practical way. This book is an essential reference for .NET developers building today's leading-edge intelligent systems."

—**John Timney, Senior Web Services Consultant,**
  British Telecom Consulting & Systems Integration

Building Intelligent .NET Applications

Building Intelligent .NET Applications

Agents, Data Mining, Rule-Based Systems, and Speech Processing

Sara Morgan Rea

Addison-Wesley

Upper Saddle River, NJ • Boston• Indianapolis • San Francisco
New York • Toronto • Montreal • London • Munich • Paris • Madrid
Capetown • Sydney • Tokyo • Singapore • Mexico City

Many of the designations used by manufacturers and sellers to distinguish their products are claimed as trademarks. Where those designations appear in this book, and the publisher was aware of a trademark claim, the designations have been printed with initial capital letters or in all capitals.

The author and publisher have taken care in the preparation of this book, but make no expressed or implied warranty of any kind and assume no responsibility for errors or omissions. No liability is assumed for incidental or consequential damages in connection with or arising out of the use of the information or programs contained herein.

The publisher offers excellent discounts on this book when ordered in quantity for bulk purchases or special sales, which may include electronic versions and/or custom covers and content particular to your business, training goals, marketing focus, and branding interests. For more information, please contact:

    U.S. Corporate and Government Sales
    (800) 382-3419
    corpsales@pearsontechgroup.com

For sales outside of the U.S., please contact:

    International Sales
    international@pearsoned.com

Visit us on the Web: www.awprofessional.com

Library of Congress Number: 2004117956

Copyright © 2005 Pearson Education, Inc.

All rights reserved. Printed in the United States of America. This publication is protected by copyright, and permission must be obtained from the publisher prior to any prohibited reproduction, storage in a retrieval system, or transmission in any form or by any means, electronic, mechanical, photocopying, recording, or likewise.

For information regarding permissions, write to:

    Pearson Education, Inc.
    Rights and Contracts Department
    One Lake Street
    Upper Saddle River, NJ 07458

ISBN 0-321-24626-8

Text printed in the United States on recycled paper at R. R. Donnelley, Crawfordsville, Indiana.
First printing, April, 2005

*This book is dedicated to my husband, Mark,
and my three children,
Christian, Justin, and Anna.*

Table of Contents

Foreword xiii
Preface. xv
Acknowledgments. xxi
About the Author. xxiii

Chapter 1: Introduction 1

Profile Box: Historical Highlights of AI. 2
The AI Effect 3
Enhanced Computing 4
Seamless Computing 6
Why Should You Consider Enhanced Computing? 7
Why Use Visual Studio.NET?. 8
How This Book is Organized 8
Profile Box: Microsoft Research (MSR). 9
What You Need 10

Chapter 2: Creating Applications That Talk 13

The Microsoft Speech Application SDK (SASDK) 14
Profile Box: SALT Forum 15
Business Benefits of Speech 19
How the Speech Engine Works 20
Installing the SASDK 21
Creating a Speech Application. 22
Profile Box: ScanSoft, Inc.. 28
Debugging and Tuning a Speech Application 38
Setting Up a Telephony Server. 41
Summary. 42

x   Table of Contents

Chapter 3:   Telephony Applications 45

Creating a Speech Application to Solve a Business Problem 46
Profile Box: Case Study: GMAC Commercial Mortgage 47
Loading the Sales Scheduling Database 48
Building a Telephony Application 51
Profile Box: Vocal Help Desk 65
Profile Box: Voice Manager Exchange, 3.0 70
Tuning User Prompts 71
Summary. 73

Chapter 4:   Multimodal Speech Applications 77

Why Create Multimodal Applications? 78
Sunrise Community College. 79
Building a Multimodal Application 81
Profile Box: Case Study: Landstar Systems 83
The Manifest File 102
Running the Application on Pocket PC 103
Applicaiton Tuning 103
Summary. 106

Chapter 5:   Data-Mining Predictions. 109

Introducing Data Mining with SQL Server 110
Savings Mart 113
Profile Box: Case Study: ComputerFleet 124
Working with Mining Models 128
Summary. 139

Chapter 6:   Applying Data-Mining Predictions 141

Working with the Sample Application 142
Generating New Shipment Schedules 145
Profile Box: Case Study: Web Usage Mining 156
Measuring Success of the New Shipment Method 157
Closed Loop Processing 166
Summary. 169

Chapter 7: An Evolving Database ... 171

Understanding Rule-based Systems ... 172
Profile Box: BizTalk Server 2004 ... 173
Zoom Lending ... 175
Building a Rule-based Application ... 176
Profile Box: Handling E-mails with Rules ... 192
Summary ... 198

Chapter 8: Building an Agent ... 201

Understanding Agents ... 202
Building a Multiple Agent Solution ... 206
Profile Box: Microsoft Agent ... 212
Summary ... 227

Chapter 9: The Future of Enhanced Computing ... 229

The Next Development Platform ... 230
Microsoft Research (MSR) ... 237
Profile Box: The Future of Speech at Microsoft ... 241
What about AI? ... 243
Profile Box: American Association
for Artificial Intelligence ... 244
Other Areas of AI ... 245
Profile Box: Sonum Technologies ... 249
Opportunities for Developers ... 252

Glossary ... 255
Bibliography ... 265
Index ... 271

Foreword

When the public talks about Artificial Intelligence, in most cases they actually think it still belongs to the science-fiction realm. The great Alan Turing predicted in 1950 that in about fifty years, "an average interrogator, after five minutes of questioning, will not have more than a 70% chance of identifying whether or not a computer is indeed a computer." However, the enthusiasm for a real "thinking machine" has slowly fizzled, and we are now taking incremental, evolutionary steps toward "smarter computers." Researchers are now tackling smaller problems than the thinking machine, but it doesn't mean that AI research hasn't produced real-world results. Neural networks technology has been used for a wide variety of tasks, from stock market prediction to computer games; speech recognition is now entering mainstream; various machine translation services are available online; handwriting recognition, as well as optical character recognition, can now translate arbitrary (type) written script into text.

Being involved in various AI-related development projects for almost 15 years, I did my share of programming in Prolog, LISP, Smalltalk, C, Java, and similar languages and development environments. Judging from my previous experience, the .NET framework and ASP.NET represent an exciting and important evolutionary step in the software development world. They provide a feature-rich application and development environment and are language and platform neutral—although more efforts will have to be invested to achive full platform independency through projects such as Mono. It is all about reducing the burden and the complexity of software creation. It is also about winning the hearts of developers all over the world through the support for collaborative projects, workspaces, and even the open-source movement, something that Microsoft has criticized strongly at times in the past. .NET does require a shift in developer mentality, but the time invested in it quickly pays off.

So it is time to put these two, Artificial Intelligence and .NET, together. Both technologies are innovative; both are ambitious. Considering the amount of hype surrounding almost all AI-related technologies, it should be easy to find your way through, right? Think again: .NET is a newcomer in this area, and don't expect to find plenty of resources on AI development using its tools and languages. Most code samples and tutorials are written using traditional AI tools, and converting them to .NET can be a slow and painstaking process. This is where Sara Rea fills a huge gap with this book and its practical, hands-on approach. The four AI-related areas she covered offer unlimited potential for business-related applications. After all, a typical professional software developer doesn't have time to reinvent the wheel and needs a focused and pragmatic guide to this vast field. From speech applications to data mining, rule-based systems and agents, this book offers a solid instructional text of basic theory, the principles from which it derives, and how it is practically applied to develop advanced products.

As I was witnessing this book being written, I quickly discovered Sara's passion for knowledge and a talent in making hard things easy. I'm sure you'll appreciate that many advanced topics are presented in an easy-to-digest form thanks to this talent. Unlike many other technical books, it will not leave you feeling overwhelmed, but motivated to apply the techniques described inside to the real-world problems. And that's what software development is all about: building better and smarter solutions. Only this time, they'll be really smart.

Denis Susac
CEO of Mono Software,
http://www.mono-software.com

Preface

Artificial Intelligence (AI) has been around almost as long as computers. It was first introduced in the 1950s, and many scientists soon developed unrealistic expectations surrounding it. Throughout the past fifty years there have been as many advances as disappointments. Most people do not realize that AI-based technologies are being utilized every day. This is because once a technology becomes mainstream, it is generally no longer considered to be AI-related.

Take the things we associate with intelligence—speaking, writing, thinking; these are actually some of the easiest forms for AI to reproduce. The real beauty of our intelligence is that, while not easily seen, it exists deep inside every living cell that performs a specific function. No individual cell is smart enough to function alone. Instead, humans are a complicated network of cells that carry the blueprints for all other cells.

AI is not an all-or-nothing situation. It achieves success through an incredible number of baby steps. The fact that we are not yet able to build a being like Data in Star Trek does not mean we cannot create some very usable applications in our professional lives. Baby steps have already been taken in the form of technological advancements, including optical character recognition (OCR), speech recognition, digital encoding of pictures and data, and smaller, faster computers. All of these are helping to pave the way for AI-based applications.

I work for a company that creates software for state and city legislatures. Our group is constantly under the gun to produce new and innovative software. To be competitive with the other vendors, we have to show that our product is better. Most important, we have to deliver the product on time.

Recently, we were up against a tight deadline and the pressure was starting to mount. People were getting testy and irritable, and everyone seemed to be waiting on the next guy to do their part. One of my colleagues jokingly informed the other developers that we would soon be installing the newly released Microsoft telepathy product. This could be used to read the minds of all the other developers and make sure everyone was on the same page.

Now, of course, there is no Microsoft telepathy software. Even with the phenomenal progress that has taken place in neuroscience, we still do not fully understand how the brain works, much less how to read one another's minds. Still, I can envision a day, not too far off, when we will have software that can anticipate what users are thinking and act on those predictions.

This book is not about reading minds. It is about utilizing a few artificial intelligence technologies to enhance the value of existing and new applications.

The four AI-related areas I cover in this book are not meant to represent everything the field of artificial intelligence has to offer. In fact, they are just a sampling of the somewhat unexplored potential for business-related applications. They are

- Agents
- Data mining
- Rule-based systems
- Speech processing

Who Is This Book For?

I wrote this book for developers who are not satisfied with "business as usual." For developers who are always looking to improve their code and their skill sets. For developers who surf development Web sites and read technical journals, hoping to make the applications they work on better.

This book is for any developer, contract or in-house, who is building enterprise-wide applications. The applications could range from those running standalone within the company to those dispersed geographically as Web applications. The companies could be of any size, large or small, but large organizations will probably find the most benefits.

Readers already familiar with Microsoft products, and especially with Visual Studio .NET, will get the most out of this book. It focuses on using AI-based techniques with Microsoft products. Readers already familiar with Microsoft SQL Server will be the most comfortable, since all of the applications utilize Transact-SQL (T-SQL) inside stored procedures.

What You Should Know

This book is not an introduction to programming with Visual Studio .NET. Many of the applications featured in the book are Web-based. It is assumed that the reader is already familiar with designing Web-based applications using ASP.NET. Readers should be familiar with such concepts as setting up a virtual directory and executing a Web application on their localhost machine. They should also understand the difference between server-side script and client-side script.

The sample applications are not intentionally complex, but they access code embedded in SQL Stored Procedures. These stored procedures contain some of the application logic in the form of T-SQL statements. The reader should have a basic understanding of T-SQL and know how to view stored procedure code using Microsoft's Enterprise Manager or Query Analyzer.

To simplify common operations such as data access and exception handling, the sample applications utilize Microsoft Application Blocks. These blocks contain code that demonstrates best practices for accessing common functionality. No additional installation steps are necessary for the reader to execute the sample code. However, readers interested in learning more about the functionality available in these blocks should visit the Microsoft Patterns and Practices Web site at http://www.microsoft.com/resources/practices/code.mspx.

A Note about Security

The sample applications in this book were designed to demonstrate key techniques presented in each chapter. **Although limited forms of security were considered, readers should not assume that the sample applications are production-ready.**

Readers interested in using the sample applications as a starting point for building their own solutions should thoroughly evaluate the code for security weaknesses. The Microsoft MSDN Web site (http://msdn.microsoft.com) contains many helpful resources for writing secure code. One resource readers may want to refer to first is a MSDN Webcast titled "Writing Secure Code—Best Practices." The Webcast, which originally played on October 12, 2004, is available through the Microsoft On-Demand Webcasts Web site at http://www.microsoft.com/seminar/events/webcasts/ondemand.mspx.

Why I Wrote This Book

I am the type of developer who is always pushing the envelope—looking for more. I eagerly await the emergence of new products and technologies, and I am always trying to make the next application I write better than the last one. That being said, I also have a limited amount of time every day to get everything done.

I wrote this book to explore and introduce some interesting technologies and products that I think are either unknown or unexplored. They all revolve around AI-based concepts that have been around for several years. This book seeks to introduce concepts that may have been viewed as too hard in the past.

The world is changing fast, and the development world even faster. Professional software developers do not have time to learn the foundation of every AI-related technology. We barely have enough time to wade through the documentation that accompanies a beta product. What we need is someone to give us an intuitive and standard way for accessing these technologies. We know that AI technologies can be useful, but we need a good way to get to them.

Sample Applications

This book introduces some AI-based concepts using Visual Studio .NET. Starting with Chapter 3, the book will present six practical applications that can be designed with Visual Studio.NET. All the code for the sample applications is available in both Visual Basic and C# versions on the book's Web site at http://www.awprofessional.com/title/0321246268 and http://www.cutsolutions.net.

The first two applications deal with the newly released Microsoft Speech Server product. This product allows you to create Web-based applications that communicate with the user through speech. Speech processing is already important to companies that want to automate their call centers. As society becomes more mobile, speech processing will be critical to enabling mobile workers. Readers interested in learning about this natural interface will want to focus on Chapters 2, 3, and 4.

Starting with Chapter 5, the book switches to utilizing Microsoft Analysis Services. Analysis Services can be used to build data-mining models against historical data in a relational database. These models can then be used to make predictions about the data. Data mining involves more than just querying a database or creating a fancy report for business executives. It involves uncovering trends and patterns in large quantities of data. In many cases, the trends and patterns discovered were not even thought to have existed.

Chapter 7 examines the concept of rule-based programming. Rules encapsulate the business logic of a program and are stored in a central repository. Each rule is assigned a priority, and the series of rules that is applied will depend on the program's input. Programs using this technique can be more reactive to their environments.

Software agents are explored in Chapter 8. Just as a sports agent represents the best interests of an athlete, a software agent is meant to represent the best interests of the user. An agent is generally independent, reactive, personalized, and communicative. Agents that are able to learn from their users are the most valuable and are thought to possess intelligent capabilities.

Why Just Microsoft Technologies?

This book deals exclusively with Microsoft technologies. The primary reason for this is that Microsoft technologies focus on the needs of businesses and therefore are in line with revenue-generating goals. Many developers today are already familiar with Microsoft tools because they serve as the building blocks of some key business applications. This instantly lowers the learning curve needed for exploring AI techniques utilizing them.

Microsoft has dedicated substantial funds to a vast research division, Microsoft Research, that reviews many current AI areas. The division has made many advances toward speech recognition and natural language processing, as will be explored in the first and last chapters.

Microsoft is generous in providing developers with knowledge. The numerous Software Development Kits (SDKs) available for free download from its Web sites are a testament to this. These kits significantly lower the learning curve associated with adopting new technologies. Since the primary goal of this book is to lower the learning curve associated with AI, it makes sense to utilize a few SDK's in the process.

This book is the start of what I hope will be a trend toward making AI-related technologies more accessible and easy to use. I hope to see more and more developers finding creative and insightful ways to harness these technologies. Have fun!

Acknowledgments

- To my husband, Mark, for providing limitless support and love. Without him this book would not have been possible.
- To Christian, Justin, and Baby Anna, for putting up with the fact that mom was always working on the book.
- To my mom, Wendy Morgan, for showing me that I need to make my own opportunities.
- To my dad, Bruce Morgan, to whom I am more alike than anyone else.
- To my incredibly creative friend Alex Cook, for submitting a fantastic book cover design and being a great sounding board for some of my ideas.
- To Stephane Thomas of Addison-Wesley for approaching me about writing this book.
- To Joan Murray of Addison-Wesley for helping me to create the best book possible.
- To Ebony Haight and Elizabeth Zdunich of Addison-Wesley for answering endless questions about all sorts of things.
- To all the reviewers who provided valuable insight into how I could improve each chapter. Most notably, thank you to Greg Binning, Marc Briand, John Christof, Peter O'Kelly, Denis Susac, and John Timney.
- To the generous employees at Microsoft who offered valuable information and insight into some of the technologies featured in this book. Most notably, thank you to Sameer Chothani, Paco Galanes, Eric Horvitz, Steve Kuyatt, John Lawrence, Jamie MacLennan, James Mastan, and Scott White.

- To CC's Coffee House and the East Baton Rouge Parish Library for providing the locations in which I wrote this book.
- To my employer, Public Systems Associates (www.publicsystems.org), for supporting me during the writing of this book and providing an excellent work environment.

About the Author

Sara Rea is a senior developer for Public Systems Associates, a Baton Rouge–based company that produces legislative software. She is an MCSD and MCDBA and is certified in SQL Server 2000 and VB.NET. She specializes in developing Web-based applications utilizing Microsoft technologies. Since graduating from Louisiana State University in 1993 with a degree in quantitative business analysis, she has been developing software for a variety of industries, including a not-for-profit hospital, a financial company offering mortgages, a retail company selling coffee, and an Application Service Provider.

In 1998 she wrote an article on stress-testing Web sites that was featured on the front cover of *MSDN Magazine*, formerly named *Microsoft Interactive Developer* (MIND). Since then she has written articles featured in *Enterprise Development* and *.NET Development*. To reference the articles Sara Rea has written, refer to www.custsolutions.net. This Web site also features her latest research efforts and is a good resource for readers who want to learn more about enhanced computing.

CHAPTER 1

Introduction

If someone casually mentions artificial intelligence (AI), several different associations may come to mind. Some may remember the movie *2001: A Space Odyssey* and the crazed on-board computer HAL. Some may think of Steven Spielberg's recent movie *AI*, which told the sad story of an orphaned robot—essentially a modern-day version of Pinocchio. Others may think of the great chess champion Garry Kasparov being defeated by IBM's Deep Blue in 1997 and of the rematch in 2003 that resulted in a tie.

What may not immediately come to mind is the fact that many aspects of AI are already in wide use in the business world—and that more applications are on the way.

There are many definitions of AI, but in general, the definitions describe machines that have the ability to think and reason like an intelligent human. Yet there is debate about exactly what makes humans intelligent. Psychologists continue to develop new definitions of intelligence and new tests to measure it. What you believe about intelligence depends a lot on the theory of development to which you subscribe. For instance, behaviorists believe that intelligence is measured by a person's ability to communicate effectively.

Furthermore, some people are intelligent in one area but not another. Abilities that constitute intelligence in one area may not be effective in other areas. Ask a brilliant mathematician to draw you a picture and you might end up with a stick figure. It gets even trickier when you consider such things as emotional intelligence, or maturity.

So how do we know if and when AI has been created? A very good question. It is one that scientists in many fields have been trying to answer for over fifty years. The sidebar titled "Historical Highlights of AI" is a synopsis of important events during this time period. In the beginning, expectations were high, but unfortunately many researchers underestimated the scope of the problem.

Although we are now closer to a definition of artificial intelligence, we are not necessarily close to producing machines with "real AI." By this I mean computer systems that are able to act and, most important, react as a human would.

We cannot build an android like *Star Trek*'s Data anytime soon. But this does not mean that we cannot design some very usable applications utilizing AI technologies in the meantime.

Historical Highlights of AI

- In 1950, Alan Turing published a paper in which he asked whether machines can think. He later proposed the famous "Turing test," which is now a litmus test for AI. The original Turing test involved placing a man and a woman in separate rooms and having a judge, who could not see them, try to determine which was which. The test was quickly modified so that a computer took the place of the woman and the judge communicated with both the man and the computer. If the judge could be fooled into identifying the computer as the person, then it passed the test.
- The term "artificial intelligence" was first used in 1956 when John McCarthy coined the phrase. This happened at a Dartmouth summer conference where several mathematicians and scientists had gathered to discuss the potential of the field. During this time, research was focused on natural language understanding and problem solving. It was believed that as soon as better hardware became available, "true" AI would be achieved.
- The 1960s and 1970s brought about a dose of reality for AI researchers. They soon realized how complex human thinking really was. Games seemed to benefit the most from AI technologies, since they involved a limited set of rules. Arthur Samuel designed a checkers game that eventually was able to beat a former state checkers champion.
- As computer usage increased in the 1980s, many companies found themselves with lots of data but no useable information. That is when expert systems made their grand appearance. All of a sudden companies like American Express were able to increase profitability by cutting down on bad credit authorizations. For the

first time, an AI-based technology offered the thing businesses were really interested in—money.
- The 1990s brought about big hardware advancements in terms of computer speed and storage capacity. This enabled many AI researchers to push past some of the physical limitations that once hindered them. Advances in speech recognition and artificial senses were becoming more common. Neural nets were being used in many financial applications, and companies like Volvo were using genetic algorithms to solve manufacturing problems.
- In the new century, the field of AI quietly continues to advance, and its techniques are used in many different industries. Large banks use AI technologies to analyze credit card transactions and detect fraudulent behavior. In attempts to build better control systems, car-makers are installing voice recognition in many of their luxury models. Some schools are experimenting with intelligent tutoring systems designed to give students individualized instruction.

The AI Effect

Many people have observed that once a technology becomes widely accepted it is no longer associated with AI. Rodney Brooks, director of MIT's AI lab, was once quoted as saying, "Every time we figure out a piece of it, it stops being magical; we say, 'Oh, that's just a computation.'" For instance, Optical Character Recognition (OCR) was once a challenge for AI researchers. Now it is simply seen as a part of document imaging. Desktop scanners and their associated software are common tools that almost everyone with a computer has, and OCR software is widely available for use with such tools.

Advances in computer-generated speech and voice recognition, once a stumbling block for AI researchers, have been numerous in the past decade. Nearly all of us have spoken numbers into a phone in an effort to retrieve our bank account information. With the introduction of the Microsoft .NET Speech SDK, even small companies can implement speech-based applications.

These advances continue to seep into our everyday lives and have come to be expected. Something once viewed as new and different quickly becomes old and outdated. Part of the reason for this effect is the tendency of some marketers to disassociate their products with AI. Therefore, an AI-based product may not be easily identifiable.

Chapter 1 Introduction

We are entering an age of amazing technical breakthroughs in which the impossible suddenly becomes ordinary. One day, even the remaining AI challenges, such as natural language understanding, will be resolved. It will be interesting to see what AI may be called then.

Enhanced Computing

I would argue for the use of a new term that I call **Enhanced Computing** (EC) to identify computer programs that enable better use of information. These applications would utilize many AI-based technologies. Table 1.1 lists in alphabetical order the areas of AI that are specifically featured in this book.

Table 1.1 Alphabetical listing of areas of AI featured in this book.

Area	Description
Agents	Agents are computer programs that perform specific tasks for their owners and may be called upon to interact with other agents. They are usually mobile, meaning that they are able to propagate themselves across networks and execute on remote computers. They also may be able to learn and act proactively. Some may be reactive and simply respond to inputs or other agents. Others may be sent out to do specific things or just gather information. Agent applications can be referenced by several different names. Many people refer to them as bots, spiders, or personal assistants. In this book we will examine an agent application for practical business uses, but the potential of this AI branch goes well beyond that.
Data mining	Data mining involves the extraction of meaningful information from data by identifying patterns within the data. Patterns discovered can be utilized to make predictions about future data. Uncovering trends in the data allows developers to build powerful applications that can anticipate future needs and streamline existing systems. In this book, Microsoft's Analysis Services is used to perform data-mining functions.

Area	Description
Rule-based systems	Rule-based systems determine what programming logic to execute by evaluating a series of rules. Rules are usually represented with IF...THEN logic and are stored in a central repository. In this book, we examine a rule-based application which is used to add fields to a SQL Server database. The application determines how and where to add the field according to the evaluation of the rules.
Speech processing	Speech recognition involves the translation of human speech into machine-readable instructions. Speech-based applications also have a voice component in which the application generates natural-sounding speech. In the last few years there have been significant advancements in the quality of machine voices. The Microsoft .NET Speech SDK, featured in this book, offers an easy and low-cost method of implementing these types of applications.

By utilizing AI technologies, traditional applications can be improved—their functionality and usefulness extended. This can include but is not limited to the following:

- Using natural interfaces, such as speech, to make the user experience optimized and more intuitive.
- Creating autonomous and personalized processes that allow users to do more with less effort.
- Creating adaptable programs that are more reactive to their environments
- Extracting meaningful information from large datasets by identifying patterns within the data.
- Incorporating learning methods so that the application's performance improves over time.

The premise of this book is that beneficial applications can be created today based on enhanced computing technologies. The sample applications provided in this book are business related because that is an area most readily amenable to useful innovations. They are also practical in nature. Interested readers may wish to customize the code and use it at their own companies.

> **NOTE:** The sample applications in this book were designed to demonstrate key techniques presented in each chapter. Although limited forms of security were considered, readers should *not* assume that the sample applications are production ready.
>
> Readers interested in using the sample applications as a starting point for building their own solutions should thoroughly evaluate the code for security and performance weaknesses.

The sample applications incorporate techniques from four AI areas (listed in Table 1.1). This does not mean that EC applications are limited to using just these technologies. Any AI-based technology that can be used to extend the capabilities of traditional applications could be included.

Seamless Computing

Seamless computing is a vision introduced by Bill Gates at Comdex in November 2003. The concept is tied closely to the release of the next operating system—now known as Longhorn. It involves removing the seams involved in modern computing and breaking down many of the barriers that currently limit users.

You may be wondering what the seams are. They are the interfaces, errors, and so on that the user sees and has to deal with. Microsoft believes that removing some of these unnecessary things will allow computing to be truly effective and useful. The goal is to make the user experience better and more streamlined. This involves better ways of connecting applications together—and in the case of Microsoft's vision, Microsoft applications specifically.

This involves but is not limited to things like:

- Automatically connecting "smart" devices without user intervention.
- Creating more natural interfaces for the user, such as those involved with speech technology.
- Creating reliable software products that are less susceptible to security attacks and internal bug failures.
- Allowing users to search for and retrieve files no matter what type they are.
- Filtering e-mail intelligently so that unwanted e-mail does not slip through.

How does seamless computing differ from enhanced computing? In many ways, they cover the same areas. Enhanced computing seeks to utilize AI technologies to extend the user's experience. In some cases this may involve the same concepts outlined in Bill Gates's vision of seamless computing. This is especially true when it comes to speech recognition—a big part of seamless computing.

However, enhanced computing can involve additional areas, such as data mining, software agents, and any other AI-based technology used to enhance traditional applications.

Enhanced computing can be accomplished using existing technologies and does not rely on the release of Longhorn or any other new Microsoft product. Longhorn is still in the very early stages and at best will not be seen until 2006.

This does not mean that the technologies and products tied to seamless computing, and particularly Longhorn, could not be used to build an enhanced application.

Why Should You Consider Enhanced Computing?

Enhanced applications can provide many long-term and short-term benefits to companies. The six sample applications presented in this book seek to make traditional applications more efficient. They take advantage of advances that have been years in the making. More developers now have the opportunity to utilize these same advances.

The most noticeable and easiest technology to implement is speech recognition. Microsoft and various other hardware and software vendors are making huge commitments toward taking speech recognition mainstream. Two applications in this book deal specifically with the newly released Microsoft **Speech Application SDK**. Speech recognition offers workers and customers a naturalistic and often more efficient access to applications. Another technology featured in this book is Microsoft SQL Servers **Analysis Services**. Analysis Services provides a way to analyze large quantities of data and extract meaningful information.

In order to remain marketable, companies must offer unique and useful services. Developers who possess the skills necessary to create these unique and useful services will be the most valuable. You are probably already familiar with some of the tools and technologies featured, so the learning curve should be small.

Why Use Visual Studio .NET?

In the early days of AI development, there were no useful tools for developing AI applications. Part of the reason was that the entire field of computer programming was itself new and concepts such as object-oriented programming had yet to be imagined. New languages were developed to assist AI developers. The most popular of these were LISP and PROLOG. Although they are both still utilized, many current AI developers have turned to other languages, such as C++ or Java.

Like C++ and Java, Visual Basic.NET and C# are object-oriented. Thus they share some of the essential features that have led developers to choose those languages. Visual Studio.NET has developed into quite a robust tool and offers performance advantages not available in earlier versions of Visual Studio (especially where Visual Basic is concerned). These advantages, along with the fact that many developers have already adopted .NET, and especially Visual Basic, make it an excellent choice for developing the applications described in this book.

Many people are critical of Microsoft because they feel it is too dominating. However, the company's size and long-term success make it a perfect impetus for enhanced computing. More than likely Microsoft will continue to be a market leader for many years to come. With the continued advances of Microsoft Research (featured in the profile box "Microsoft Research (MSR)"), it will contribute to the advancement of technology. This book will identify some of the Microsoft tools and technologies already available to developers. In the final chapter, we will review new technologies on the horizon.

How This Book is Organized

- Chapter 2 introduces Microsoft Speech Server 2004 and focuses primarily on the Speech Application SDK (SASDK). The wizards and controls that make the SASDK so easy to utilize will be reviewed.
- Chapter 3 presents a sample telephony (voice-only) application intended to supplement an existing solution for remote salespeople. This application allows salespeople to access constantly changing customer and product data with their mobile phones.
- In Chapter 4, the Speech Application SDK is used again to create a multimodal student registration application for a community college.

How This Book is Organized

> **Microsoft Research (MSR)**
>
> In 1991, under the direction of Nathan Myhrvold, Microsoft founded its own research division, Microsoft Research (http://research.microsoft.com). The idea was that Microsoft's products could only benefit from research done by the brightest minds in the country. So that is what Microsoft has been assembling for the past thirteen years. Today, MSR employs over seven hundred people in more than fifty areas, such as data mining, machine learning, natural language processing, and speech recognition. Although the main research facility is located in Redmond, Washington, there are adjunct facilities located in San Francisco, Silicon Valley, Beijing, and Cambridge, England.
>
> MSR researchers have received many prestigious honors, including the Kyoto Prize in Advanced Technology and the Turing Award of the Association for Computing Machinery. Many of the researchers have been recruited from top universities and maintain their academic ties by routinely publishing papers for peer review. MSR is able to attract such top researchers by offering them something that not every company can—freedom to work on what they want, while still having access to abundant resources.
>
> To maintain the close connection between research and product development, MSR sponsors an annual event to demonstrate the latest advances to Microsoft developers—a geek fest appropriately named "TechFest." Many of the technologies that began at MSR have made their way into current Microsoft products. Analysis Services and the Speech Application SDK are both direct results of this research.
>
> When describing the goals of MSR, Bill Gates, chairman and chief software architect at Microsoft, stated:
>
> "We're focusing more on research than ever. We're building the technology that will enable computers to see, listen, speak and learn so people can interact with them as naturally as they interact with other people."

The application not only gives students an alternative and more efficient means of registration, but demonstrates that the college is proactive in implementing new technology.
- Chapter 5 introduces SQL Servers Analysis Services as a tool for making predictions with a large quantity of data. This chapter will identify the different types of mining models available and the reasons why each may be utilized.
- Chapter 6 presents a real-world scenario in which Analysis Services could be utilized. The scenario involves a fictional retailer in need of a

more efficient distribution schedule. The chapter steps through the use of Analysis Services to create a mining model based on a randomly generated database.
- Chapter 7 introduces a rule-based application designed to handle how new fields are added to a database. A threshold value is used to determine whether the field to be added is similar to any existing fields. The chapter identifies the four phases in the implementation of this type of application.
- In Chapter 8 an example of multiple software agents is presented. It involves creating multiple applications that allow remote salespeople to access files held in the home office. It also notifies them of new sales opportunities and utilizes a Web service to retrieve data from the central office.
- The final chapter will identify possible directions for the field of computing in the next few years. It will specifically look at promising areas of research in development at Microsoft Research. It will identify additional resources you may want to refer to for more information. In addition, it will examine a few branches of AI that may be of further interest to the reader.
- All the sample applications, available in both Visual Basic and C# versions, are provided in their entirety on the book's Web site at http://ww.awprofessional.com/title/0321246268

What You Need

Minimum System Requirements

Processor	Pentium III class—600 MHz or higher
RAM	256 MB or higher
Operating system	Windows 2000, service pack 3
	Windows 2003 Server
	Windows XP Professional, service pack 1
Hard disk space	To install all SDK's, code samples, and databases included on the book's Web site, you will need a minimum of 950 MB available hard disk space.
Soundcard	Speakers are optional
Microphone	Headset with close-fitting microphone

What You Need   **11**

Overall Software Requirements

Description	Install Location
All available service packs and critical updates from Microsoft Windows Update	http://windowsupdate.microsoft.com
Microsoft English Visual Studio .NET 2003 Professional, Enterprise Architect, Enterprise Developer, or Trial Edition (60-day trial available for download from MSDN	http://go.microsoft.com/fwlink/?LinkID=15120
Microsoft Internet Information Services, version 5.1 or higher	http://www.microsoft.com/downloads/search.aspx?displaylang=en
Microsoft Internet Explorer, version 6.0, service pack 1 or higher	http://www.microsoft.com/downloads/search.aspx?displaylang=en
Microsoft .NET Framework Class Library 1.1 SP2 or greater	Installed with Visual Studio .NET 2003. Service pack updates available at http://www.microsoft.com/downloads/search.aspx?displaylang=en
Microsoft SQL Server 2000, Standard, Personal or Enterprise Edition	
SQL Server 2000 Service Pack 3a	http://www.microsoft.com/sql/downloads/2000/sp3.asp

Software Requirements for Chapters 2, 3, and 4

Description	Install Location
Microsoft Speech Application SDK (SASDK), version 1.0	http://www.microsoft.com/downloads/details.aspx?FamilyId=5DAAE9C4-188C-4547-A9D6-1671132A39A1&displaylang=en
Microsoft Enterprise Instrumentation	Available with the extracted SASDK files in the Prerequisites\EnterpriseInstrumentation directory
Chapter 3 Solution File	Chapter3\Code\Chapter3\Chapter3.sln
Chapter 3 SQL Database	Chapter3\Database\SalesScheduling_Data.mdf and SalesScheduling_Log.ldf
Chapter 4 Solution File	Chapter4\Code\Chapter4.sln
Chapter 4 SQL Database	Chapter4\Database\SCC_Data.mdf and CC_Log.ldf

Software Requirements for Chapters 5 and 6

Description	Install Location
Microsoft XML Parser (MSXML) 4.0 or greater	http://www.microsoft.com/downloads/search.aspx?displaylang=en
Microsoft XML for Analysis Specification 1.1	http://www.microsoft.com/downloads/search.aspx?displaylang=en
Microsoft ADO for multi-dimensional objects (ADOMD.NET), version 8.0	http://www.microsoft.com/downloads/search.aspx?displaylang=en
Chapter 5 Solution File	Chapter5\Code\LoadSampleData\LoadSampleData.sln
Chapter 5 SQL Database	Chapter5\Database\SavingsMart_Data.mdf and SavingsMart_Log.ldf
Chapter 6 Solution File	Chapter6\Code\LoadSampleData\LoadSampleData.sln
Chapter 6 SQL Database	Chapter6\ Database\SavingsMart_Data.mdf and SavingsMart_Log.ldf

Software Requirements for Chapter 7

Description	Install Location
Microsoft Office XP Primary Interop Assembly	http://www.microsoft.com/downloads/search.aspx?displaylang=en
Chapter 7 Solution	Chapter7\Code\Chapter7.sln
Chapter 7 SQL Database	Chapter7\Database\ZoomLending_data.mdf and ZoomLending_Log.ldf

Software Requirements for Chapter 8

Description	Install Location
Microsoft Background Intelligent Transfer Service, version 1.5	http://www.microsoft.com/downloads/search.aspx?displaylang=en
Chapter 8 Solution File	Chapter8\Code\Agent\Agent.sln
Chapter 8 SQL Database (NOTE: Utilizes the same database used in Chapter 3)	Chapter3\Database\SalesScheduling_Data.mdf and SalesScheduling_Log.ldf

CHAPTER 2

Creating Applications That Talk

In 1939, Bell Labs demonstrated a talking machine named "Voder" at the New York World's Fair. The machine was not well received because the voice was robotic and unnatural sounding. Since then, many advances have been made in the area of speech synthesis—specifically in the last five years. Also known as text-to-speech, speech synthesis is one of two key technologies in the area of speech applications.

The second technology is speech recognition. For decades, science fiction movies have featured talking computers capable of accepting oral directions from their users. What once existed only in the thoughts of writers and filmmakers may soon become part of everyday life. In the last few years many advances have been made in the area of speech recognition by researchers such as the Speech Technology Group at Microsoft Research.

Speech-based applications have been slowly entering the marketplace. Many banks allow customers to access their account data through automated telephone systems, also known as Interactive Voice Response (IVR) systems. Yahoo and AOL have set up systems that read e-mail to their users. The National Weather Service (NOAA) has an application that reads the weather.

Speech processing is an important technology for enhanced computing because it provides a natural and intuitive interface for the user. People communicate with one another through conversation, so it is comfortable and efficient to use the same method for communication with computers.

Recently Microsoft released Speech Server as part of an effort to make speech more mainstream. Microsoft Speech Server (MSS) has three main components:

1. Speech Application SDK (SASDK)
2. Speech Engine Services (SES)
3. Telephony Application Services (TAS)

All three components are bundled into both the Standard Edition and the Enterprise Edition. The primary difference between the two depends on how many concurrent users your application must support.

Speech Engine Services (SES) and Telephony Application Services (TAS) are components that run on the Speech Server. The Speech Server is responsible for interfacing with the Web server and the telephony hardware. Web-based applications can be accessed from traditional Web browsers, telephones, mobile phones, pocket PC's, and smart phones.

This chapter will focus primarily on specific components of the SASDK, since this is the component most applicable to developers. The installation files for the SASDK are available as a free download from the Microsoft Speech Web site at http://www.microsoft.com/speech/. Chapters 3 and 4 will expand on the use of the SASDK and will introduce two fictional companies and the speech-based applications they developed.

The Microsoft Speech Application SDK (SASDK)

The Microsoft Speech Application SDK (SASDK), version 1.0 enables developers to create two basic types of applications: telephony (voice-only) and multimodal (text, voice, and visual). This is not the first speech-based SDK Microsoft has developed. However, it is fundamentally different from the earlier ones because it is the first to comply with an emerging standard known as Speech Application Language Tags, or SALT (refer to the "SALT Forum" profile box). Run from within the Visual Studio.NET environment, the SASDK is used to create Web-based applications only.

Speech-based applications offer more than just touch-tone access to account information or call center telephone routing. Speech-based applications offer the user a natural interface to a vast amount of information. Interactions with the user involve both the recognition of speech and the reciting of static and dynamic text. Current applications can be enhanced by offering the user a choice to utilize either traditional input methods or a speech-based one.

Development time is significantly reduced with the use of a familiar interface inside Visual Studio.NET. Streamlined wizards allow developers to quickly build grammars and prompts. In addition, applications developed for telephony access can utilize the same code base as those accessed with a Web browser.

The SASDK makes it easy for developers to utilize speech technology. Graphical interfaces and drag-and-drop capabilities mask all the complexities behind the curtain. All the .NET developer needs to know about speech recognition is how to interpret the resulting confidence score.

SALT Forum

Founded in 2001 by Cisco, Comverse, Intel, Microsoft, Philips, and ScanSoft, the SALT Forum now has over seventy contributors and adopters. Their collaboration has resulted in the creation and refinement of the Speech Application Language Tags (SALT) 1.0 specification. SALT is a lightweight extension of other markup languages such as HTML and XML. The specification standardizes the way devices such as laptops, personal digital assistants (PDA's), phones, and Tablet PC's access information using speech. It enables multimodal (text, voice, and visual) and telephony (voice-only) access to applications.

The forum operates a Web site at www.saltforum.org which provides information and allows individuals to subscribe to a SALT Forum newsletter. The site also provides a developer forum that contains a download of the latest specification along with tutorials and sample code. Membership is open to all, and interested companies can download a SALT Adopters agreement.

SALT is based on a small set of XML elements. The main top-level outputs/inputs are as follows:

- <prompt...>—A prompt is a message that the system sends to the user to ask for input. This tag is used to specify the content of audio output and can point to prerecorded audio files. It contains the subqueue object used to specify one or more prompt objects.
- <listen...>—Input element used for speech recognition or audio recording. It contains the grammar element used to specify the different things a user can say. The record element is used to configure the recording process.
- <dtmf...>—Short for Dual Tone Multi-Frequency tones. Element used in telephony applications. It is similar to the listen element in that it specifies possible inputs. Like the <listen> element, its main elements are grammar and bind.
- <smex...>—Short for Simple Messaging Extension. Asynchronous element used to communicate with the device. Can be used to receive XML messages from the device through the received property.

(continued)

> SALT supports different browsers by allowing for two modes of operation, object and declarative. The object mode exposes the full interface for each SALT element but is only supported by browsers with event and scripting capabilities. The declarative mode provides a limited interface and is supported by browsers such as those found on portable devices.

NOTE: VoiceXML, 2.x is simple markup language introduced by the World Wide Web (W3C) Consortium (http://www.w3.org). Like SALT, it is used to create dialogs with a user using computer-generated speech. They are both based on W3C standards.

The VoiceXML specification was created before SALT and was designed to support telephony applications. SALT was designed to run on a wide variety of devices, including PDA's, smartphones, and Tablet PC's.

SALT has a low-level API, and VoiceXML has a high-level API. This allows SALT a finer-level control over the interface with the user.

VoiceXML does not natively support multimodal applications and is used primarily for limited IVR applications. Because of this, Microsoft Speech Server does not support VoiceXML. But everything that can be accomplished with VoiceXML can be accomplished with SALT.

Telephony Applications

The Microsoft Speech Application SDK enables developers to create telephony applications, in which data can be accessed over a phone. Prior to the Speech Application SDK, one option for creating voice-only applications was the Telephony API (TAPI), version 3.0, that shipped with Windows 2000. This COM-based API allowed developers to build interactive voice systems. The TAPI allowed developers to create telephony applications that communicated over a Public Switched Telephone Network (PSTN) or over existing networks and the Internet. It was responsible for handling the communication between telephone and computer.

Telephony application development would further incorporate the use of the SAPI (Speech Application Programming Interface), version 5.1, to provide speech recognition and speech synthesis services. This API is COM based and designed primarily for desktop applications. Like TAPI, it does not offer the same tools and controls available with the new .NET version. Most important, the SAPI is not SALT compliant and therefore does not utilize a common platform.

Telephony applications built with the SASDK are accessed by clients using telephones, mobile phones, or smartphones. They require a third-party Telephony Interface Manager (TIM) to interpret signals sent from the telephone to the telephony card. The TIM then communicates with Telephony Application Services (TAS), the Speech Server component responsible for handling incoming telephony calls (see Figure 2.1). Depending on which version of Speech Server is used, TAS can handle up to ninety-six telephony ports per node, with the ability to add an unlimited number of additional nodes.

Telephony applications can be either voice-only, DTMF (Dual Tone Multi-frequency) only, or a mixture of the two. DTMF applications involve the user pressing keys on the telephone keypad. This is useful when the user is required to enter sensitive numerical sequences such as passwords or account numbers. In some cases, speaking these types of numerical sequences might entail a security violation, because someone might overhear the user.

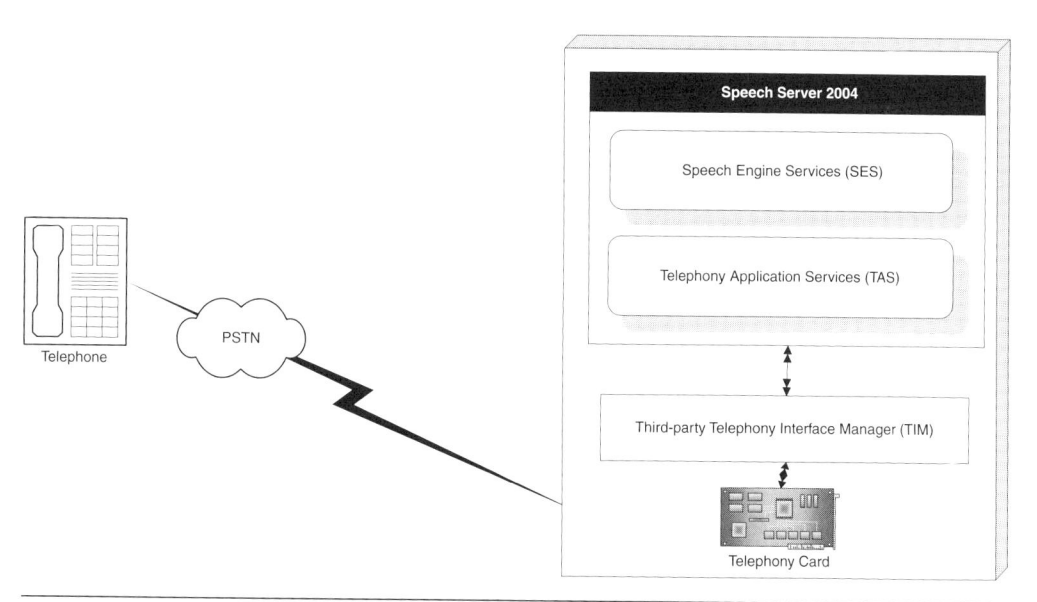

Figure 2.1 The main components involved when telephony applications are received. The user's telephone communicates directly with the server's telephony card across the public telephone network. The Third-party Telephony Interface Manager (TIM) then communicates with Telephony Application Services (TAS), a key component of Speech Server 2004.

Call centers typically use telephony applications to route calls to appropriate areas or to automate some basic function. For instance, a telephony application can be used to reset passwords or request certain information. By automating tasks handled by telephone support employees, telephony applications can offer significant cost savings.

Telephony applications can also be useful when the user needs to iterate through a large list of information. The user hears a shortened version of the item text and can navigate through the list by speaking certain commands. For example, if the telephony application is used to recite e-mail, the user can listen as the e-mail subjects of all unread e-mails are recited. A user who wants to hear the text of a specific e-mail can speak a command such as "Read e-mail." The user can then navigate through the list by speaking commands such as "Next" or "Previous."

Multimodal Applications

Multimodal applications allow the user to choose the appropriate input method, whether speech or traditional Web controls. The application can be used by a larger customer base because it allows the user to choose. Since not all customers will have access to microphones, the multimodal application is the perfect way to offer speech functionality without forcing the user into a corner.

Multimodal applications are accessed via Microsoft Internet Explorer (IE) on the user's PC or with IE for the Pocket PC (see Figure 2.2). Both versions of IE require the installation of a speech add-in. Users indicate that they wish to utilize speech by triggering an event, such as clicking an icon or button.

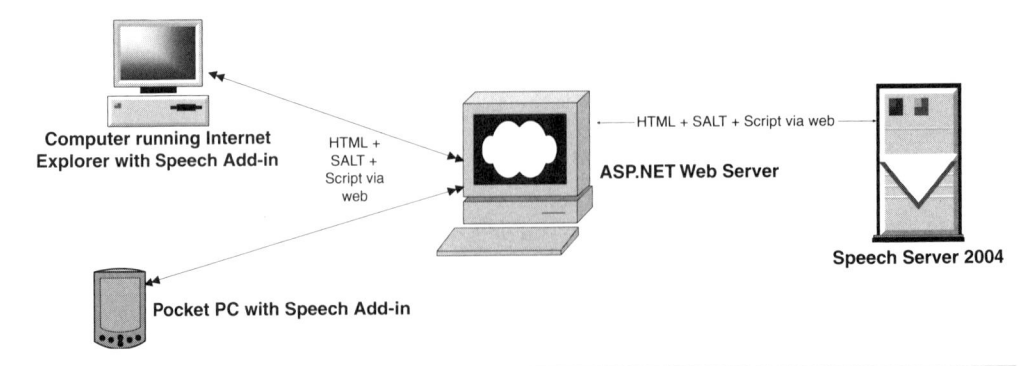

Figure 2.2 The high-level process by which multimodal applications communicate with Speech Server. The ASP.NET application is accessed either by a computer running Internet Explorer (IE) with the speech add-in or by Pocket IE with the speech add-in.

The speech add-in for IE, necessary for interpreting SALT, is provided with the SASDK. It should be installed on any computer or Pocket PC device accessing the speech application. In addition to providing SALT recognition, the add-in displays an audio meter that visually indicates the volume level of the audio input.

Business Benefits of Speech

Self-service applications are on the rise in just about every industry. Customers rarely tolerate anything less than 24/7 access to their information. Speech makes it easier and sometimes faster for customers to get to that information. This can be accomplished using either telephony or multimodal applications.

Telephony applications are great for automating call center functionality. They generally result in increased customer satisfaction and lower costs. If designed properly, a telephony application can reduce the number of telephone transfers or menu layers that a customer must navigate. Telephony applications can also reduce the hold time for customers because they will not have to wait on the availability of a limited number of customer service agents. Best of all, you can be sure that the customer is always treated courteously. You do not have to worry about the customer reaching a rude or untrained customer service agent.

Multimodal applications offer the better of two worlds. They increase customer satisfaction by allowing customers to select the input method that works best for them. For applications that execute on small devices like a PDA or a smartphone, being able to swap between speech and GUI access can speed access time.

Both multimodal and telephony applications can automate certain processes. For instance, an information services department can use a speech-based application to reset passwords, access e-mail, or customer contact information.

Hands-free access is not only useful for busy remote workers, but can be vital to handicapped individuals. Best of all, mobile workers are not limited to using only stylus pens when entering data.

The benefits of speech processing are numerous, especially for businesses. Hardware and software limitations that once hindered the technology are being lowered or removed everyday. Products like Microsoft Speech Server will increase the number of developers with the skills to build these types of applications. As companies search for innovative ways to increase customer satisfaction and decrease costs, speech-based applications should become more and more common.

How the Speech Engine Works

If you have ever utilized a dictation program to create documents, you know that the program requires a training process to accurately interpret your speech. The training process usually consists of several sessions where the user reads prompts slowly and clearly. The speech engine matches the sounds recorded to the words in the prompt script. Unfortunately, this process usually discourages the use of speech-based products.

The speech engine that is part of the Speech Application SDK works differently. It utilizes what are called grammar rules to interpret what the user is saying. Rather than requiring the engine to be open to any spoken text, the speech application is restricted to certain phrases defined in multiple grammar files. Each grammar file is associated with a particular user interaction.

While this enables the application to accurately interpret the user's speech without a training process, it does require more work by the application developer. The developer must try to anticipate every spoken phrase the user may utter. This is not as much of an issue for the sample application in this chapter. Trained employees and not the general public will use the telephony application. Therefore, it is easier to anticipate and restrict what phrases are appropriate.

The Speech Application SDK allows for the use of dynamic grammars. This is necessary when the content is not known ahead of time, as when the user is reading values from the database. This process will be even more relevant in Chapter 4, where an application used to register students will be examined.

In general, applications built with the Speech Application SDK are least like "real AI," in which the system can act and react like a human would. Even though they offer the user a natural interface, the inputs and outputs must be defined in advance. Nevertheless, they are still an important step toward better enabling mobile workers. These applications offer an enhanced method for accessing data that would not be available using traditional applications.

Installing the SASDK

To run the samples provided in the next two chapters, you will need to install the SASDK. You will first need to download the SDK from the Microsoft Speech Web site at http://www.microsoft.com/speech/. Installation will require completion of the following steps:

1. Ensure that you have a minimum of 702 MB of free hard disk space. This will be needed for the contents of the Setup directory.
2. Double-click **SASDK_V1_Full.exe** and allow it to extract files to C:\SpeechSDK.
3. Double-click the **SASDK_Extract.exe** file to extract additional installation files to C:\SpeechSDK.
4. Go to a command prompt by clicking **Start** and **Run**, type **CMD**, and then click **OK**.
5. Browse to the C:\SpeechSDK directory and type '**SASDK_ExtractAll.cmd C:\SpeechSDK\Setup**' This step will create the setup directory and extract all the necessary installation files. This step may take several minutes to execute.
6. Execute **Setup.exe** from the newly created C:\SpeechSDK\Setup directory and click **Install the Speech Application SDK**.
7. From the Installation Guide dialog box click, **Detect and Install Prerequisites**. The Prerequisites dialog (see Figure 2.3) will list all the necessary components along with either a checkmark indicating that the component is found or a red x to indicate that the component was not found. Click the red x icon to begin updating your computer.
8. Once all the prerequisites have been installed, click **Install the Speech Application SDK** and follow the wizard steps for a complete install until the SDK installation is finished. The installation will take several minutes to complete.
9. Click the **Check for the latest Service Release** link. Requiring an Internet connection, this step will direct the user to the area where all speech-related downloads are located.
10. Once all the steps have been completed, click **Exit** to leave the installation wizard.

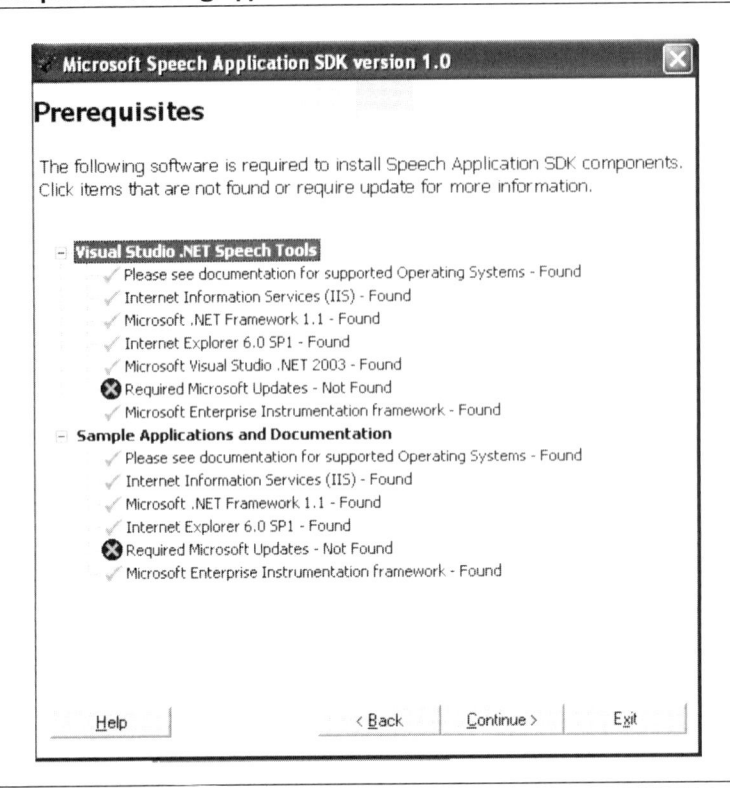

Figure 2.3 Screenshot of the Prerequisites dialog featured in the SASDK installation wizard. This dialog not only allows users to determine which components are missing from their computer, but provides a link to the installation for the missing component. In this example the wizard indicates that one of the required updates was not found.

Creating a Speech Application

The SASDK provides a template for creating new speech applications with Visual Studio .NET. It also provides visual editors for building the prompts (words spoken to the user) and grammars (words spoken by the user). This section will examine the basics of creating a speech application with the SASDK.

To utilize the template provided with the SASDK, open Visual Studio.NET and execute the following steps:

1. Click **File**, **New**, and **Project**. From the **New Project** dialog box, select the desired Project Type and click the **Speech Web Tem-**

plate icon in the Templates window. This template was created when you installed the SASDK. Change the value in the location dropdown box to the desired project name and click **OK**.
2. You can either accept the setting defaults and click **Finish**, or select **Application Settings** and **Application Resources** to specify custom settings.
3. The default application mode is voice-only, so if you want to create a multimodal application, you can change the mode from the Application Settings tab.
4. The Application Resources tab allows you to specify that a default grammar library file will be created and the name it will be called. From here you can also indicate that a new prompt project will be created and specify what the name for it will be.
5. Click Finish at any time to build the new project.

If you choose to build a voice-only application, the project will include a Web page named **Default.aspx**. This page contains two speech controls, AnswerCall and SemanticMap. These are basic controls used in every voice-only application. Their specific functions will be covered in the section titled "Using Speech Controls." The default project will also include a folder named **Grammars** that contains two grammar files, Library.grxml and SpeechWebApplication1.grxml. For voice-only applications the prompt project and Grammars folder are included by default.

If you choose to build a multimodal application, the Default.aspx page is included, but it will contain no controls. There will be a Grammars folder, but no prompt project will be created.

By default, the Manifest.xml file is included for both project types. It is an XML-based file that contains references to the resources used by the project. References include grammar files and prompt projects. Speech Server will preload and cache these resources to help improve performance.

The Prompt Editor

Microsoft recommends that you prerecord static prompts because voice recordings are more natural than the result of the text to speech engine. The prompt editor (see Figure 2.4) is a tool that allows you to specify potential prompts and record wave files associated with each prompt.

The utterance "Welcome to my speech application" represents a single prompt. For voice-only applications, you need to make sure you include a

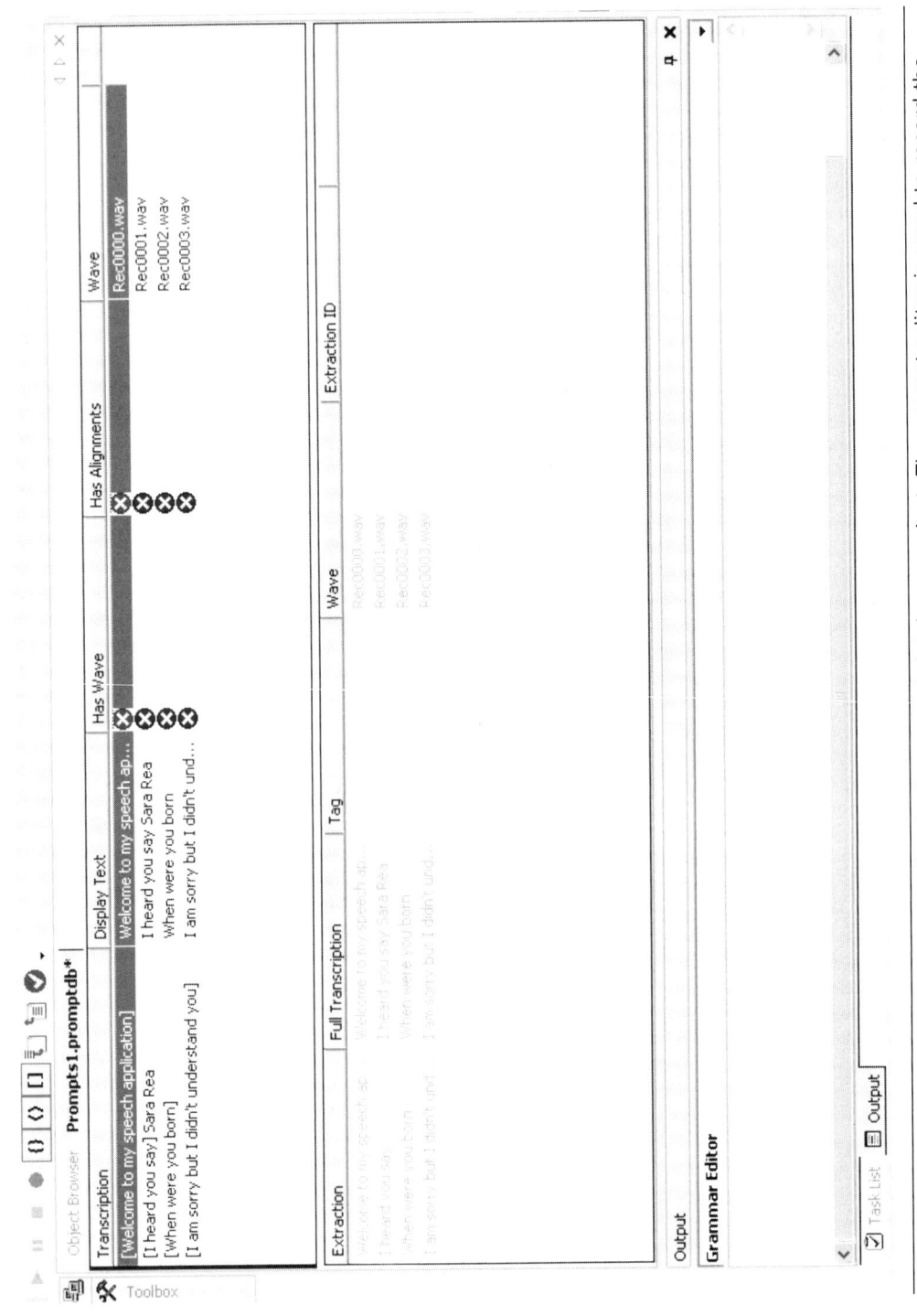

Figure 2.4 Screenshot of the prompt editor in the prompt database project. The prompt editor is used to record the wave files associated with each prompt. The screenshot includes four different prompts.

wide range of prompts. Since the user relies on these prompts to understand how the application works, they need to be clear and meaningful.

The Prompt Database

An application built with the Speech SDK wizard adds a prompt database project by default. If you choose to add another prompt database, it can be done by using the **File** menu and selecting **Add Project** and **New Project** (see Figure 2.5). The new project will be based on the Prompt Project template. Once the project is added, a new Prompt Database can be added by right-clicking the prompt project and then selecting **Add** and **Add New Item**. The Prompt Database item opens up a data grid style screen that allows you to specify all the potential prompts.

The prompt database contains all the prerecorded utterances used to communicate with the user. An application can reference more than one prompt database. One reason for doing this is ease of maintenance. Prompts that change often can be placed in a separate prompt database. By restricting the size of the prompt database, the amount of time needed to recompile is minimized.

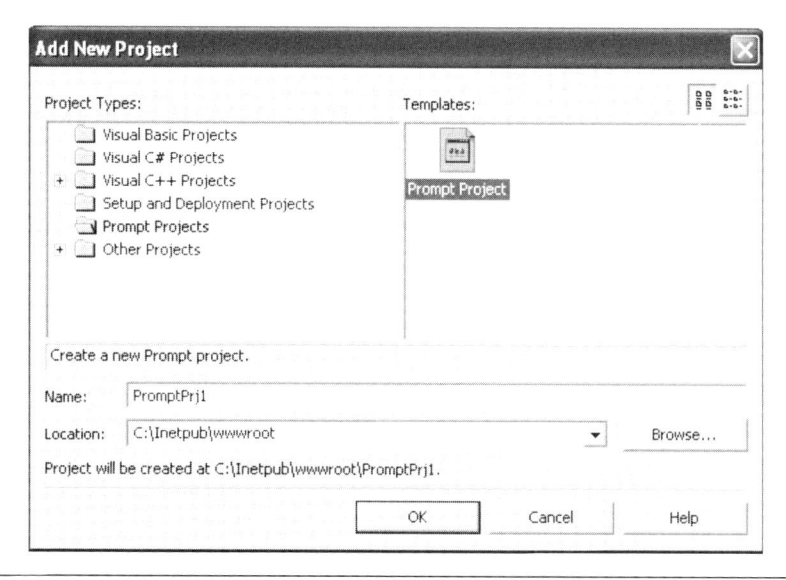

Figure 2.5 Screenshot of the dialog used to add a new prompt project to your speech application. This dialog is accessed by clicking Add project from the File menu and then clicking New Project.

If you followed the instructions in the last section to create a new speech project, you can now open the default prompt database by double-clicking the prompts file from **Solution Explorer**.

Transcriptions and Extractions

Figure 2.6 is a screenshot of the recording pane in the prompt project database. There are two grids in a prompt project. The top one contains transcriptions, and the bottom one extractions. Transcriptions are the individual pieces of speech that relate to a single utterance. Extractions combine transcription elements to form phrases. Extractions are formed when you place square brackets around the transcription elements.

Sometimes a prompt can involve one or more transcription elements, such as "I heard you say Sara Rea." In this case, the two elements are "I heard you say" and "Sara Rea." In some cases employee names may also be prerecorded in the prompt database. This adds an additional burden, because every time a new employee is added to the database, someone needs to record the employee's name. However, by doing this, we prevent the speech engine from utilizing text-to-speech (TTS) to render the prompt. This is preferred because using recordings results in a more natural-sounding prompt.

Prompts are controlled from prompt functions. These functions programmatically indicate what phrases are spoken to the user. When the speech engine is passed a phrase from the function, it first searches the prompt database to see if any prerecorded utterances are present. It searches the entire database for matches and will string together as many transcription elements as necessary to retrieve the entire phrase.

Because the speech engine parses transcription elements together to form phrases, you can break phrases up to prevent redundancy. For instance, the phrase "Sorry, I am having trouble hearing you. If you need help, say help" may be spoken when an application encounters silence. The phrase "Sorry, I am having trouble understanding you. If you need help, say help" is used whenever the speech engine does not recognize the user's response. Therefore, the subphrase "If you need help, say help" can be recorded as a separate phrase in the prompt database. This means that the subphrase will only have to be recorded once. In addition, the size of the prompt database is minimized.

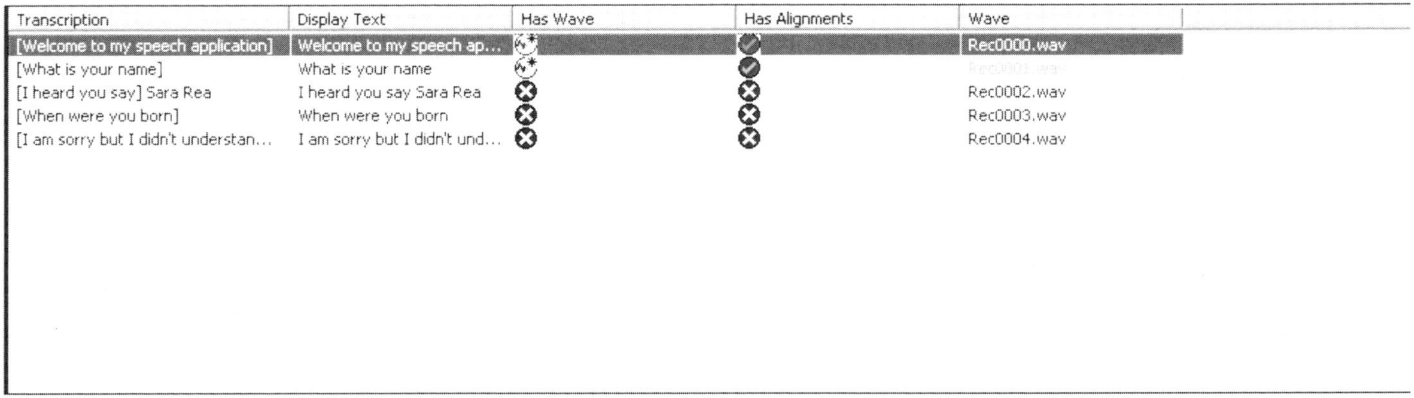

Transcription	Display Text	Has Wave	Has Alignments	Wave
[Welcome to my speech application]	Welcome to my speech ap…	✱	✱	Rec0000.wav
[What is your name]	What is your name	✖	✖	Rec0001.wav
[I heard you say] Sara Rea	I heard you say Sara Rea	✖	✖	Rec0002.wav
[When were you born]	When were you born	✖	✖	Rec0003.wav
[I am sorry but I didn't understan…	I am sorry but I didn't und…	✖	✖	Rec0004.wav

Figure 2.6 Contents of the Recording pane in the prompt database project. Transcriptions are the individual pieces of speech that can be prerecorded. No utterances have been recorded for prompts with a red X in the Has Wave column.

The Recording Tool

The Recording Tool can be accessed by clicking the red circle icon above the Transcription pane or by clicking **Prompt** and then **Record All**. The text from the transcription item selected is displayed in the Display Text textbox (see Figure 2.7). After clicking **Record**, the person making the recording should speak clearly into the microphone. Click **Stop** as soon as the entire phrase is spoken. Try to select a recording location where background noise is minimized.

In some cases, you may want to utilize professional voice talent to make recordings. There are third-party vendors, such as ScanSoft (see the "ScanSoft" profile box), that can provide professional voice talent and assistance with recordings. Wave files created in a recording studio can be associated with a specific transcription element by clicking **Import** and browsing to the file's location.

If the speech engine is unable to find a match in any of the prompt databases, it utilizes TTS. The result is a machine-like voice that may go against the natural interface you are trying to create. Speech Server comes bundled with ScanSoft's Speechify TTS engine (see the "ScanSoft" profile box), but at present the results from a text-to-speech engine are not as natural-sounding as a recorded human voice. On the other side, it will not always be possible or manageable to prerecord all utterances. You will have to weigh these options when designing your speech application.

ScanSoft, Inc.

In 2003, ScanSoft, Inc. (www.scansoft.com) merged with SpeechWorks to become one of the largest suppliers of speech-related applications and services. SpeechWorks, one of the original founders of the SALT Forum, offered ScanSoft expertise in the areas of speech recognition, text-to-speech (TTS), and speaker verification.

ScanSoft, a publicly traded company (NASDAQ:SSFT), was already a large supplier of popular products, such as Dragon's NaturallySpeaking, which allows users to dictate into any Windows-based application up to 160 words per minute. The merger made the company a dominant force in the area of speech technology.

ScanSoft offers a broad range of products, but also offers such services as assistance in deployment and configuration of speech solutions. In addition, it provides voice talent for companies that wish to have their prompts professionally recorded.

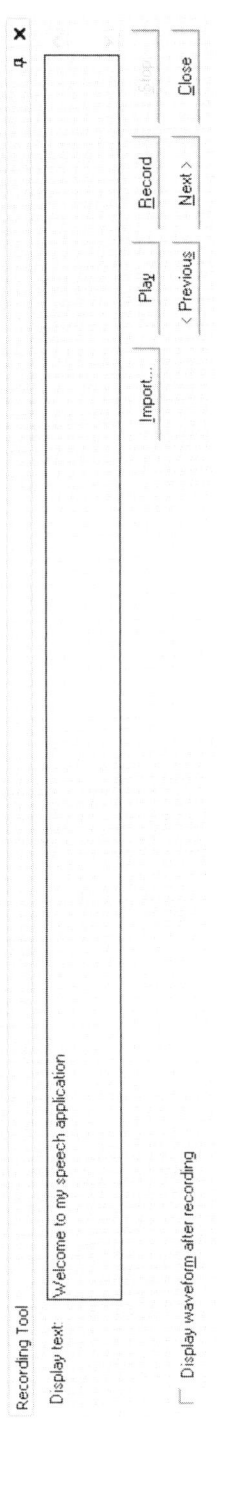

Figure 2.7 The Recording tool allows you to directly record each prompt associated with a transcription. Prompts can also be recorded by professional voice talent in a studio, made into wave files, and imported.

> ScanSoft has deployed speech-based solutions to a broad range of industries, including financial services, government, health care, and retail.
>
> Microsoft first licensed the Speechify text-to-speech engine with its Microsoft Speech API (SAPI) 5.0 product in 2001. This was done because of the high quality of the Speechify text-to-speech voice.
>
> In 2002, SpeechWorks and Microsoft formed a strategic alliance which ensured that the Speechify text-to-speech engine would be included with the Microsoft Speech Server product. The Speechify TTS engine is SALT-based and is included out-of-the-box with Speech Engine Services.
>
> Including the Speechify product was important not only because it provides a natural-sounding voice, but also because it supports multiple languages and performs well. Utilizing ScanSoft's TTS engine, Microsoft was able to focus more on perfecting the speech-recognition engine.
>
> At the time of the alliance, SpeechWorks agreed to add support for its OpenSpeech Recognizer (OSR) product. The OSR product is a high-performance recognition engine that can be purchased separately from ScanSoft and then included with the Enterprise Edition of Speech Server.
>
> ScanSoft and the ScanSoft logo are registered trademarks of ScanSoft, Inc.

The recording of prompts is a major consideration when designing a speech-enabled application. If professional talent is used, you will want to try to minimize the need for multiple recording sessions. If the application requires the utilization of text-to-speech for most prompts, you may want to consider purchasing a third-party TTS add-in.

The Grammar Editor

Grammar, the reverse of prompts, represents what the user says to the application. This is a key element of voice-only applications because they rely completely on accurate understanding of the user's commands. The grammar editor builds Extensible Markup Language (XML) files that are used by the speech-recognition engine to understand the user's speech. What is nice about the grammar editor is that you drag-and-drop controls to build the XML instead of having to type it in directly. This helps to reduce the time spent building grammars.

A grammar is stored in the form of an XML file with a grxml extension. Each of its Question/Answer (QA) controls, representing an interaction with the user, is associated with one or more grammars. A single grammar file will contain one or more rules that the application uses to interpret the user's response.

TIP: In order to increase the speed of the application, grammars can be compiled into .cfg files using the grammar compiler. This is typically done after the application is deployed, because that is when you will obtain the most benefit. Using compiled grammar files instead of text files reduces the size of files and thus the amount of time required to download them. Most important, it allows the speech engine to load files into memory faster.

Grammars are compiled with a command-line utility named SrGSGc.exe. It is installed by default in Program Files\Microsoft Speech Application SDK 1.0\SDKTools\bin. The tool can be accessed by clicking Start|Programs|Microsoft Speech Application SDK 1.0|Debugging Tools|Microsoft Speech Application SDK Command Prompt. From the command prompt, type SrGSGc.exe followed by the name of the output file (.cfg) and then the name of the input file (.grxml).

Clicking **Add New Item** from the **Project** menu accomplishes adding a grammar file. From there, select the category **Grammar File** and name the file accordingly. Existing grammars can be viewed by expanding the Grammar folder within Solution Explorer. By default, two grammar files are added when you create a voice-only or multimodal application. The first file, named library.grxml, contains common grammar rules you may need to utilize. For instance, it includes a rule for collecting yes/no responses (see Figure 2.8). It also includes rules for handling numbers, dates, and even credit card information. Rules embedded within the library grammar file can be referenced in other grammar files through the RuleRef control.

The second grammar file is named the same as the project file by default. This is where you will place the grammar rules associated with your application. Although you could store all the rules in a single file, you may want to consider adding subfolders within the main Grammars folder. You can then create multiple grammar files to group similar types of grammar rules. This helps to organize code and makes referencing grammar rules easier.

Grammar rules are built by dragging elements onto the page. Controls are available in the **Grammar** tab of the toolbox. Figure 2.9 is a screenshot of these grammar controls. Most rules will consist of one or all of the following:

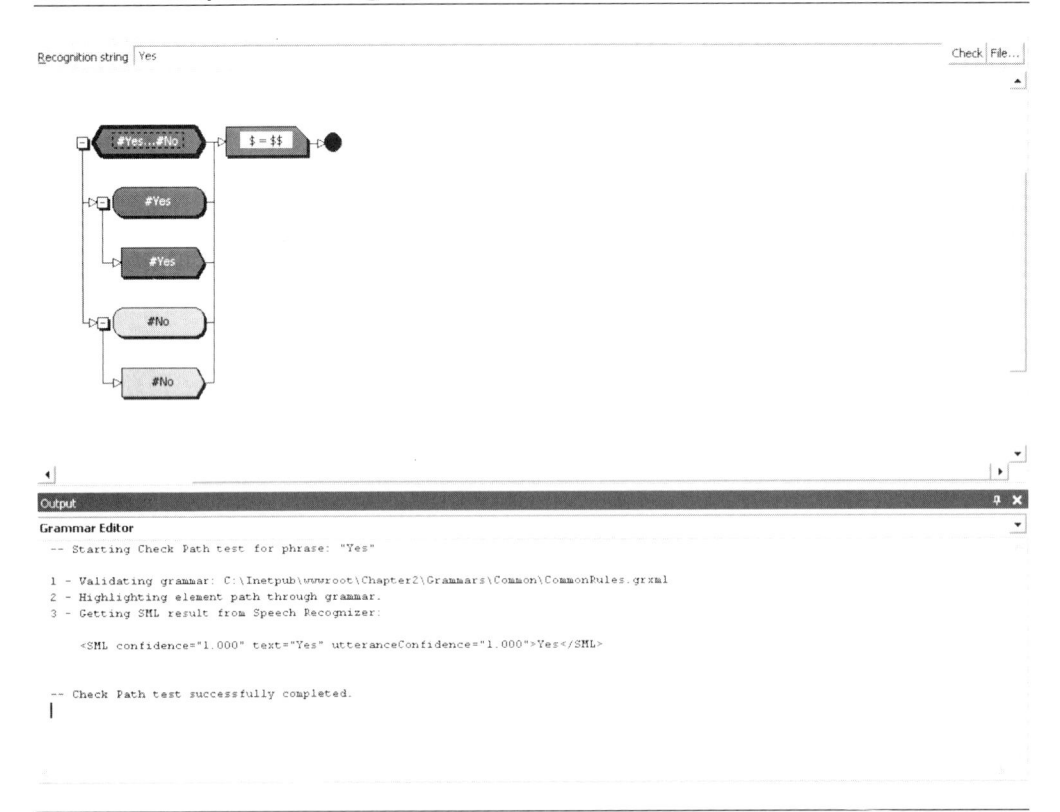

Figure 2.8 Screenshot displaying the yes/no rule inside the grammar editor. This is one of several rules included by default with the Library.grxml file.

Figure 2.9 Screenshot of the Grammar tab, available in the toolbox when creating a new grammar. The elements you will use most often are the List, Phrase, RuleRef, and Script Tag elements.

- Phrase—represents the actual phrase spoken by the user.
- List—contains multiple phrase elements that all relate to the same thing. For instance, a yes response could be spoken as "yeah," "ok," or "yes please." A list control allows you to indicate that all these responses are the same as yes.
- RuleRef—used to reference other rules through the URI property. This is useful when you have multiple grammar files and want to reuse the logic in existing rules.
- Group—used to group related elements. It can contain any element, such as a List, Phrase, or RuleRef.
- Wildcard—used to specify which words in a phrase can be ignored.
- Halt—used to stop the recognition path.
- Skip—used to indicate that a recognition path is optional.
- Script Tag—used to get semantic information from the grammar.

The grammar editor (see Figure 2.8) contains a textbox called **Recognition String**. When dealing with complex rules, it can be used to test the rule without actually running the application. This is very useful when you are building the initial grammar set. To use this feature, just enter text that you would expect the user to say and click **Check**. The output window will display the Semantic Markup Language (SML), which is the XML generated by the speech engine and sent to the application. If the text was recognized, you will see "Check Path test successfully complete" at the bottom of the output window.

TIP: Do not use quotation marks when entering text in the Recognition String textbox. Doing so will cause the speech engine not to recognize the text.

The Script tag element is used to value a semantic item with the user's response. The properties for a script tag include an ellipsis that brings you to the Semantic Script Editor. This editor helps you to create an assignment so that the correct SML result is returned. You can also switch to the Script tab and edit the script directly. Figure 2.10 is a screenshot of the Semantic Script Editor.

When building grammars you will probably not anticipate all the responses on an initial pass. Therefore, grammars require fine-tuning to make the application as efficient and accurate as possible. This process is eased since grammar files are not compiled and instead are available as XML reference files. For this reason, you would not want to compile

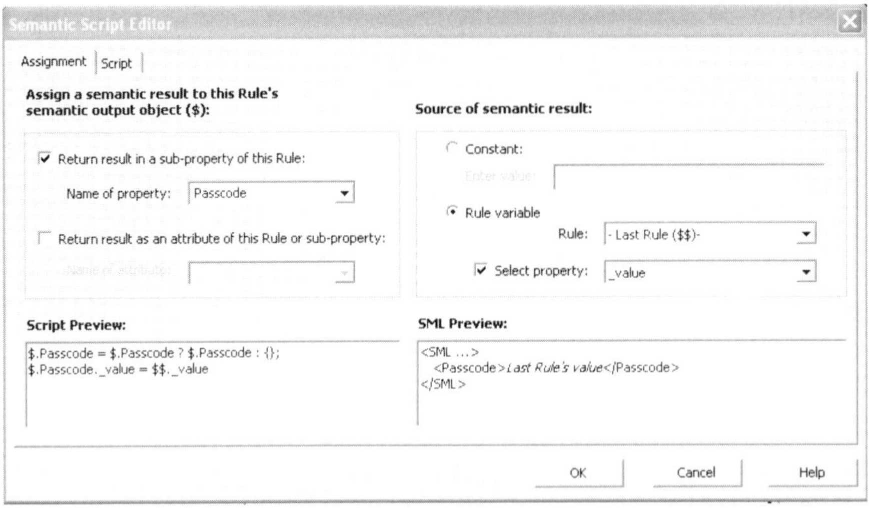

Figure 2.10 Screenshot of the Semantic Script Editor that is available when you use a Script Tag element. The Script Tag is used whenever you need to value a semantic item with the user's response.

grammar files until after the application has been thoroughly tested and is ready to deploy.

Using Speech Controls

A voice-only application has no visible interface. It runs on IIS as a Web page and is accessed with a telephone. When developing and debugging the application, it is executed within the Web browser, and the Speech Debugging Console is used to provide the developer with information about the application dialog. The user will never see the page created, so it is not important what is placed on it visually. Therefore, the only elements on the page will be speech controls, and they will be seen only by the developer.

The Speech Application SDK includes several speech controls that are visible from the Speech tab in the Toolbox. These controls will be dragged onto the startup form as the application is built. Figure 2.11 is a screenshot of the speech controls available in the speech tab of the toolbox. Speech controls are the basic units for computer-to-human interac-

Creating a Speech Application

```
Toolbox
Speech
   Pointer
   SemanticMap
   QA
   Command
   SpeechControlSettings
   ListSelector
   DataTableNavigator
   AlphaDigit
   CreditCardDate
   CreditCardNumber
   Currency
   Date
   NaturalNumber
   Phone
   SocialSecurityNumber
   YesNo
   ZipCode
   SmexMessage
   AnswerCall
   TransferCall
   MakeCall
   DisconnectCall
   CompareValidator
   CustomValidator
   RecordSound
   Listen
   Prompt
```

Figure 2.11 Screenshot of all the speech controls available in the speech tab of the toolbox. The QA control is the most basic unit and is utilized in every interaction with the user. SmexMessage, AnswerCall, TransferCall, MakeCall, RecordSound, and DisconnectCall are only applicable for telephony applications.

tion, and the SASDK contains two varieties of controls: dialog and application speech controls.

Dialog Speech Controls

Table 2.1 is a listing of the dialog speech controls used for controlling the conversational flow with the user. A QA control, the most commonly used control, represents a single interaction with the user in the form of a prompt and a response.

Table 2.1 Dialog Speech Controls are used for controlling the conversational flow with the user.

Control Name	Description
Semantic Map	Collection of SemanticItem controls where a SemanticItem control represents a single piece of information collected from the user, such as a last name.
QA	Question/Answer control. This represents one interaction with the user in the form of a question and then a response.
Command	Often used to navigate the application with unprompted commands such as Help or Main Menu.
SpeechControlSettings	Specify common settings for a group of controls.
SmexMessage	Sends and receives messages from a computer-supported telephony application (CSTA) that complies with European Computer Manufacturers Association (ECMA) standards.
AnswerCall	Answer calls from a telephony device. Used for inbound telephony applications.
TransferCall	Transfers a call.
MakeCall	Initiates a new call. Used for outbound telephony applications.
DisconnectCall	Ends a call
CompareValidator	Compares what the user says with some value
CustomValidator	Validates data with client-side script
RecordSound	Records what the user says and copies it to the Web server so it can be played back later.
Listen	Represents the listen element from the SALT specification. Considered a basic speech control.
Prompt	Represents the prompt element from the SALT specification. Considered a basic speech control.

Speech Application Controls

Speech Application Controls are extensions of the basic speech controls. They are used to anticipate common user interaction scenarios. Refer to Table 2.2 for a listing of the application controls included with the SASDK. For instance, the Date control is a speech application control that expands on the basic QA control. It is used to retrieve a date and allows for a wide range of input possibilities. Application controls can reduce development time because much of the user interaction is built directly into them.

Table 2.2 Speech Application Controls available in the Speech tab of the toolbox. These controls can reduce development time by building in typical user interactions.

Control Name	Description
ListSelector	Databound control that presents the user with a list of items and asks user to select one.
DataTableNavigator	Databound control that the user navigates with commands such as Next, Previous, and Read.
AlphaDigit	Collects an alphanumeric string.
CreditCardDate	Collects a credit card expiration date (month and year); does not ensure that it is a future date.
CreditCardNumber	Collects a credit card number and type. Although it does not validate the number, it ensures that the number matches the format for the particular type of credit card.
Currency	Collects an amount in U.S. dollars that falls within a specified range.
Date	Used to collect either a complete date or one broken out into month, day, and year.
NaturalNumber	Collects a natural number that falls within a specified range.
Phone	Collects a U.S. phone number where area code is three numeric digits, number is seven numeric digits, and extension is zero to five numeric digits.
SocialSecurityNumber	Collects a U.S. Social Security number.
YesNo	Collects a yes or no answer.
ZipCode	Collects a U.S. zip code where the zip code is five numeric digits and the extension is four numeric digits.

Creating Custom Controls

If no control does everything you need, you have the option of creating a custom control. Custom controls allow you to expand on the functionality already available with the built-in speech controls. Utilizing the concept of inheritance, custom controls are created using the ApplicationControl class and the IDtmf interface. The developer will create a project file that is compiled into a separate DLL for each custom control.

The Samples solution file, installed with the SASDK, includes a project titled ColorChooserControl. The ColorChooserControl project by itself is installed by default in the C:\Program Files\Microsoft Speech Application SDK 1.0\Applications\Samples\ColorChooserControl directory. This project can serve as a template for any custom control you wish to create. The Color Chooser control is a complex control that consists of child QA controls used to prompt the user for a color and then confirm their selection. The grammar and prompts associated with the control are built directly in. This particular control supports voice-only mode.

The ColorChooserControl is a custom control used to control the dialog flow with the user. It demonstrates what considerations must be made when building these types of controls. It is an excellent starting point for anyone wanting to create custom controls.

Debugging and Tuning a Speech Application

The SASDK provides several tools that can be used to debug and fine-tune your application. These tools allow developers to simulate the user's environment, which is important not only when developing the application, but during testing and deployment. The SASDK also includes logging and reporting tools that can be used to evaluate the impact and effectiveness of the application.

Speech Debugging Console

The Speech Debugging Console is a tool essential for building voice-only applications. It allows you to simulate the user's experience while displaying important information. Figure 2.12 shows a screenshot of the tool.

The **Options** menu allows you to toggle on and off the following: Break on Listen, Break on DTMF, Play prompts, Edit SML, and Show/Hide other windows. When building your application you will typi-

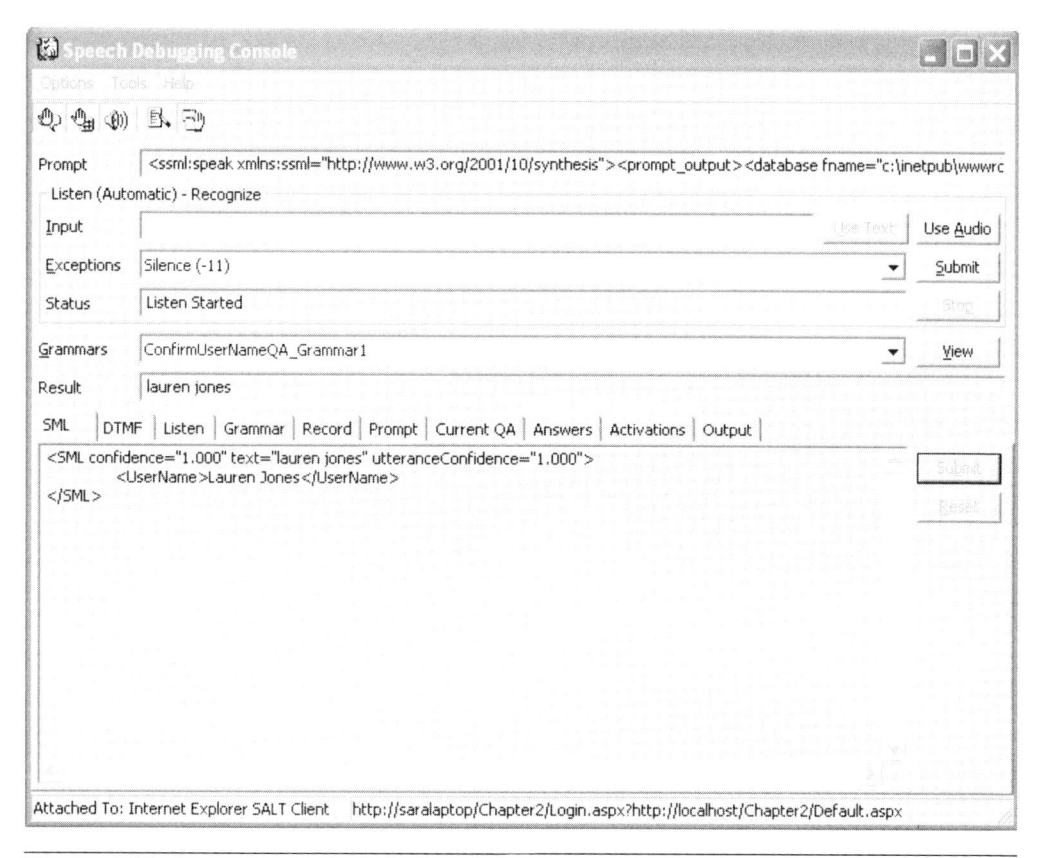

Figure 2.12 Screenshot of the Speech Debugging console after it has processed a QA control. The SML tab contains the SML created by the speech recognition engine. Since text was used instead of real speech in this situation, a confidence score of 1.0, or 100 percent, was assigned.

cally have all these options turned on. Break on Listen and Break on DTMF are important because they allow you time to inspect results within the tabs without being interrupted. Otherwise, your delays would be interpreted as silences and certain events might be triggered.

The Speech Debugging console offers the developer useful debugging information. The **Output** tab is shown by default and will contain a stream of messages returned from the Web server. These messages are critical if you experience an error or unexpected result. You can trace through the output to understand the application's dialog flow.

For each control that is activated, an entry is made inside the **Activations** tab. Whenever the RunSpeech engine tries to activate a control it places a node inside this tab. From here you can expand the nodes and determine the state of the semantic items associated with each activation step.

The **SML** tab shows the SML for the last semantic item processed. This can be useful when you are trying to determine why the speech engine did not recognize the grammar correctly. It will also show you the confidence level the item was recognized at. For the example in Figure 2.12, the confidence score was 1.000, or 100 percent. The SML tab also allows the developer to edit the SML output and therefore can be used to simulate different outcomes.

Telephony Application Simulator (TASim)

Available with the SASDK, TASim allows you to simulate the client experience for telephony applications. Where Speech Debugging Console is used to design and debug your application, TASim is used for testing and deploying it. You access TASim from the **Debugging Tools** submenu beneath the Microsoft Speech Application SDK 1.0 programs menu item. Go to **File** and **Open URL** to specify the http path to your application. Figure 2.13 is a screenshot of the Telephony Application Simulator.

When debugging telephony applications, TASim is the only way to enter DTMF input or numerical digits. The DTMF tab is not available when using the Internet Explorer Add-in client. In order to execute within TASim, a Web page must contain an AnswerCall control to initiate

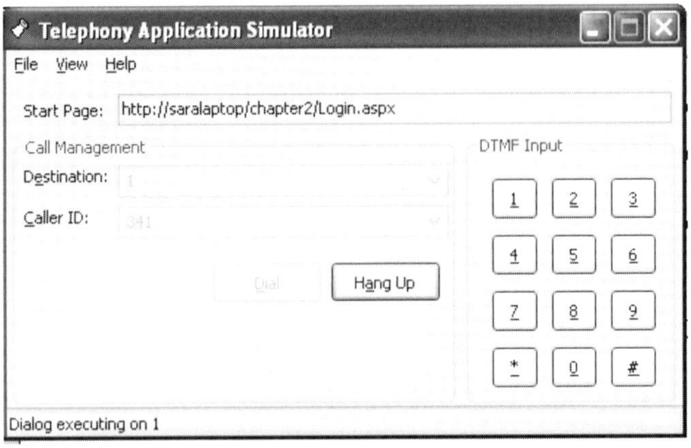

Figure 2.13 Screenshot of the Telephony Application Simulator used to simulate the client experience.

the call. With TASim, it is not necessary to install Speech Server in order to build, debug, and test telephony applications.

Analysis and Reporting

MSS provides two primary means for analysis and reporting:

1. **Call Viewer**—Allows the developer to analyze the results of one or more calls. This tool is generally used by developers to identify problem areas, such as the grammar or the confidence threshold.
2. **Speech Application Reports**—Built on Microsoft SQL Server Reporting Services, they are used to analyze data for multiple calls. Used by both developers and IT decision-makers, they include a few predesigned reports that anticipate common analysis needs.

Each call is logged to the Windows Event Trace Log and stored in a log file with an .etl (event log tracing) extension. This file is then imported into a SQL database using a prebuilt SQL Server Data Transformation Services (DTS) package. Both the Call Viewer application and the Speech Application Reports access the SQL database to analyze imported data.

Several utilities provided with the SASDK allow the developer to extract data from .etl files. In addition, the developer can install the speech application log analysis tools, available by default in the C:\SpeechSDK\Setup\Redistributable Installers\Microsoft Log Analysis Tools for Speech Application directory. This directory should have been created if you followed the instructions in the section titled "Installing the SASDK." After executing **Setup.exe**, you should be able to access the Call Viewer application by browsing to **Microsoft Speech Application SDK 1.0** and **Log Analysis Tools**.

Setting Up a Telephony Server

The Telephony Server provides the interface between the Web server and the telephone network. This enables phone access to SALT applications. For speech applications that run on a Web browser (multimodal), an Internet Explorer (IE) plug-in is available to interpret SALT tags. For telephony applications, the server itself acts as the SALT interpreter.

The Telephony Server can be a standard server machine running Windows 2003. It will include Telephony Application Services (TAS), third-party interface software, or the Telephony Interface Manager (TIM), and a telephony board. It will communicate directly with the Private Branch Exchange (PBX) or the Public Switched Telephone Network (PSTN). The telephony board provides the physical connection to the network. TAS is the piece that interprets SALT tags. And finally, the TIM is what connects the telephony board to TAS.

There are many considerations when setting up a telephony server, such as how many ports to use and whether to use analog or digital connections. You may want to consider working with a Microsoft Speech partner to set up your telephony server. This should reduce the amount of time it takes to deploy your telephony application. A list of current Microsoft partners can be found on the Microsoft Speech Server Web site at http://www.microsoft.com/speech.

Summary

- In the spring of 2004, Microsoft released Speech Server as part of an initiative to make speech applications mainstream. The Speech Application SDK (SASDK), version 1.0, is the component that allows Visual Studio.NET developers to create two types of applications—telephony and multimodal. The SASDK complies with an emerging standard, Speech Application Language Tags or SALT. SALT is a lightweight extension of other markup languages such as HTML and XML that standardizes the way devices use speech.
- Telephony or voice-only applications are accessed by a standard telephone, mobile phone, or smartphone. They can accept input in the form of spoken text or numerical digits pressed on the keypad. Telephony applications have typically been used to make call centers more efficient. The built-in controls offered in the SASDK give them the potential to offer much more.
- Multimodal applications are accessed by either a desktop PC or a pocket PC device. They allow users to select the input mechanism they prefer, whether traditional Web controls or spoken text. A speech add-in installed with Internet Explorer (IE) allows the client to access speech applications.
- There are many opportunities for voice-only applications in today's society. These applications will lower the barriers between human and com-

puter interaction. They will also provide cost-efficient alternatives to traditional information-retrieval methods. The problems that once plagued these applications are being removed, and development has been eased by tools like the Microsoft Speech SDK.

- The speech engine recognizes what the user says by applying predefined grammar rules. Although this requires more effort by the developer, it results in more accurate recognition.
- Once the SASDK is installed, a new speech application is created using the template type for a Speech Web application. Depending on the application type selected (multimodal or telephony), certain files are included by default.
- The prompt editor is a tool for managing an applications prompt database. This database contains prerecorded phrases used throughout the application to prompt the user for input. If phrases are not recorded in the prompt database, the text-to-speech (TTS) engine will speak the phrase. Unfortunately the TTS engine is not very natural sounding, so it is usually best to prerecord prompts.
- As prompts represent what is spoken to the user, grammars represent what the user says. An application consists of several grammar files that each specify a range of possible responses. This increases the efficiency and accuracy of the speech engine, since it knows what to expect.
- A series of speech controls represent the content of a single page. Since the voice-only application has no visible interface, it relies on these controls to direct the user flow. The question/answer (QA) control is the main control used; it represents a single interaction with the user.
- The Telephony Application Simulator (TASim) and the Speech Debugging Console are both used when developing and debugging a voice-only application. The TASim is used to simulate the client experience for telephony applications, and the Speech Debugging Console allows developers to view specifics of the dialog flow.
- Call Viewer and Speech Application Reports are two tools provided with Microsoft Speech Server that allow you to analyze and report on call event data. The developer does not need to install Speech Server to access these tools. They can be accessed from the Redistributable Installers directory that is part of the SASDK installation files.
- Once a voice-only application is developed and tested, it is deployed on a telephony server. The Microsoft Speech Server is the piece that allows phones to access voice-only applications. The telephony server is integrated with Windows and works to interpret the SALT tags for the application.

CHAPTER 3

Telephony Applications

Within the past few years the mobility market has exploded. Not everyone has a personal computer, but almost everyone has a cell phone. Competition has escalated, and most providers offer free phones to users who sign an extended service agreement.

The devices themselves are improving at a steady pace. Users can purchase phones that take pictures or function as a phone and a handheld Personal Digital Assistant (PDA). Providers offer a variety of service plans that include Internet connectivity for phones that function as a PDA and a mobile phone. The barriers that once limited mobile workers are lowering everyday. We have become a mobile society.

A next step to better enabling mobile workers is through speech recognition. Workers with the ability to access critical data through voice commands can react quickly and efficiently. Hands-free earpieces have enabled drivers and those people juggling multiple items to continue talking while moving. The very same earpieces can be used with cell phones or PocketPC's and the Microsoft Speech SDK to enhance traditional mobile applications.

This chapter will present a fictitious company named Slugger Sports that recently invested in a solution for its mobile salesforce. The main application does not always meet the company's needs, but management does not want to start over with a new solution. It wants to supplement its existing solution with a telephony solution.

This chapter will examine the source code for this simple telephony application. Because the SASDK utilizes built-in controls for Visual Studio.NET, very little code is needed to implement a voice-only application. Complete code along with a database file can be found on the book's Web site at http:// www.awprofessional.com/title/0321246268.

The chapter includes a case study involving a real company named GMAC Commercial Mortgage. This company recently replaced a speech application it was using with one developed with the SASDK. The new application scales better and is easier for the company's development staff to support.

Also included is a profile box which features a company selling a pre-bundled speech-based application that accesses information in Microsoft Exchange. There is also a profile box featuring a product named the Vocal Help Desk. This packaged software runs on Microsoft Speech Server and can be used by network users to reset their Windows passwords over the phone.

Creating a Speech Application to Solve a Business Problem

A Remote Business Problem

Slugger Sports produces a wide variety of sports equipment for T-ball and youth baseball games. It employs dozens of regional sales representatives who work almost entirely on the road. Eighteen months ago management had the information technology department implement a remote scheduling and ordering application. The company also purchased laptops and PocketPC devices for all of its sales representatives.

Every morning, the representatives access the application with their laptops to retrieve potential sales leads and build their daily schedule. Once the contact list is downloaded, they transfer the data to their PocketPC devices via ActiveSync. The system works great as long as everything goes exactly as planned.

Unfortunately, sales reps often encounter unforeseen glitches. Appointments may be rescheduled at the last minute or traffic jams make them miss opportunities. Existing customers sometimes ask about the availability of items they have never ordered. Quite often a representative is tipped off to a new lead during the day and feels the opportunity requires a schedule adjustment. Representatives may miss good information when new leads are added to the database after they have retrieved their daily schedules.

The representative often has to call back to the home office for information. In some cases the rep wastes time looking for an Internet connection in order to reconnect the laptop to the customer-scheduling application. The company is not willing to go back to the drawing board for a new solution, but wishes to supplement the existing one.

> **Case Study: GMAC Commercial Mortgage**
>
> GMAC Commercial Mortgage, one of the nation's largest loan originators, recently replaced a speech-based application used by its executives. The original application was used to access e-mails, contacts, and schedules from Microsoft Outlook.
> The application was a success initially, since remote executives could use it to listen to and respond to e-mails using their cell phones. Some executives were able to clear out their in-boxes while driving to work.
> The first problem was that the application was limited to twelve analog lines, so it did not scale well for the number of users who required it. Second, it was hard to debug and required that the developer make an actual call into the production server. Finally, it limited the dialog between user and application. Users were asked to speak one piece of information at a time.
> The new speech-based application was written with the Speech Application SDK and runs on a Microsoft Speech Server. The new version still allows remote executives to access their information from Microsoft Outlook. However, it can now handle a 24-channel digital T1 connection.
> The new application was developed quickly because GMAC's IT people were already experienced with Microsoft .NET. Debugging is no longer an issue since the developers can use the emulators to recreate errors and then step through the code till they locate the problem. Developers can resolve problems using their own development machines.
> GMAC likes the new application because it fits well with the company's current environment and allows it to take advantage of emerging technologies. Busy executives like the application because they can manage their e-mails and schedules no matter where they are, saving them valuable time. The new application has improved the dialog between user and application since it can now manage phrases with multiple commands.
> For more information about this case study, visit the case studies section on the Microsoft Speech Server Web site at http://www.microsoft.com/speech/evaluation/casestudies.

A Telephony Solution

The Microsoft Speech SDK (SASDK) 1.0, part of Microsoft Speech Server, enables developers to create telephony applications. These are applications in which the user will access data over a phone. This chapter will examine the source code for a telephony application built with the SASDK. The application should help Slugger Sports resolve problems with unexpected scheduling changes. It will allow sales representatives to dial in using their cell phones and to access product and opportunity information with voice commands. Because it is entirely voice based, the application can be accessed while the salesperson is driving or walking between meetings.

Since Slugger Sports is already utilizing Microsoft .NET, and the Speech SDK is free, the software costs will be minimal. Of course, there will be development costs. However, for experienced .NET developers, the time needed to develop a speech application should be lower than if a proprietary speech-development tool was utilized. Hardware costs are also small because each salesperson already owns a cell phone. The largest cost may come with setting up the telephony server.

> **NOTE:** This chapter examines a telephony or voice-only solution. Keep in mind that a multimodal solution, as discussed in Chapter 2 and featured in Chapter 4, could also work well for Slugger Sports. The company's sales representatives could use the PocketPC devices they already own to access the solution.

Loading the Sales Scheduling Database

To run the code accompanying this chapter, you will need to create a database in **Microsoft SQL Server** named **SalesScheduling**. The book's Web site contains a database file named SalesScheduling.mdf that can be attached to a SQL Server installation.

To attach the SQL database, execute the following steps:

1. Copy the SalesScheduling.mdf and SalesScheduling.ldf files from the book's Web site to a local directory on the server where Microsoft SQL Server is installed.
2. Open **Microsoft Enterprise Manager**
3. Right-click the **Databases** node and click **All Tasks...** and **Attach Database...**

4. From the **Attach Database** dialog (see Figure 3.1), browse to the directory where you copied the database files in step 1 and select the SalesScheduling.mdf file. Click **OK**.
5. Click **OK** to attach the database.
6. To see the newly added database, you will need to click **Action** and **Refresh**.

The database is simple and consists of nine tables, but two of them (Statuses and ZipRegions) are for reference purposes only. Figure 3.2 shows a diagram of the database to illustrate the relationship between tables.

Marketing and sales people at the home office utilize an in-house application to add contact opportunities to the Leads table. When a new lead is entered, it is assigned the status value of 'N' to indicate it is new. As the regional salespeople build their schedules, new items are added to the ScheduledItems table. As leads are reviewed, the value of status is changed to either 'S' for scheduled or 'B' for bypassed.

Leads become customers only after an order has been placed. For every customer, there is a corresponding lead record, but not all leads become customers. The ZipRegions table is used to group postal codes within a 100-mile radius. This helps regional salespeople identify which leads are in their area. The Statuses table contains all the possible stages that an order can be in.

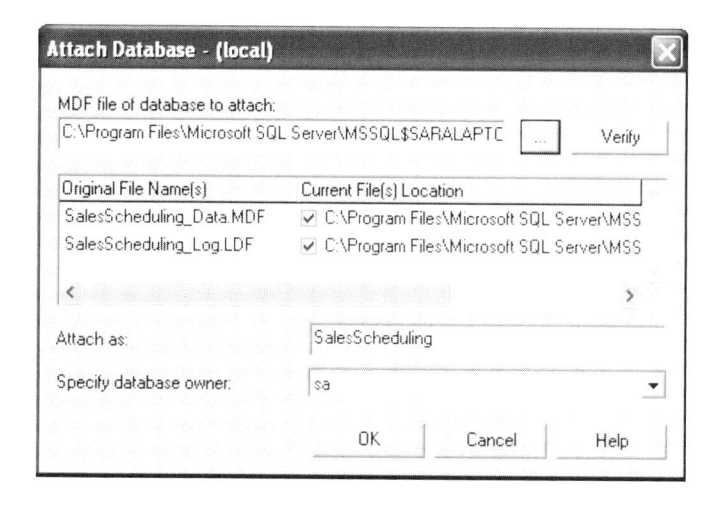

Figure 3.1 Screenshot of the Attach Database dialog inside Microsoft Enterprise Manager. This dialog is used to attach the SalesScheduling database to your local SQL Server.

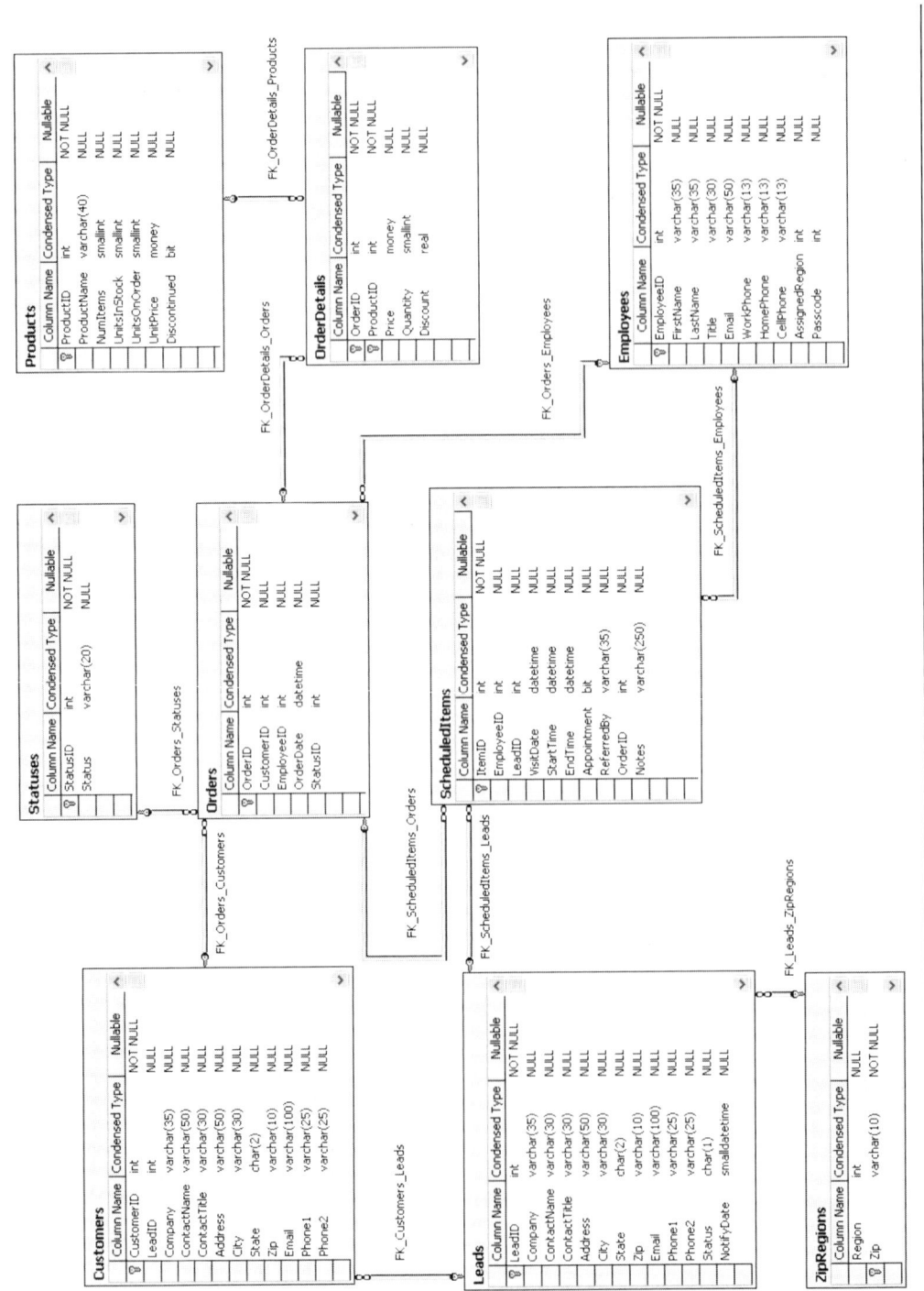

Figure 3.2 SQL Server 2000 database used by Slugger Sports. The database is named SalesScheduling. The primary table that drives the sample telephony application is ScheduledItems.

To ensure consistent data access, the application will utilize the Microsoft Data Access Application Block, version 2. Available as a free download from the Microsoft Patterns and Practices Web site at http://www.microsoft.com/resources/practices/code.mspx, the Data Access Block is one of several projects Microsoft offers. Each project contains efficient and well-proven methods for accomplishing common tasks. The application also utilizes the Exception Management Application block to log encountered exceptions to the Web server's event log.

Building a Telephony Application

Designing a User Navigation Path

Before jumping in and writing code for a voice-only application, it is a good idea to determine the exact user navigation paths. Microsoft Visio was used to design the navigation flow for this chapter, but any tool that allows you to graphically design program functionality would work fine.

The Slugger Sports application allows the salesperson to retrieve two crucial types of information: new opportunities and product information. For telephony applications, the user is guided through the application with a series of questions and answers; therefore it is important to design simple and intuitive navigation.

Figure 3.3 illustrates the possible paths a salesperson can take. After being welcomed to the system, the salesperson will be prompted to say a first and last name. The application will then repeat the name it recognized and ask if it is correct. If the response is yes, the salesperson will be asked to enter a password code.

NOTE: For the sample application, users are asked to say their first and last names in order to identify themselves. Since Slugger Sports is a small company with a limited number of salespeople, this is a viable method. For large companies that support hundreds or thousands of employees, it may be more practical to ask the user to say a unique identifier, such as an employee number.

The password code can be entered via the keypad or spoken as text. Allowing the user to enter via the keypad prevents anyone from overhearing the password code if it is spoken in a public area.

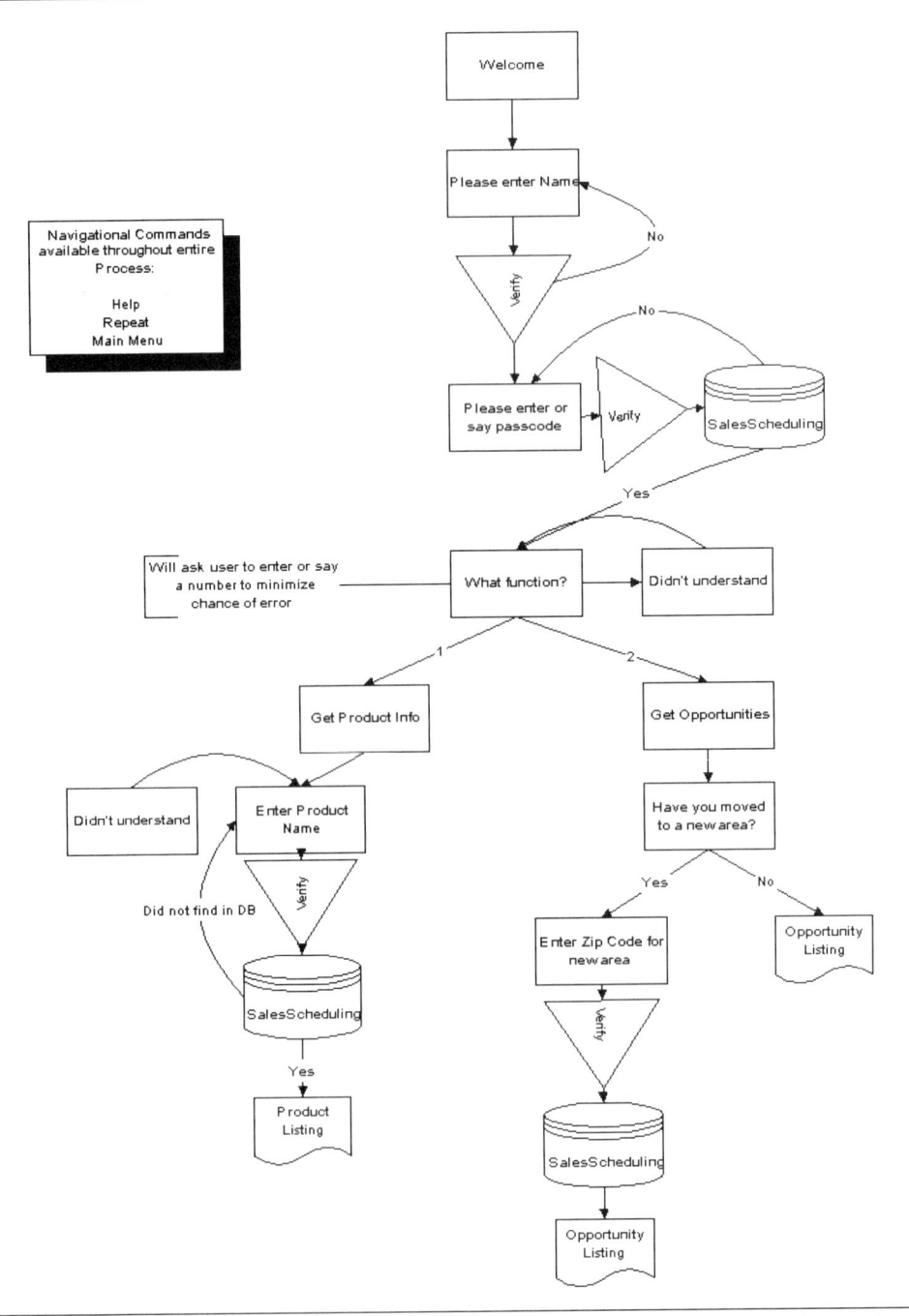

Figure 3.3 User flow for the voice-only sample application. By determining the navigation path before code is written, you can reduce the need for rewrites and determine what prompts are needed. Each shaded box represents an opportunity to both prompt a user and receive a response.

If the password code entered exists in the database, the salesperson is directed to the main menu. The salesperson is then asked what function they wish to perform. The system will list the possible functions and ask the user to respond with a

- '1' for Get Product Info
- '2' for Get Opportunities

NOTE: Asking the salesperson to specify numbers instead of complete commands reduces the chance of error. However, utilizing numbered responses instead of voice commands makes the application less natural. This is a tradeoff to consider when designing a voice-only application.

A salesperson who wishes to get product info is asked for a product name. If the product name is found in the database, all current product information is listed. This information includes the number of units in stock, number of units on order, and unit price.

A salesperson who wishes to get new opportunities is first asked whether he or she has moved to a new area. Unexpected events can sometimes cause this to happen. If the salesperson is in the same area, the system looks for all leads in that area with a status of 'N'.

All functions end with a listing recited to the salesperson. To navigate through this listing, the salesperson can use the commands Next, Previous, and Read.

Determining the flow before the code is written can help reduce the need for code rewrites. Documented flows, even if handwritten, can also help to determine what recorded prompts are needed. This can be especially helpful when designing the prompt database.

Loading the Sample Application

Table 3.1 contains a listing of the two project files that comprise the sample application. To execute the sample code provided on the book's Web site, you will need to execute the following steps:

1. If IIS has already been installed on the machine, then by default you will have a directory named C:\Inetpub\wwwroot. Create a new folder in this directory named Chapter3 and copy the contents of the code directory for Chapter 3 (located on the book's Web site) to this location.

2. You will then need to open the Internet Information Services Manager and browse to the **Default Web Site** node. Right-click the newly created Chapter3 folder and click **Properties**. From the Directory tab, click the **Create** button. When finished, click **OK** and exit Internet Information Services Manager.
3. To enable dynamic grammars (discussed later in this section), you will need to grant the ASPNET account file access permissions to the grammars subdirectory. This is done using Microsoft Windows Explorer. Start by locating the grammar subdirectory (which should be located at C:\Inetpub\wwwroot\Chapter3\grammars), right-clicking the subdirectory, and clicking **Properties**. From the Security Tab, click the **Add** button. Enter the ASPNET account name and click **OK** to return. Select the **Modify** checkbox to allow the ASPNET account to write to the files located in this subdirectory.
4. As long as Visual Studio .NET has already been installed on your machine, you can open the code sample by double-clicking the solution file named Chapter3.sln from the C:\Inetpub\wwwroot\Chapter3 directory using Microsoft Windows Explorer.
5. After opening the solution file, you will need to set the start page. This is done by right-clicking the start page, **Login.aspx**, from Solution Explorer and clicking **Set as Start Page**.

Table 3.1 Code Listing for Chapter3 and SalesPrompts, the two projects that represent the sample application for this chapter. The files can be accessed by opening the Chapter3.sln file.

Project	File Name	Description
Chapter3	Chapter3.sln	Solution file
	Components/Dynamic Grammar.vb	Contains server-side Visual Basic code used to build all dynamic grammars.
	Components/Login.vb	Contains server-side Visual Basic code used by the Login.aspx page.
	Components/ Opportunity.vb	Contains server-side Visual Basic code used by the GetOpportunities .aspx page.
	Components/Product.vb	Contains server-side Visual Basic code used by the ProductList.aspx page.

Project	File Name	Description
	Grammars	Contains all the grammar files used in the sample application. The files are grouped into subdirectories.
	Common.ascx	User control that contains commonly accessed speech controls. This file is included on most pages.
	CommonFunctions.js	JScript file that contains commonly accessed client-side JScript functions used in most pages.
	Disconnect.aspx	Web page called when the user decides to exit the program. Contains a QA control that will thank the user for calling and then disconnect.
	Error.aspx	Web page called when an exception is encountered. Contains a QA control that will play once and inform the user that an error has occurred. It will then disconnect the user.
	GetOpportunities.aspx	Web page used to retrieve a list of opportunities for a specific salesperson.
	GetProductInfo.aspx	Web page used to request information for a specific product. The user will be redirected to the ProductList.aspx page after speaking the product name.
	GetProductInfo.pf	Prompt file that contains client-side Jscript code used by the GetProductInfo.aspx page.
	Login.aspx	Start page used to login to the system
	Login.pf	Prompt file that contains client-side Jscript code used by the Login.aspx page.
	MainMenu.aspx	Web page used to navigate to GetOpportinities.aspx or GetProductInfo.aspx
	MainMenu.pf	Prompt file that contains client-side Jscript code used by the MainMenu.aspx page.

(continued)

Table 3.1 *Continued*

Project	File Name	Description
	Manifest.xml	XML-based file that contains a listing of resources that can be preloaded by Speech Server.
	ProductList.aspx	Web page used to select a product from a list and then redirect to the GetProductInfo.aspx page.
	ProductList.pf	Prompt file that contains client-side Jscript code used by the ProductList .aspx page.
	PromptGenerator.js	JScript file that contains commonly accessed client-side JScript functions used in most pages to generate prompts.
SalesPrompts	SalesPrompts1.promptdb	Prompt Database file used to hold all recorded prompts used by the Chapter3 project.

Examining the Startup Web Page

The startup page for the sample application is **Login.aspx**. This page will handle the initial validation of the salesperson by asking for a user name and password code. Validation is accomplished by executing server-side code and calling the VerifyPasscode function. VerifyPasscode, found in the Login.vb code file, executes the VerifyLogin SQL Server–stored procedure. Once validated, the user will be redirected to the MainMenu.aspx page.

The first control associated with Login.aspx (see Figure 3.4) is a user control that references the **Common.ascx** file. This control groups together the common navigational commands Help, Repeat, and Main Menu. The commands are placed in a user control so they can be reused in other pages. This group also contains Include statements that point to JScript files containing commonly used client-side functions.

The second control on the page is the SemanticMap. This control contains information about all the semantic items used on the page. Normally there will be one semantic item associated with each piece of information retrieved from the user. For the login page, there will be two: siUserName and siPasscode. Semantic items can be viewed and ed-

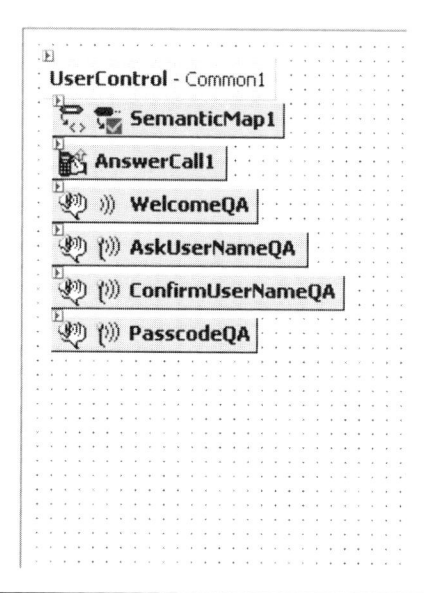

Figure 3.4 Partial Screenshot of the Design view for Login.aspx (the startup Web page). Since the sample application is voice-only, no visible controls are needed.

ited by selecting the control and clicking the **Property Builder** link inside of **Properties**.

The first control that initiates an interaction with the user is the AnswerCall control. The next control, named WelcomeQA, is used to read a welcome message one time. This control is the only one that utilizes an Inline prompt. All the other controls will utilize prompt functions. Although you have the option of using an Inline prompt for all controls, it is recommended that you not do so. Inline prompting involves hard-coding the prompt used for the control. It is inflexible and can present a maintenance problem in your application.

Using Prompt Functions

A voice-only application will typically contain several prompt functions. Prompt functions represent client-side Jscript code that is used to generate dynamic prompts depending on the flow of dialog.

For our sample application, the control that begins the first dialog with the user is AskUserNameQA. To view the prompt associated with this control, click on the **PropertyBuilder** link at the bottom of the

Properties box. Click the **General** tab under Voice Output. From here, you will see that the control uses a prompt function named AskUserNameQA_prompt (see Figure 3.5). You can go directly to the code for this function by clicking **Edit prompt function file**. You can also access the function by double-clicking the file **Login.pf** from Solution Explorer.

NOTE: By default, the SASDK creates a prompt function file (with a .pf extension) with the same name as the Web page. This is done the first time the developer clicks <New...> from the Prompt Options dialog (see Figure 3.5).

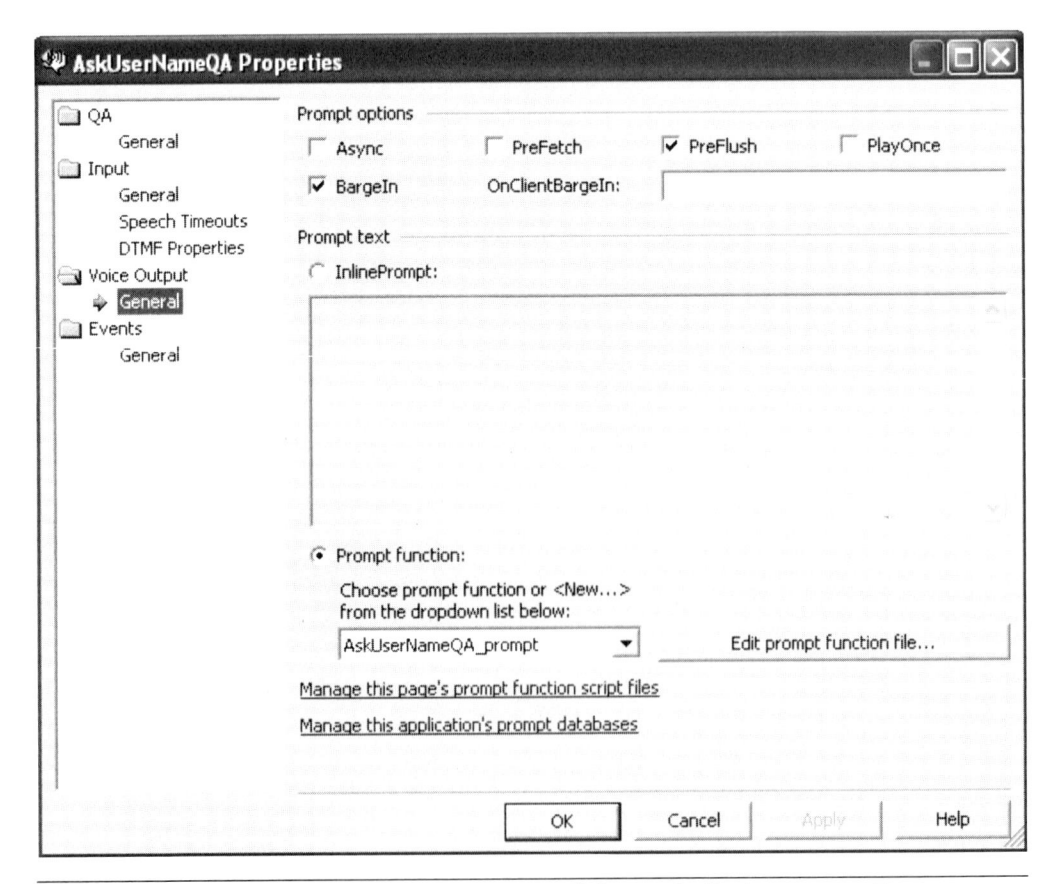

Figure 3.5 Screenshot of the Property Builder dialog as it displays properties for the AskUserNameQA control. This control uses a prompt function named AskUserNameQA_Prompt.

Building a Telephony Application

To prevent code redundancy, the application utilizes a file named **PromptGenerator.js**. This javascript class includes code used by all QA controls to generate prompts. Utilizing the Generate function makes it unnecessary to include code for handling commands such as Help and Repeat within each prompt function.

```
function PromptGenerator.Generate(History, text, help)
{

   switch (History[History.length - 1])
   {
    case "NoReco":
      if (History.length > 1)
        return "Sorry, I still don't understand you. " + help;
      else
        return "Sorry, I am having trouble understanding you. If you
          need help, say help. " + text;
    case "Silence":
      if (History.length > 1)
        return "Sorry, I still don't hear you. " + help;
      else
        return "Sorry, I am having trouble hearing you. If you need
          help, say help. " + text;
    case "Help":
       PromptGenerator.RepeatPrompt = help;
       return help;
    case "Repeat":
       return "I repeat: " + PromptGenerator.RepeatPrompt;
    default:
       PromptGenerator.RepeatPrompt = text;
       return text;
   }
}
```

The function accepts three parameters: history, text, and help. These parameters allow you to control what prompts are displayed depending on the user's response. A user who does not respond before the InitialTimeout property expires will be prompted with "Sorry, I am having trouble hearing you. If you need help, say help." For subsequent silence periods, it will respond with "Sorry, I still don't hear you" along with the help string from the calling prompt function.

Prompt functions allow you to vary what is prompted to the user depending on the situation. This helps to create a more dynamic and natural-sounding dialog. Instead of hearing the same phrase repeated endlessly, the user will get different prompts.

Building a Dynamic Grammar

The QA control represents a specific interaction with the user. This includes not only the prompt but the grammar as well. The grammar associated with the AskUserNameQA control is username.grxml. This is seen by viewing the **Grammar** tab in Property Builder. Since the user name is the name of the employee, and employee turnover at Slugger Sports is high, this grammar is created dynamically. The **username.grxml** file is rewritten every time the login page is loaded.

Since dynamic grammars will be utilized more than once in this application, a central function named LoadGrammarFile was placed in the **DynamicGrammars** class file (available within the Components folder of **Solution Explorer**).

LoadGrammarFile accepts three parameters: the file location, the node name to be used in the grammar file, and the SQL Server–stored procedure name used to access the data from the SalesScheduling database. By utilizing a central function, we do not have to repeat identical code throughout the application. Dynamic grammars will be used when requesting the user names and product names.

The following code snippet shows the contents of the LoadGrammarFile method. This method accepts as parameters the file location, the name to be shown in the SML, and the stored procedure used to access the data.

```
Public Shared Sub LoadGrammarFile(ByVal fileloc As String, _
        ByVal Name As String, ByVal sp As String)
'Define location for resulting grammar file
Dim xmlFileOutputLoc As String = fileloc

Dim sb As New StringBuilder

'Define the high level tags used in the grammar file
sb.Append( _
  "<grammar xml:lang=""en-US"" tag-format=""semantics-ms/1.0"" " _
  & "version=""1.0"" root=""" + Name + "Rule"" mode=""voice"" " _
  & "xmlns=""http://www.w3.org/2001/06/grammar"">")
```

```
sb.Append("<rule id=""" + Name + "Rule"" scope=""public"">")

'Define one-of elements which indicates a list
sb.Append("<one-of>")

Dim dr As SqlDataReader = SqlHelper.ExecuteReader( _
   ConfigurationSettings.AppSettings("Chapter3.Connection"), _
   CommandType.StoredProcedure, sp)

'Loop through the Datareader
Do While dr.Read()
sb.Append(DynamicGrammar.ConvertGrammarItem(Name, _
   dr.GetString(0)))
Loop

'Closing tags
sb.Append("</one-of>")
sb.Append("</rule>")
sb.Append("</grammar>")

'Write out the new file
Dim xDoc As XmlDocument = New XmlDocument
xDoc.LoadXml(sb.ToString)
xDoc.Save(xmlFileOutputLoc)

End Sub
```

This function builds an XML stream needed for the grammar file. It then calls the ExecuteReader function of the SqlHelper class to execute the stored procedure name passed in as a parameter. Once all the grammar items are loaded into the stream, it writes the output to disk.

NOTE: In order for the function to write the XML file, you will have to grant the ASPNET account write access to the file located at Server.MapPath(Request.ApplicationPath + "/Grammars/UserNames.grxml"). The exact file location depends on where the Chapter3 application is installed on your Web server.

The username.grxml file is necessary in order for the speech engine to recognize the employee's name. Every time the speech engine processes input from the user, it returns an SML stream that indicates what was recognized. The SML contains the text interpreted by the speech engine along with a confidence score (a score of 1.0 indicates a 100 percent confidence). Controls can be configured to only accept results above a certain confidence score. I would recommend setting an initial confidence score of .70 and then adjusting it if necessary.

LoadGrammarFile also calls a function named ConvertDataItem, seen as follows, which is used to format the record values as XML.

```
Public Shared Function ConvertGrammarItem(ByVal Name As String, _
    ByVal GrammarItem As String) As String

    ' Build the grxml <item> element
    Dim s As New StringBuilder

    s.Append("<item>")
    s.Append("<item>")
    s.Append(GrammarItem)
    s.Append("</item>")
    s.Append("<tag>$." + Name + " = """ + _
       GrammarItem + """</tag>")
    s.Append("</item>")

    Return s.ToString()

End Function
```

Other Page Controls

The sample application in this chapter utilizes a user control named common.ascx. This control is placed on every page and contains Include statements pointing to common files such as PromptGenerator.js. It also contains QA controls for our global commands Help and Repeat. Otherwise, we would have to duplicate these controls on every page. Finally, it contains a SpeechControlSettings control used to define common properties for certain types of controls.

The Semantic Map control defined the semantic item associated with the user name. The value spoken by the user is stored in a session variable named UserName and can be referenced in other areas of the code. The AskUserNameConfirm QA control is used to repeat the user name to the user and ask if the value is correct. Since it is possible for the speech engine to recognize the user name incorrectly, this allows the user to start over if necessary.

The confirmation control utilizes a grammar named **YesNo.grxml** and is an example of using the RuleRef control (see Figure 3.6). The root node for this grammar file contains references to two other rules: Yes and No. By using rule references, complex grammars can be broken down into more manageable units and then assembled into one root rule (the root rule is the one loaded by default). The rule can be referred to with the pound sign and rule name after the grammar file name. For example, the src property for the grammar tag would contain the value Grammars/Common/YesNo.grxml#YesNoRule.

The final control on the Login page is the PasscodeQA. This control is responsible for prompting the user for the password code and then recognizing the digits entered on the phone keypad. DTMF stands for Dual Tone Multi-Frequency tones, and it represents tones resulting from pressing a keypad. The PasscodeQA control references both the **Passcode.grxml** and **PasscodeSpoken.grxml** files. The Passcode.grxml file is of mode DTMF. This is specified in the Mode property for the QA control. The PasscodeSpoken.grxml file is used for spoken digits, such as "one" or "two." The application allows the user the choice of speaking the password code or keying it in via the phone pad. This helps to ensure the security of the password code when the user is in a public area.

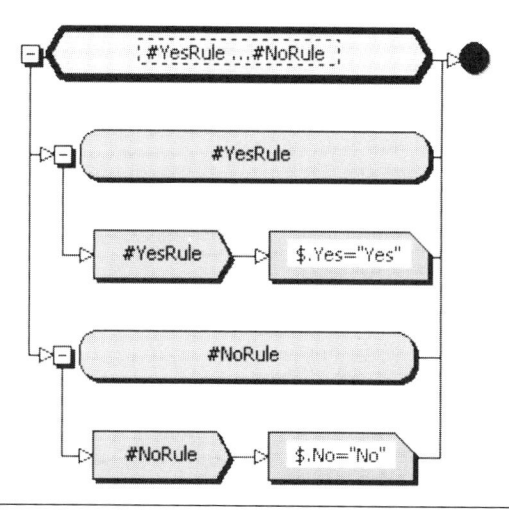

Figure 3.6 Partial screenshot of the Grammar Editor as it displays the YesNoRule. This rule utilizes a RuleRef control to reference the Yes and No rules. The rule name is preceded with a pound sign.

Figure 3.7 Screenshot of the Grammar Editor as it displays part of the PasscodeRule. This is the root rule used to evaluate the user's spoken passcode. The rule will collect six digits since the Max Repeat and Min Repeat properties are both set with a value of 6.

The root rule PasscodeRule (see Figure 3.7) for both grammars references a rule named digit. Since a passcode should be exactly six digits long, we will set the Max Repeat and Min Repeat properties with a value of 6. Once six digits are entered, the speech engine interprets the result and writes out the SML.

Posting Back to the Server

Once the last control is evaluated, a postback to the server will occur automatically, and code in the page_load (as follows) will call the VerifyPasscode function.

```
Dim _DynamicGrammar As CDynamicGrammar
Dim _Login As CLogin
Try
   If Page.IsPostBack Then
     If siPasscode.Text <> "" Then
        Dim apasscode As String() = siPasscode.Text.Split(" ")
        Dim spasscode As String = ConvertNumtoDigits(apasscode)
        Dim ipasscode As Integer = Convert.ToInt32(spasscode)
        _Login = New CLogin
        If _Login.VerifyPasscode(ipasscode, siUserName.Text) Then
           'Save this for later
           Session("UserName") = siUserName.Text
           Server.Transfer("MainMenu.aspx")
        Else
           'Reset the state b/c we are going to
           'prompt the user for the passcode again
           siPasscode.State = "Empty"
        End If
     End If
   Else
```

```
      Dim strPath As String = _
      Server.MapPath(Request.ApplicationPath _
        + "/Grammars/Login/UserNames.grxml")
        _DynamicGrammar.LoadGrammarFile(strPath, _
        "UserName", "GetUserNames")
    End If
Catch ex As Exception
    ExceptionManager.Publish(ex)
    Server.Transfer("Error.aspx")
Finally
    _Login = Nothing
    _DynamicGrammar = Nothing
End Try
```

The VerifyPasscode function accepts the values stored in the semantic items siUserName and siPasscode. It then executes the VerifyLogin stored procedure to determine whether the user name matches the password code in the database. If it does, the user is redirected to the MainMenu.aspx page.

If an error is encountered, the error handler will log the exception to the server's application event log. The application will then redirect the user to the **Error.aspx** page. The Error.aspx page contains a QA control and a DisconnectCall control. The QA control is responsible for informing the user that an error has occurred and it is necessary to contact the Main Office for further assistance. The message will play only once and then the user will be disconnected by the DisconnectCall control.

TIP: This chapter utilizes the Exception Management Application block available from the Microsoft Patterns and Practices Group. By default, the exception manager will log all exceptions to the server's application event log.

Readers interested in learning more about the different options available for exception handling should refer to the Microsoft Web site at http://msdn.microsoft.com/library/default.asp?url=/library/en-us/dnbda/html/emab-rm.asp

---

Vocal Help Desk

Solar Software (www.solarsoftware.net), located in Columbus, Ohio, was the first Microsoft Speech partner to demonstrate a working application. Powered by Microsoft Speech Server, Vocal Help Desk 1.0 allows users to access the Vocal Help Desk application by phone and reset their network passwords.

> Automating and speech-enabling this frequently required task not only frees up valuable time for network administrators, but it gets users back to work quicker. Solar Software estimates that the application can reduce calls to the IT help desk by as much as 30 percent.
>
> Network administrators can also use Vocal Help Desk to reboot servers, restart services, and disable accounts.
>
> Vocal Help Desk is just one example of how functionality exposed through the Active Directory can be speech-enabled.

The Main Menu

The MainMenu.aspx page is used to determine what function the user wishes to perform and then direct the user to the appropriate page. Only one QA control is needed for the MainMenu.aspx page. It contains a reference to the Common user control and a Semantic Map control. The semantic map holds one item: siMainFunction. The QA control for the page is named MainMenuQA, and the prompt function it uses is MainMenuQA_prompt.

The Function to Get Product Info

Function 1, Get Product Info, allows the user to say a product name and retrieve information about the product. The information that can be retrieved includes the number of items in stock, the number of items on order, and the unit price. This allows the salesperson to quickly reference the latest product information while at a customer's location.

Ordering Speech Controls

Speech controls are activated according to their order on the Web page. Another alternative is to assign a value to the SpeechIndex property for the QA control. This allows you to specify an order different from the physical order. The **GetProductInfo.aspx** page demonstrates the use of the SpeechIndex property. The ProductNameConfirm control physically resides on this page before the ProductNameQA control and by default would be activated first. The activation order for this page can be viewed by going to **View** and **Speech Controls Outline** (see Figure 3.8). Be-

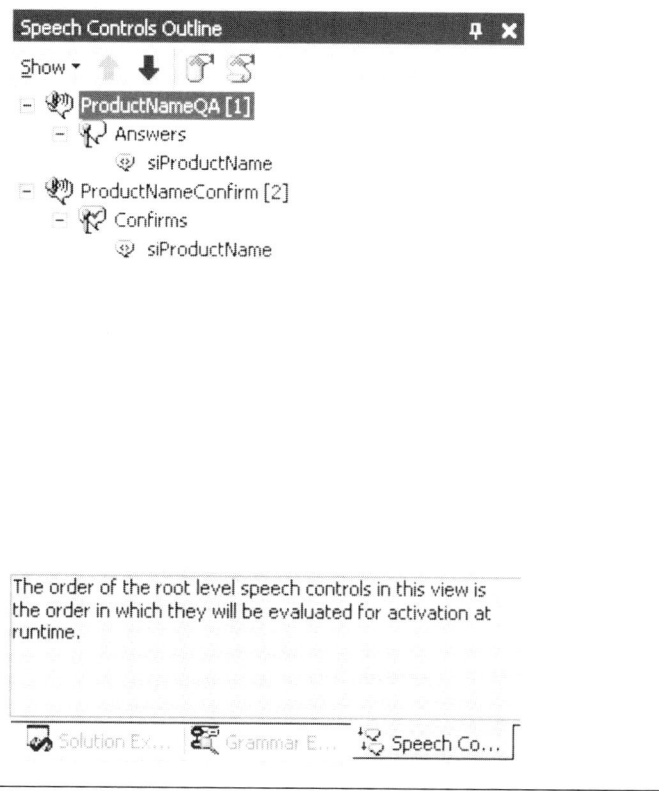

Figure 3.8 Screenshot of the Speech Controls Outline dialog box. This allows you to alter the order in which controls on a page will be evaluated.

cause the SpeechIndex property was utilized, the order indicates that the ProductNameQA control will be activated first instead.

Retrieving the Product Information

The GetProductInfo.aspx page is similar to the Login.aspx page in that it uses a dynamic grammar. This is used to get product names that are not discontinued. Once the product name is confirmed, the user is directed to the **ProductList.aspx** page. The ProductList.aspx page loads with a call to the GetProductList stored procedure, which is used to retrieve product information from the SalesScheduling database. The data values returned from the stored procedure call are then appended, as follows, into a string that is returned from the GetProductList function.

```
'Set and value input parms
Dim params(0) As SqlParameter
params(0) = New SqlParameter("@prodname", SqlDbType.VarChar, 50)
params(0).Value = prodname

'Use the parameters in a command
Dim dr As SqlDataReader
dr = SqlHelper.ExecuteReader(AppSettings("Chapter3.Connection"), _
 CommandType.StoredProcedure, MethodInfo.GetCurrentMethod.Name, params)

Dim sb As New StringBuilder
Do While dr.Read
   sb.Append("Product " + prodname + " consists of ")
   sb.Append(Convert.ToString(dr("numitems")) + " items, has ")
   sb.Append(Convert.ToString(dr("unitsinstock")) + " items in stock, ")
   sb.Append(Convert.ToString(dr("unitsonorder")))
   sb.Append(" items on order and lists for ")
   sb.Append(Convert.ToString(dr("unitprice")))
Loop

Return sb.ToString
```

The string returned from the GetProductList function will be used to assign a value to a semantic item used in the prompt function for the ProductInfoReview QA control. Finally, the user is asked whether they want to get another product. If the answer is yes, the user is redirected to the GetProductInfo page. Otherwise, the user is redirected to the MainMenu page.

The Function to Get Opportunities

Another main menu option is get opportunities. By selecting this option, the salesperson is redirected to the **GetOpportunities.aspx** page. The first question asks whether the salesperson's area code has changed. If the reply is a yes, the salesperson is asked for the new area code. Otherwise, the GetOpportunityList stored procedure is used to return a dataset containing opportunities for the current day. The data returned from the stored procedure call is then formatted and returned in a new dataset. It is this dataset that is used to populate a DataTableNavigator application control.

The DataTableNavigator control has built-in functionality that allows the user to navigate several rows of data. Navigation commands such as "Next" and "Read" are specified through control properties. This control greatly simplifies the process of reviewing data.

Building a Telephony Application

For the GetOpportunityList function, the content results are formatted as one string which is then returned as a field in a dataset (as follows).

```vb
'Split the name into a first and last name
Dim uname As String() = username.Split(" ")
Dim firstname As String = uname(0).ToString
Dim lastname As String = uname(1).ToString

'Set and value input parms
Dim params(1) As SqlParameter
params(0) = New SqlParameter("@firstname", SqlDbType.VarChar, 30)
params(1) = New SqlParameter("@lastname", SqlDbType.VarChar, 30)
params(0).Value = firstname
params(1).Value = lastname

'Use the parameters in a command
Dim dr As SqlDataReader
dr = SqlHelper.ExecuteReader(AppSettings("Chapter3.Connection"), _
 CommandType.StoredProcedure, MethodInfo.GetCurrentMethod.Name, params)

'Define a Data table used to hold the formatted results
Dim dTable As New DataTable
Dim colCompany As DataColumn = New DataColumn("company", _
  System.Type.GetType("System.String"))
dTable.Columns.Add(colCompany)
Dim colOppString As DataColumn = New DataColumn("oppstring", _
  System.Type.GetType("System.String"))
dTable.Columns.Add(colOppString)
Dim rowTable As DataRow
Do While dr.Read
  rowTable = dTable.NewRow
  rowTable("company") = Convert.ToString(dr("company"))
  Dim strDesc As String
  If dr("appointment") = 1 Then
    strDesc = "Appointment starts at " + _
        Convert.ToString(dr("starttime"))
  Else
    strDesc = "Opportunity starts at " + _
        Convert.ToString(dr("starttime"))
  End If
  strDesc = strDesc + " and ends at " + Convert.ToString(dr("endtime"))
  strDesc = strDesc + " notes are " + Convert.ToString(dr("notes"))
  strDesc = strDesc + " and it was referred by "
```

```
    strDesc = strDesc + Convert.ToString(dr("referredby"))
    rowTable("oppstring") = strDesc
    dTable.Rows.Add(rowTable)
Loop

Dim ds As New DataSet
ds.Tables.Add(dTable)
dr = Nothing
dTable = Nothing
colCompany = Nothing
colOppString = Nothing

Return ds
```

> **Voice Manager Exchange, 3.0**
>
> HeyAnita Inc (www.heyanita.com) is a Microsoft Speech partner based out of Los Angeles. It provides messaging solutions to telecommunication operators like Verizon Wireless and Sprint PCS.
> Voice Manager Exchange is one of the products it offers as part of the Voice Manager Suite. This application allows remote users to access their Microsoft Exchange e-mails, calendars, and contacts through a phone.
> This is a great way for mobile workers to get hands-free access to vital contact information while they are literally "on the road." Once a contact is located by voice, the mobile worker can dial it by just saying his or her name.
> In the case study involving GMAC Commercial Mortgage, the company's IT staff built a customized speech application to give remote executives voice access to their e-mails. For companies not able or willing to develop their own solution, Voice Manager Exchange may be a better alternative to getting voice access to e-mail.

Navigating the Application

At any point after login, the salesperson has the option of returning to the main menu page by saying "Main Menu" or ending the call by saying "Disconnect." These commands are available through the common.ascx file.

The Common user control contains four global commands that can be called from any page: Help, Repeat, Main Menu, and Disconnect. All four controls are contained within a panel Web control to identify their scope.

Since the Speech Engine will read the grammars for these controls every time a page is activated, you want to limit the number of global commands.

The MainMenuCmd and DisconnectCmd are different from the other global commands because they execute a triggered event when activated. The triggered events call server routines that redirect to either MainMenu.aspx or Disconnect.aspx.

```
Private Sub DisconnectCmd_Triggered(ByVal sender As System.Object, _
   ByVal e As Microsoft.Speech.Web.UI.CommandTriggeredEventArgs) _
   Handles DisconnectCmd.Triggered
       Server.Transfer("Disconnect.aspx")
End Sub

Private Sub MainMenuCmd_Triggered(ByVal sender As System.Object, _
   ByVal e As Microsoft.Speech.Web.UI.CommandTriggeredEventArgs) _
   Handles MainMenuCmd.Triggered
         If Session("UserName") <> "" Then
       Server.Transfer("MainMenu.aspx")
     End If
End Sub
```

The triggered event for the Main Menu command ascertains whether the public variable that stores the user name contains a value. If the variable contains a blank value, then we know the user has not been validated and thus should not be directed to the main menu page. The session variable UserName is set in the code of Login.aspx only after the user has been successfully validated.

Tuning User Prompts

The **Prompt Editor**, introduced in Chapter 2, is a tool that allows you to specify prompts and record the wave files associated with each of them. To view the prompt database for Slugger Sports, open the Chapter3 solution file and expand the node labeled **SalesPrompts**. Double-click the Salesprompts1.promptdb file.

Figure 3.9 is a screenshot of the prompt project database for Chapter 3. There are two grids in a prompt project; the top one contains transcriptions, and the bottom one extractions. **Transcriptions** are the individual pieces of speech that relate to a single utterance. **Extractions** combine transcription elements to form phrases.

72 Chapter 3 Telephony Applications

Transcription	Display Text	Has Wave	Has...
[I'm sorry but I did not find that product in our database]	I'm sorry, but I did not find that product in our database	~	O
[You asked to get new opportunities is this correct]	You asked to get new opportunities, is this correct?	~	O
[Have you moved to a new area]	Have you moved to a new area?	~	O
[Please say a zip code for a new area]	Please say a zip code for a new area	~	O
[You asked to get order statuses is this correct]	You asked to get order statuses, is this correct?	~	O
[Please say the customer name]	Please say the customer name	~	O
[I'm sorry but I did not find that customer in our database wo...	I'm sorry, but I did not find that customer in our database, would...	~	O
[Say 1 to get a listing of all orders for customer] John Doe	Say 1 to get a listing of all orders for customer John Doe	~	X
[Say 2 to look for orders on a specific date]	Say 2 to look for orders on a specific date	~	O
[Please say an order date for customer] John Doe	Please say an order date for customer John Doe	~	X
[I'm sorry but I didn't understand you please repeat the order...	I'm sorry, but I didn't understand you, please repeat the order d...	~	O
[I'm sorry but there are no orders on that date for customer] ...	I'm sorry, but there are no orders on that date for customer Joh...	~	X
[To review listings use the commands Next to go to the next r...	To review listings use the commands, Next to go to the next reco...	~	O
[At any time you may say Help Repeat or Main Menu]	At any time you may say Help, Repeat, or Main Menu	~	O
[I'm sorry my fault again]	I'm sorry, my fault again	~	O
[I heard you say] Lauren Jones [Please confirm that this is co...	I heard you say Lauren Jones Please confirm that this is correct ...	~	X
[lauren jones]	lauren jones	~	O
[russel biggs]	russel biggs	~	O
[janet marshall]	janet marshall	~	O
[Is this correct yes or no]	Is this correct yes or no	~	O
[Your passcode is a six-digit code that was sent to you with t...	Your passcode is a six-digit code that was sent to you with the in...	~	O
[If you don't know your passcode please contact the main offi...	If you don't know your passcode, please contact the main office	~	O

Extraction	Full Transcription	Tag	Wa
I heard you say	I heard you say Lauren Jones Please confirm that this is correct ...		Re

Figure 3.9 Screenshot of the Prompt Editor that includes the transcriptions and extractions used by the Chapter 3 sample application.

All the prompts listed in Figure 3.9 are associated with a wave file (confirmed with a blue squiggly-line icon in the **Has Wave** column) and marked as aligned (confirmed with a checkmark icon in the **Has Alignments** column). Alignment is the process by which words in the transcription element are matched to words in the wave file. Alignments are formed automatically when a wave file is imported or recorded using the prompt editor. If the speech engine was unable to form the alignment, then a red X icon will appear in the Has Alignments column of the Transcription pane. In these cases, the developer will want to use the Wave Editor to manually form the alignment.

NOTE: If the text is spoken slowly and clearly, there should be no need to tune prompts using the Wave Editor. In most cases, the speech-recognition engine will be able to accurately detect word boundaries. The Wave Editor will be most useful after you have deployed your application and receive feedback from the users. You may find that some users are not hearing a prompt correctly, and if so you will probably decide that an adjustment is necessary. Although you could rerecord the prompt, there may be some cases where this is not an option.

The Wave Editor (see Figure 3.10) allows you to adjust the alignment associated with a wave file. To access the Wave Editor, double-click the icon in the Has Wave or Has Alignments column for the associated element. Figure 3.10 displays the Wave Editor which lists the spoken text "Welcome to the Slugger Sports Remote Sales Application."

In this example, the text was spoken slowly and at the same volume level. The words at the bottom of the figure show what matched in the alignment process. If you wanted to listen to the recording for one particular word, you could click the arrow next to it.

The Wave Editor can be used to adjust the word boundaries, which are the starting and ending points for each word. You can mark an area to adjust by clicking and dragging at the point you wish to change. The area marked can then be moved by right-clicking and selecting **Cut** and **Copy** or deleted by selecting **Delete**.

The Wave Editor can also be used to insert an area of silence. This can be useful when a phrase was spoken too quickly and is hard to understand.

Summary

- Since so many members of today's workforce are mobile, there is a crticial need for remote applications that are flexible and easy to deploy. This chapter examines a voice-only application used by mobile sales workers via their existing cell phones. The solution utilizes the newly released Microsoft Speech SDK (SASDK). This SDK allows for two types of Web-based applications, voice-only, or telephony, and multi-modal (discussed in the next chapter).

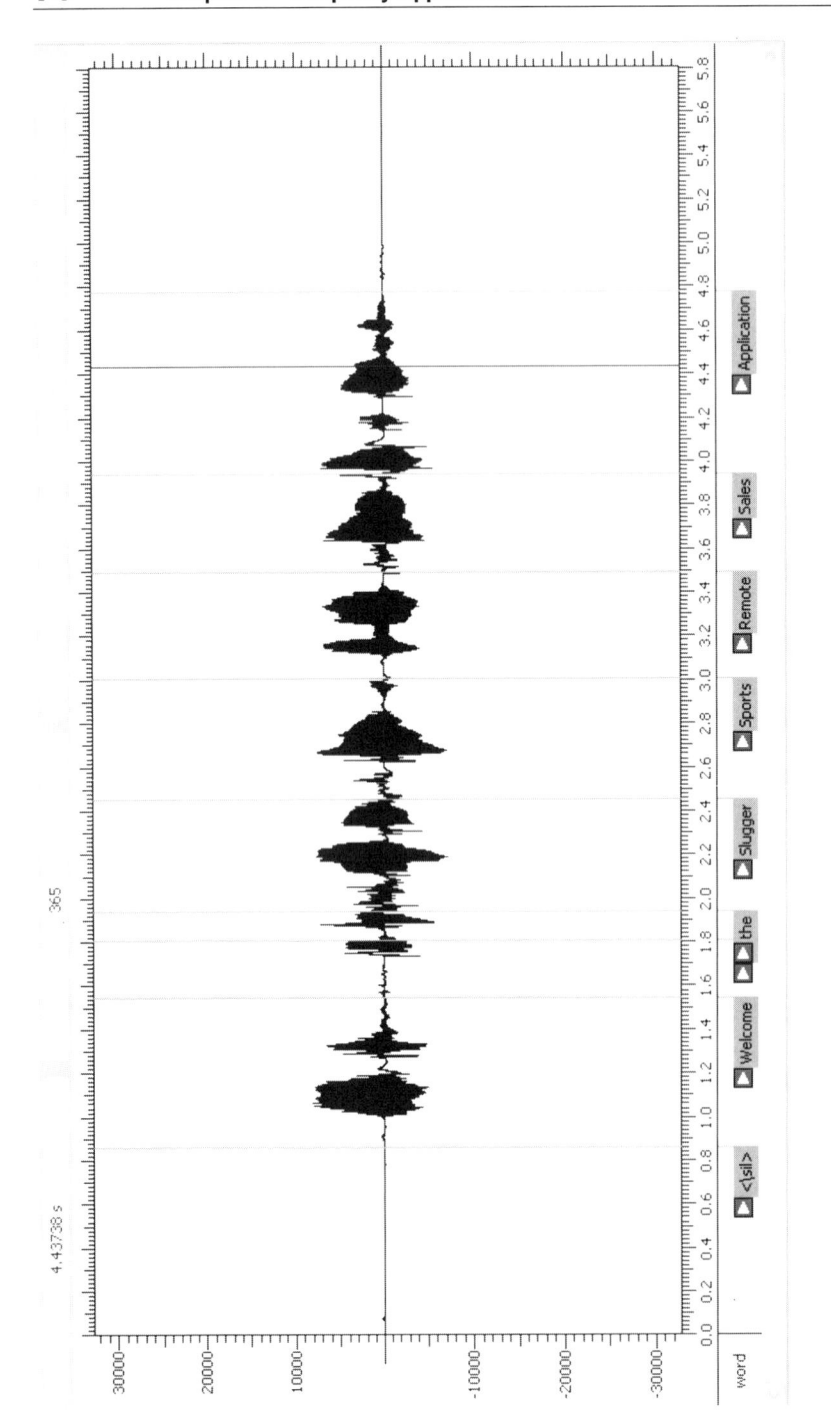

Figure 3.10 Screenshot of the Wave Editor as it displays the spoken text "Welcome to the Slugger Sports Remote Sales Application." The horizontal axis reflects time in seconds, and the vertical axis reflects amplitude.

- For the sample application, the startup page, Login.aspx is responsible for getting the user's name, verifying the user's password, and redirecting the user to the MainMenu.aspx page. From here the user is asked which one of two functions is desired: (1) Get Product Info, or (2) Get Opportunities.
- As prompts are recorded or imported, the Speech Engine automatically matches the text for each prompt with what was spoken. This process is known as alignment. Although the Speech Engine does a good job of aligning prompts, the developer has the option of adjusting these values with the Wave Editor.
- There are many opportunities for voice-only applications in today's society. These types of applications will lower the barriers between human and computer interaction. They will also provide cost-efficient alternatives to traditional information-retrieval methods. The problems that once plagued these applications are being removed, and development is eased with tools like the Microsoft Speech SDK.

CHAPTER 4

Multimodal Speech Applications

The World Wide Web exploded in the late 1990s, culminating in the presence of Web sites for nearly every company. Since then Web sites have been continually stabilized and enhanced. Web-based applications are often the preferred method of access to information. It is not enough to offer a dynamic Web site. To attract new users, you must offer something unique and customer oriented.

Chapter 3 utilized the Microsoft Speech SDK (SASDK) to create a telephony, or voice-only, application. The SASDK can also be used to develop what are known as multimodal applications. These are similar to traditional Web-based applications, but they are unique in that they offer the user a choice of input mechanisms.

Multimodal applications execute on an IIS Web server and are rendered by clients running the Speech add-in for Microsoft's Internet Explorer. There is also an add-in available for PocketPC Internet Explorer, so you can easily create speech-enabled mobile applications. What makes these applications unique is that the user is in control and can choose to utilize speech by clicking a button or icon. At that point, speech text can be used to navigate the application more efficiently than traditional point-and-click methods.

This chapter will examine a multimodal application designed for a fictional community college. The college wishes to offer students an alternative and high-tech way of registering for the upcoming semester.

The chapter also features a case study involving a real company named Landstar systems. Landstar has used the SASDK to build a multimodal application that it expects will increase call-routing efficiency and reduce agent turnover.

Why Create Multimodal Applications?

Telephony applications are the only choice for companies that wish to offer voice-only access to information through a telephone. There is, however, a growing trend toward creating multimodal applications in which the user can enter information using speech, typed text, or point-and-click methods. Interaction with a multimodal application can also involve text spoken to the user.

> **NOTE:** In addition to speech and graphical user interfaces, multimodal applications can also involve interaction through other methods, such as pens, vision, and gestures.
>
> The Multimodal Interaction Working Group is a subgroup of the W3C that is responsible for establishing standards for the development of multimodal applications.
>
> In September 2004, the group released a working draft on the use of a markup language for ink known as InkML. Readers interested in learning more about this input method can refer to the draft at http://www.w3.org/TR/2004/WD-InkML-20040928.

As opposed to telephony applications, which have been around for several years in the form of IVR's, multimodal applications have emerged just recently. This development was made possible primarily by the introduction of a wide variety of mobile computing devices, such as PDA's, Tablet PC's, and smartphones. Multimodal applications are very well suited for these types of devices because speech is an easier and more efficient method of input than a small keypad or a stylus pen.

Multimodal applications are useful for Web-based applications that need to integrate speech with traditional point-and-click methods. They are a good way to introduce speech non-obtrusively. Since there is a choice of input mechanisms, users are not forced to use only one modality. A user's decision about which input mechanism to use may change depending on the environment. For instance, if a user is in a noisy environment, speech may not be a practical choice. However, a user trying to juggle multiple items may find a hands-free access method such as speech the obvious and best choice.

The Microsoft Speech Server SDK is ideal for companies that have already adopted Visual Studio.NET as a development tool. As opposed to learning a new language or using some proprietary development tool, the company may be able to utilize code already developed when creating speech-based applications. This would be so for both telephony and multimodal applications. However, for multimodal applications, there is the added benefit of being able to add speech abilities to an existing interface.

Companies that have invested valuable time in creating interfaces that work well for their customers and employees do not want to abandon them. Multimodal applications allow developers to add speech processing to particularly well suited areas of their Web applications. By doing so they can enhance and extend the capability of their current applications.

Sunrise Community College

Sunrise Community College (SCC) is a fictional community college that opened its doors three years ago. It offers accredited college courses taught in a small-classroom setting.

Attendance at SCC has steadily risen over the past three years, but the administration would like to see it grow faster. Results from a marketing survey indicate that some students believe SCC cannot offer the same level of technical sophistication as the state university. In an effort to reverse this opinion and facilitate quicker student registration, SCC plans to offer an enhanced preregistration centered on a multimodal mobile application.

In the past, student registration took place in one day. Although students could browse through online or printed course catalogs, the final class assignments were not determined until the actual registration day. This resulted in long waiting times and many frustrated students.

SCC has already developed a preregistration system available through its public Internet site. In addition, SCC recently installed a wireless network on its entire campus. Many of the students already own wireless-capable PocketPC devices, and the number is expected to increase steadily. Allowing students to access a portion of the preregistration system through their PocketPC devices seemed an obvious next choice. However, SCC would like to make the mobile-based application even more appealing by adding speech capabilities. One day, so it is envisioned, students will be able to use their mobile devices to query the course catalog as they walk through the campus. Once they locate the courses they want, they will simply add them to their schedule. If the desired course is not available, they could add their names to the course waiting queue.

> **NOTE:** The sample application presented in this chapter is intended for demonstration purposes only. It is not meant to represent a system used by an actual college. A real college registration system would very likely contain more functionality.
>
> The sample code, available for download from the books Web site contains code with which users can login, speak a query, and review the detail for a specific course. They can then add the course to their schedule.

The application will offer options for querying the course catalog. Students can utilize traditional search methods by selecting values from drop-down boxes, or perform natural and streamlined searches using the built-in microphones on their PocketPC devices. Questions such as "Give me all available classes in the biology department that start after 6 pm" will result in both a printed listing and a text-to-speech rendering of the same list.

The SCC administration hopes that offering a technically sophisticated application will improve the image of the college. They also hope to increase student satisfaction by offering two methods for preregistration: (1) using the publicly available preregistration system already available, and (2) using the streamlined catalog search functionality available through the new mobile-based speech application

Loading the SCC Database

To execute the sample code included with this chapter, you will need to create a database file in Microsoft SQL Server named SCC. The book's Web site contains a database file named SCC.mdf that can be attached to a SQL Server installation. To attach the SQL database, execute the following steps:

1. Copy the SCC.mdf and SCC.ldf files from the books website to a local directory on the server where Microsoft SQL Server is installed.
2. Open **Microsoft Enterprise Manager**
3. Right-click the **Databases** node and click **All Tasks…** and **Attach Database…**
4. From the **Attach Database** dialog, browse to the directory where you copied the database files in step 1 and select the SCC.mdf file. Click **OK**.
5. Click **OK** to attach the database.
6. To see the newly added database, you will need to click **Action** and **Refresh**.

Figure 4.1 is a diagram of the SCC database. All current and past courses are maintained in the Courses table. Courses for the current semester are identified through the CurrentSemester field in the Semesters table. The sample application for this chapter will only be concerned with courses in the current semester. Each course is assigned a subject that belongs to one of the departments listed in the Departments table. Courses are also assigned to a unique location and a unique day pattern, such as Monday, Wednesday, and Friday or Tuesday and Thursday.

The StudentSchedules table is used to track the courses assigned to each individual student. A record is written to this table every time a student preregisters for an available course. If the student attempts to register for a course that is not available, a record is written to the CourseQueue table.

Students logging into the application will enter a unique login and a six-digit password. These values are validated against the Students table. The Student ID value will be assigned to a session variable. By default, session variables in **Internet Information Services** (IIS) will expire after twenty minutes. Once logged in, students can query the course catalog. If they attempt to browse to a page without logging in or if their session times out after twenty minutes of inactivity, they will be redirected back to the Login page.

Students viewing a specific course can attempt to add it to their schedule. If the value in the CurrentClassSize field is less than the value in StudentLimit, a record will be added to the StudentSchedules table and the value of CurrentClassSize will be incremented by 1. Otherwise, the student can be added to the CourseQueue table to be eligible for the class waiting list.

Building a Multimodal Application

Design Considerations

Encouraging users to speak commands means offering them incentives to do so. You cannot simply speech-enable a traditional point-and-click application. It is not enough to place microphone icons next to each input control and hope for the best. As opposed to a voice-only application, the user can choose to never utilize spoken commands. The application has to be designed in a manner that simplifies the process of using it if one utilizes speech.

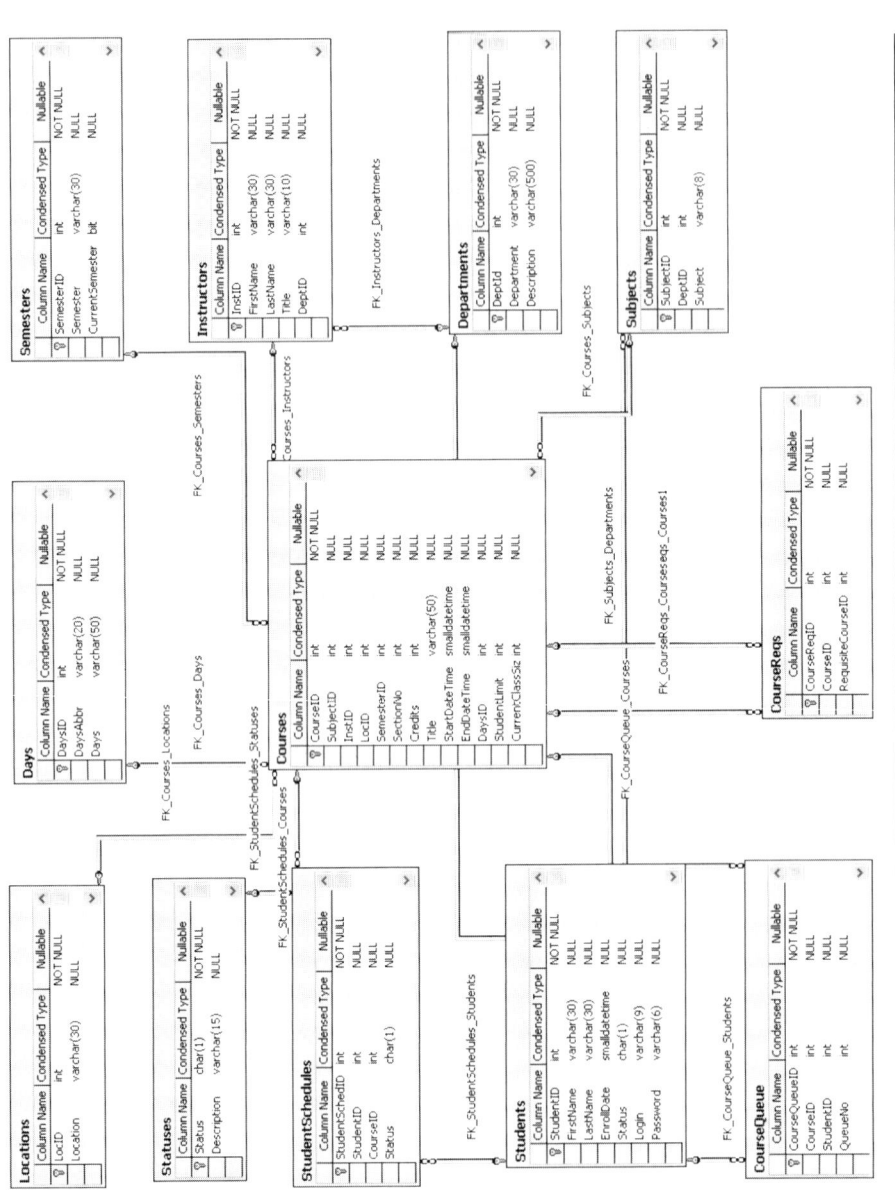

Figure 4.1 Diagram of the SCC database. The database centers around the Courses table, which contains a record for each course offered at the college. The StudentSchedules table is written to when a student preregisters for an available course. If the course is not available, a record is added to the CourseQueue table instead.

The easiest way to accomplish this is to allow users to specify multiple pieces of information with one spoken phrase. For the SCC application a user might say, "List all courses where Mr. Jones is the teacher and the classes are on Tuesday and Thursday." The alternative would be to find Mr. Jones's name in a drop-down box, type Tuesday, Thursday into a text box, and click the search button. Once the user becomes comfortable with the system, the first alternative will be much quicker. And, in the case of mobile applications, speech is an ideal input mechanism because it frees the hands from using the stylus.

> **Case Study: Landstar Systems**
>
> Landstar Systems is a national trucking company that represents thousands of independent sales agents and truck or fleet owners. Unlike the fictional company featured in this chapter, Landstar is a real business that recently developed a multimodal solution using Microsoft Speech Server.
>
> In 2002, Landstar implemented an Interactive Voice Response (IVR) solution that allowed agents to send voice messages to one another's cell phones. The system was better than the manual one the company began with but still did not address all of its business problems.
>
> Since Landstar's IT staff already had expertise in Microsoft .NET, they decided to start over and develop a multimodal application named the Compliance Inbound Assistance Application (CIAA).
>
> Built with the Microsoft Speech Application SDK, CIAA is expected to improve call-routing efficiency and reduce turnover rates. This will result in a tremendous savings for the trucking company.
>
> By allowing agents and truck owners to choose the input method that works best for them, Landstar envisions a smoother-running communication system that offers greater flexibility
>
> For more information about Landstar and the CIAA application, visit the case studies section on the Microsoft Speech Server Web site at www.microsoft.com/speech/evaluation/casestudies.

Loading the Sample Application

Table 4.1 contains a listing of the single project that comprises the sample application. To execute the sample code provided on the book's Web site, you will need to execute the following steps:

1. If IIS has already been installed on the machine, then by default you will have a directory named C:\Inetpub\wwwroot. Create a new folder in this directory named Chapter4 and copy the contents of the code directory for Chapter 4 (located on the book's Web site in the Chapter4/Code directory) to this location.
2. You will then need to open the Internet Information Services Manager and browse to the **Default Web Site** node. Right-click the Chapter4 folder and click **Properties**. From the Directory tab, click the **Create** button. When finished, click **OK** and exit Internet Information Services Manager.
3. To enable dynamic grammars (discussed later in the section "Understanding the Grammar"), you will need to grant the ASPNET account file access permission to the grammars subdirectory. This is done using Microsoft Windows Explorer. Start by locating the grammar subdirectory (which should be located at C:\Inetpub\wwwroot\Chapter4\grammars), right-clicking the subdirectory, and clicking **Properties**. From the Security Tab, click the **Add** button. Enter the ASPNET account name and click **OK** to return. Select the **Modify** checkbox to allow the ASPNET account to write to the files located in this subdirectory.
4. As long as Visual Studio .NET has already been installed on your machine, you can open the code sample by double-clicking the solution file named Chapter4.sln from the C:\Inetpub\wwwroot\Chapter4 directory using Microsoft Windows Explorer.
5. After opening the solution file, you will need to set the start page. This is done by right-clicking the start page, **Login.aspx** from Solution Explorer and clicking **Set as Start Page**.

Table 4.1 Code Listing for the Chapter4 project. The files can be accessed by opening the Chapter4.sln file. Multimodal applications, unlike telephony applications, do not utilize prompts, so there is no Prompt database project for this solution.

Project	File Name	Description
Chapter4	Chapter4.sln	Solution file
	Components/DynamicGrammar.vb	Contains server-side Visual Basic code used to build all dynamic grammars.
	Components/Login.vb	Contains server-side Visual Basic code used by the Login.aspx page.

Project	File Name	Description
	Components/Course.vb	Contains server-side Visual Basic code used by the CourseDetail.aspx page.
	Components/Review.vb	Contains server-side Visual Basic code used by the Review.aspx and ReviewResults.aspx pages.
	Grammars	Contains all the grammar files used in the sample application. The Library.grxml file contains commonly accessed grammar rules and is included by default when a new speech project is created.
	CourseDetail.aspx	Web page used to graphically display the detail information for a selected course.
	Header.ascx	User control included at the top of each Web page and containing the "SCC Online Registration" header banner. This control also contains code that checks to see if the session variable containing the Student ID is valued. If it is not, and the page is not the Login page, the user is redirected to the Login page and asked to login.
	Login.aspx	Web page used to login to the application. Once validated, the user is redirected to the MainMenu.aspx page.
	Manifest.xml	XML-based file that contains a listing of resources that can be preloaded by Speech Server.
	Review.aspx	Web page displayed when the user clicks "Search Courses" from the MainMenu.aspx page. For the sample application in this chapter, this is one of two pages that contain speech controls. This page also is used to list all courses resulting from the user's search query. The results are spoken back to the user and also displayed in a Datagrid Web control.

Examining the Sample Web Pages

Login.aspx simply retrieves the login and password and then validates the student against the database. This page does not offer speech as an input option. The reason is that the login is private information and someone might overhear the login and password being spoken. Once it is confirmed that the student is in the database and has an active status, they are redirected to the **MainMenu.aspx** page.

TIP: Readers executing the sample application can use the following login and password values to login:

Login – JONESA
Password – 030478

The main menu, which offers only two choices, Query Course Catalog and View My Schedule, is also not an appropriate place for speech processing. It is just as fast for the user to click a button as to speak a command phrase.

Main Query Page

The query page (**Review.aspx**), however, is a good place to offer speech capabilities. Available when the user clicks Query Course Catalog, this page offers five options to narrow the search: course title, department, instructor, days, and start time. Figure 4.2 is a screenshot of the Review.aspx page as it appears on the client device. From this page, the student can click the **Speak Query** button and begin speaking a query. The sample application allows a combination of two of the search criteria.

NOTE: It would have been possible to allow for more combinations, but this would have expanded the size and complexity of the grammar file. For demonstration purposes, we held to a limit of two combinations.

When designing a grammar file, developers should consider the size of the grammar file. A large grammar file is cumbersome to debug. Moreover, even when preloaded, it may slow the processing of the Web application. This is a tradeoff to consider when designing applications of this type.

For tips on how to write effective grammars, refer to the Technical FAQ's section of the Microsoft Speech Web site at http://www.microsoft.com/speech/techinfo/faq/speechsdk.asp.

Creating a Query Script

Building grammars with the Grammar editor was introduced in Chapter 2. This chapter utilizes a complex grammar for querying the course catalog. It can be helpful to make a list of possible queries before beginning the grammar-building process.

Figure 4.2 Screenshot of the Query Course Catalog page, Review.aspx. To speak a query, the user must click the Speak Query button. The student can also listen to detailed instructions by clicking the Instructions button.

Listing 4.1 lists potential queries for the **Review.aspx** page. Brainstorming a list of queries helps to identify the complexity of the grammar. Creating such a list also provides a testing script that can be used later to confirm the grammar rules.

NOTE: The queries in Listing 4.1 are meant to identify the different forms that queries can take and not every conceivable query that could be produced.

Controls Used on the Query Page

The Query Page, **Review.aspx,** contains Listen and Prompt controls. These controls are hidden from the user, but are activated when the user clicks one of two command buttons. When a user clicks the **Speak Query**

Listing 4.1 Potential search queries

```
I want all courses for Financial Accounting 1
List classes where Doctor Jones is the teacher
List all classes for Jan Jessup that start before nine a.m.
Give me classes starting after two o'clock
List all classes in the English department
Show classes on Tuesday and Thursday that start after noon
List Business classes scheduled for Monday, Wednesday and Friday
List all classes in the Math department that start after six p.m.
```

button, a client-side Jscript function is used to invoke the Start method for the Listen control.

```
function SpeakQuery() {
    Listen1.Start();
}
```

As opposed to the voice-only application in Chapter 3, the multimodal application relies on visible controls and not prompts to initiate dialogs. An exception is the instructional prompt, available when the user clicks the Instructions button.

Instructional prompts are useful for providing detailed information to the user and minimizing the amount of screen space necessary for such instructions. When the user clicks **Instructions** on Review.aspx, the Prompt control is initialized and the following text is read to the user:

> To search the catalog with a spoken question, first click the Speak Query button. You may then ask a question, such as Show me classes where Doctor Davis is the instructor or List all classes in the English department scheduled for Tuesday and Thursday.

Understanding the Grammar

The Listen control uses a grammar file to identity valid user responses. For the query page, the Listen control references the SpeakQuery.grxml grammar file. The root rule for this grammar is named TopLevel. It is referenced in the src property for the grammar control as follows:

```
<speech:Grammar Src="Grammars/SpeakQuery.grxml#TopLevel"
            ID="Listen1_Grammar1">
```

To keep the grammar file organized and readable, it is broken down into component grammar files. The additional grammars are then referenced through RuleRef elements. Since there are five query choices, each is represented by a separate grammar file.

Most of the grammar files are built dynamically because they involve matching values in a changing database. Introduced in Chapter 3, dynamic grammars involve the creation of XML-based grammar files at the time of application execution. This is useful when the grammar contains content that is likely to change. As opposed to grammar files designed by

Building a Multimodal Application

the developer using the Grammar Editor, dynamic grammars are rewritten as often as necessary. The following code is used to build grammar files containing department names:

```
'** Example of programmatically defining the grammar

Dim sb As New StringBuilder

'Define the high level tags used in the grammar file
 sb.Append( _
  "<grammar xml:lang=""en-US"" tag-format=""semantics-ms/1.0"" " _
  & "version=""1.0"" root=""" + Name + "Rule"" mode=""voice"" " _
  & "xmlns=""http://www.w3.org/2001/06/grammar"">")
 sb.Append("<rule id=""" + Name + "Rule"" scope=""public"">")

'Define one-of elements which indicates a list
sb.Append("<one-of>")

Dim dr As SqlDataReader = SqlHelper.ExecuteReader( _
  AppSettings("Chapter4.Connection"), _
  CommandType.StoredProcedure, sp)

'Loop through the Datareader
Dim _DynamicGrammar As New DynamicGrammar
Do While dr.Read()
  sb.Append(_DynamicGrammar.ConvertGrammarItem(Name, _
    dr.GetString(0), dr.GetValue(1)))
Loop
_DynamicGrammar = Nothing

'Closing tags
sb.Append("</one-of>")
sb.Append("</rule>")
sb.Append("</grammar>")

'Write out the new file
Dim xDoc As XmlDocument = New XmlDocument
xDoc.LoadXml(sb.ToString)
xDoc.Save(fileloc)

'release resources
If Not dr.IsClosed Then
   dr.Close()
```

```
End If
dr = Nothing
sb = Nothing
```

The dynamic grammar code is used to create an XML-based file that if viewed with a text-editor would appear as follows:

```
<grammar xml:lang="en-US" tag-format="semantics-ms/1.0"
version="1.0" root="DepartmentRule" mode="voice"
xmlns="http://www.w3.org/2001/06/grammar">
  <rule id="DepartmentRule" scope="public">
    <one-of>
      <item>
        <item>Business</item>
        <tag>$.Department = "5"</tag>
      </item>
      <item>
        <item>English</item>
        <tag>$.Department = "4"</tag>
      </item>
      <item>
        <item>Liberal Arts</item>
        <tag>$.Department = "2"</tag>
      </item>
      <item>
        <item>Math</item>
        <tag>$.Department = "1"</tag>
      </item>
      <item>
        <item>Science</item>
        <tag>$.Department = "3"</tag>
      </item>
    </one-of>
  </rule>
</grammar>
```

To improve scalability, the grammar files will be built once the application session is initialized, as opposed to every time the query page is loaded. In the page_load function for Review.aspx, a public variable named blnQueryGrammarsLoaded is checked. If it contains a value of false, the dynamic grammars for title, department, and instructors are built and the session variable is assigned a value of true.

Preambles and Postambles

Since the user's query will probably be phrased as a question, the grammar needs to account for unnecessary language. In the phrase "List classes where Doctor Jones is the teacher," the application is only interested in "Doctor Jones" and not the other words in the phrase. Optional words in a spoken phrase are known as preambles and postambles. A special grammar file is created for each of these.

In the case of preambles, the PreambleRule contains three optional lists that contain possible words or subphrases. In Visual Studio.NET, the PreambleRule can be viewed by double-clicking the **QueryPreamble .grxml** file in the Grammars subdirectory of **Solution Explorer**. From the Grammar Explorer window, double-click PreambleRule.

Figure 4.3 shows the contents of the PreambleRule. Note that a circular icon and the numbers 0..1 appear at the top of the list. This indicates that the entire list is optional. All three lists are optional for this rule. To specify an optional element, the Max Repeat property is set to 1 and the Min Repeat property is set to 0.

The preamble rule should be used with other rules in which the phrases are not optional. In this manner, spoken phrases that include any of the members in the PreambleRule will still be recognized. The recognition engine will consider the phrase valid and will not include the optional words as part of the SML passed back to the application.

For example, if the user spoke the query "Give me all classes for Doctor Davis," the following SML would be returned:

```
<SML confidence="1.000" text="Give me all classes for Doctor Davis" utteranceConfidence="1.000">
    <Instructor confidence="1.000">
        <InstructorTitle>Doctor</InstructorTitle>
        <InstructorLastName>Davis</InstructorLastName>
    </Instructor>
</SML>
```

In this case, the query was typed into the Recognition string textbox inside the Grammar editor. Therefore, the speech recognition engine ranked the confidence score as 1.000, or 100 percent. The confidence score is a value ranging from zero to one. It indicates how confident the speech recognizer is that the result was interpreted accurately. Since the result was typed in and not spoken, we can expect the confidence to be at the highest level, or 1.000. If you used a microphone to speak the query

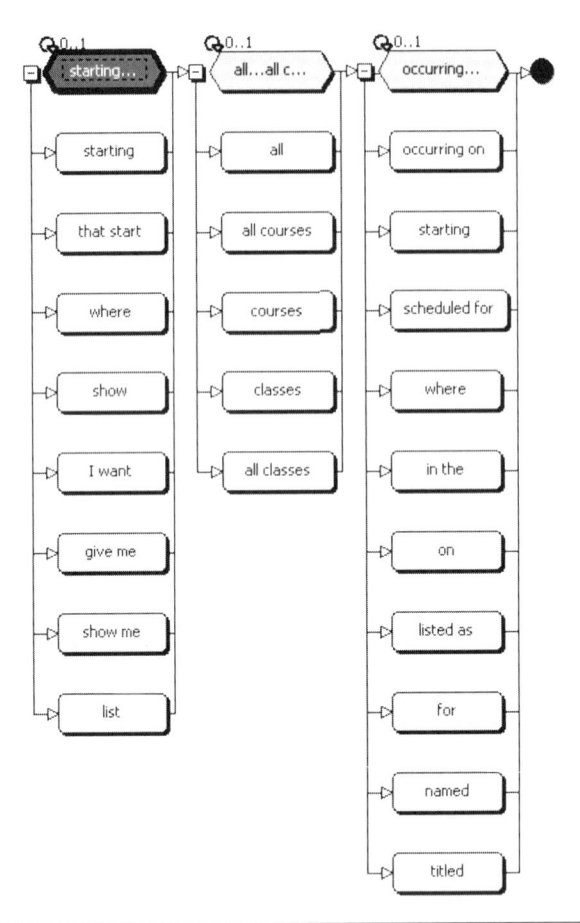

Figure 4.3 Screenshot of the PreambleRule as seen in the Grammar Editor inside Visual Studio. Preambles represent optional words spoken at the beginning or middle of a student's query.

while debugging the application using the Speech Debugging Console, the result may be lower. The exact value will depend on the quality of the microphone, the speaker's clarity, and the level of background noise.

The SML also contains values for two semantic items, InstructorTitle and InstructorLastName. Alternatively, if the user spoke the query "Courses for Doctor Davis," the same two semantic items would be returned. In the case of the second query, items from only two of the lists used in the preamble rule were considered. This is because all three of the lists that appear in the preamble rule are optional (as indicated by the circular icon and the numbers 0..1). In the first query, "List all classes for Doctor Davis": "List," "all classes," and "for" are items in each of the three lists. In the second query, "Courses for Doctor Davis," we only look at items from the second and third lists. Both queries are valid because the preamble rule does not require any of the items to be present.

The PostambleRule, part of the QueryPostamble.grxml file, works in much the same way as the PreambleRule. In this case, optional words are spoken after the key words. Since these words are optional, a phrase such as "Doctor Davis please" is considered just as valid as "List all classes for Doctor Davis."

Base Rules

The TitleRule, DepartmentRule, InstructorRule, DayRule, and StartTimeRule are base rules included in SpeakQuery.grxml. For each of the page elements, such as title and department, there is a corresponding base rule. If you look at the TitleQuery rule in grammar editor (see Figure 4.4), you will see that the PreambleRule and PostambleRule are both referenced. The TitleRule, which lies in the middle, is dynamically built and contains an entry for each current course title in the database.

Once the base rules were built, the TopLevel rule was formed with different combinations of the base rules (see Figure 4.5). In the "Design Considerations" section it was established that the application would allow the student to combine no more than two search criteria. Since the student could combine each pair of criteria in two different ways, several different combinations would have to be accounted for. For example, the student could choose to ask for title and then days or days and then title. Alternatively, the student could request a single criterion, such as instructor.

All together there are twenty-five possible combinations. Each combination is represented in the TopLevel rule, as seen in Figure 4.5. The list element at the top of the editor contains all twenty-five subrules. The first five represent searches that include only one criterion. The next twenty are combinations of two search criteria.

From here, all possible phrases can be tested inside the grammar editor. Phrases from the potential search query list created in the section titled "Creating a Query Script" can be entered into the recognition string textbox. If the phrase is valid, the SML will appear in the output window. If an error is encountered or the phrase is not recognized, an error message will appear in the output window.

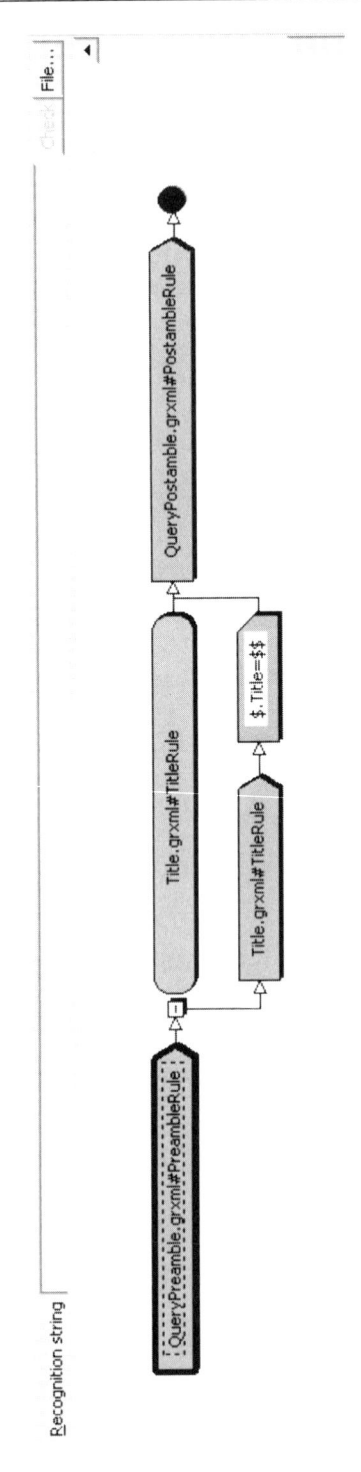

Figure 4.4 Screenshot of the grammar editor as it displays the TitleQuery rule which is referenced in SpeakQuery.grxml.

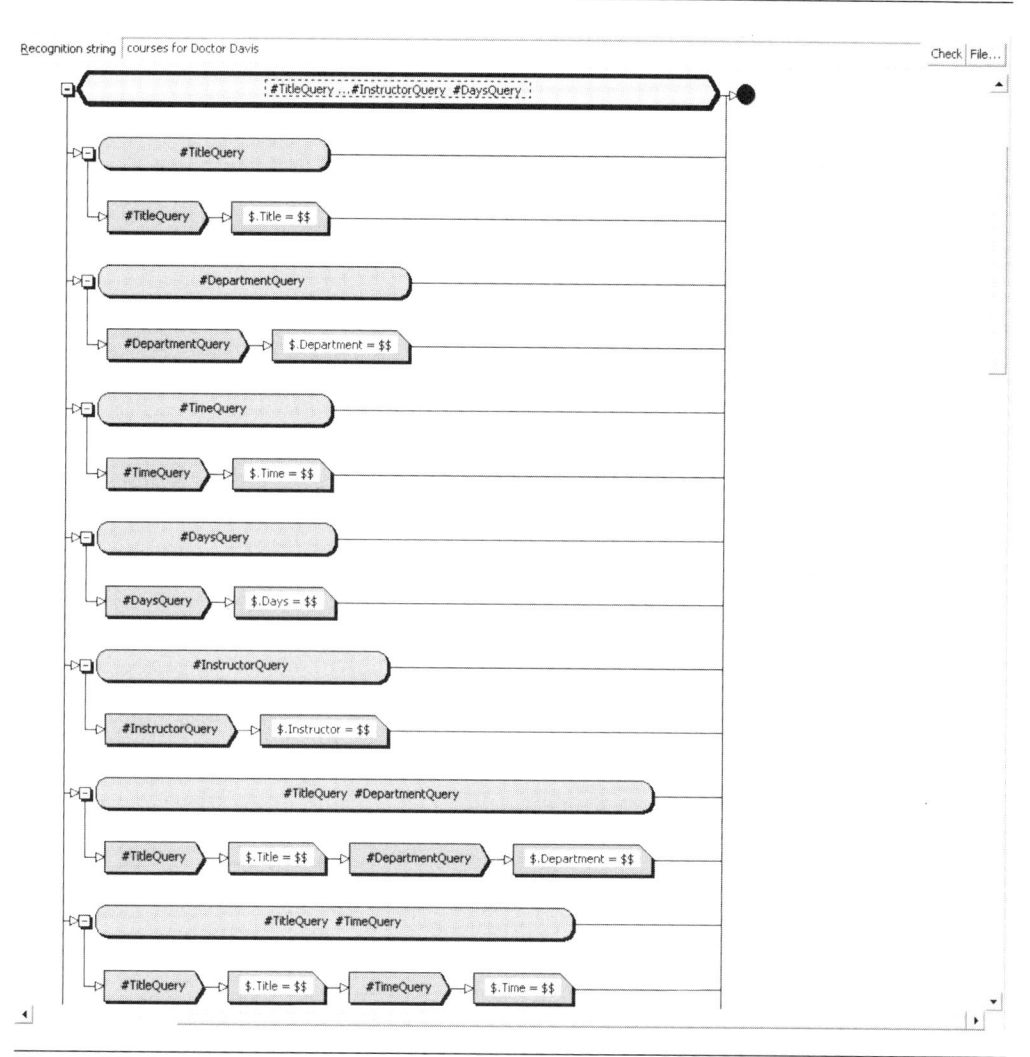

Figure 4.5 Screenshot of the grammar editor as it displays the TopLevel rule. Phrases can be tested directly from here through the recognition string.

Retrieving Query Results

Using Speech Debugging Console

Readers executing the sample application will notice that the **Speech Debugging Console** application is initiated when Review.aspx is first loaded. A query can be spoken only after the user clicks the **Speak Query** button.

At that point a client-side Jscript function is used to invoke the Start method for the Listen control. Readers should then notice that the background of the Input textbox in the Speech Debugging Console will change to white, which indicates that the textbox is available (see Figure 4.6). At this point, a query can be typed into the Input textbox and submitted by clicking the **Use Text** button. Alternatively, readers with a microphone can choose to click the **Use Audio** button and speak their query.

Setting Values for Semantic Items

When a query is spoken (which means that the user has clicked Speak Query), the search criteria will come from semantic items instead of Web

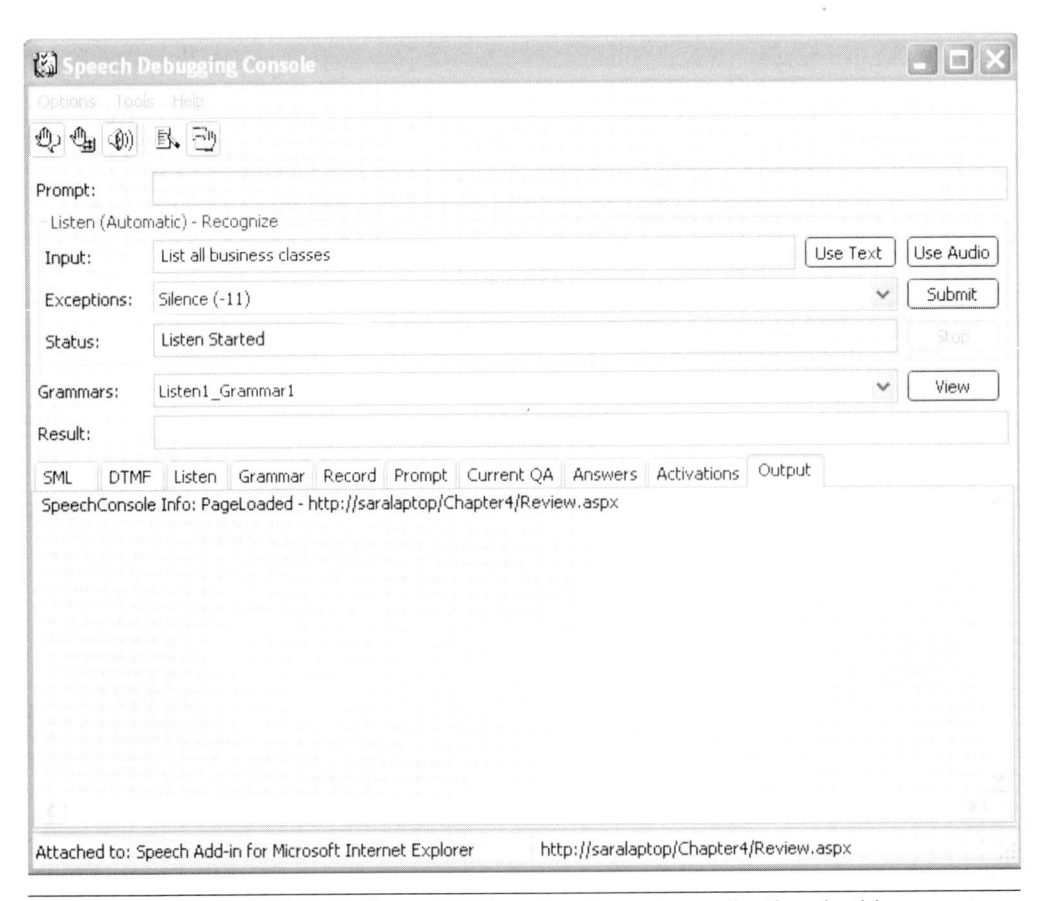

Figure 4.6 Screenshot of the Speech Debugging Console application. In this screenshot the user has typed the query "List all business classes." To submit this query, the user will need to click Use Text.

Building a Multimodal Application

controls. The Bindings collection stores the semantic items for Review.aspx, as seen below. The collection contains separate items for each criterion. You can edit or view the Bindings collection for the Listen control by right-clicking the control from Design view and selecting the ellipsis for the Bindings property. Alternatively, you can view the collection through the HTML tab for the Designer view. The HTML code containing the Listen control is as follows:

```
<speech:listen id="Listen1"
   style="Z-INDEX: 101; LEFT: 16px; POSITION: absolute; TOP: 256px"
   runat="server" AutoPostBack="true">
  <Grammars>
<speech:Grammar Src="Grammars/SpeakQuery.grxml#TopLevel"
      ID="Listen1_Grammar1">
</speech:Grammar>
 </Grammars>
 <Bindings>
   <speech:Bind TargetAttribute="value" Value="SML/Title/Title/Title"
     TargetElement="txtTitle"></speech:Bind>
   <speech:Bind TargetAttribute="value"
      Value="SML/Department/Department/Department"
      TargetElement="cboDept"></speech:Bind>
   <speech:Bind TargetAttribute="value"
    Value="SML/Instructor/Instructor/InstructorTitle"
    TargetElement="txtInstTitle"></speech:Bind>
   <speech:Bind TargetAttribute="value"
    Value="SML/Instructor/Instructor/InstructorFirstName"
    TargetElement="txtInstFName"></speech:Bind>
   <speech:Bind TargetAttribute="value"
    Value="SML/Instructor/Instructor/InstructorLastName"
    TargetElement="txtInstLName"></speech:Bind>
   <speech:Bind TargetAttribute="value" Value="SML/Days/Days/Day1"
     TargetElement="txtDay1"></speech:Bind>
   <speech:Bind TargetAttribute="value"
    Value="SML/Days/Days/Day2" TargetElement="txtDay2"></speech:Bind>
   <speech:Bind TargetAttribute="value"
    Value="SML/Days/Days/Day3" TargetElement="txtDay3"></speech:Bind>
   <speech:Bind TargetAttribute="value"
    Value="SML/Time/Time/Operator"
    TargetElement="txtOperator"></speech:Bind>
   <speech:Bind TargetAttribute="value"
    Value="SML/Time/Time/Time/Hour"
     TargetElement="txtHour"></speech:Bind>
   <speech:Bind TargetAttribute="value"
```

```
    Value="SML/Time/Time/Time/Minute"
     TargetElement="txtMinute"></speech:Bind>
 </Bindings>
</speech:listen>
```

Note that the criteria for Instructor, indicated by the bolded items, are broken into three semantic items: InstructorTitle, InstructorFirstName, and InstructorLastName. This results in more data values being collected.

Executing the Search

The Search routine, seen as follows, will execute a different version of the overloaded method QueryCourses depending on whether the query was spoken or typed in. If the query was spoken, the method will be passed additional parameters. Additional parameters are necessary to account for all the semantic item values.

```
Dim ds As DataSet
Dim _Review As CReview
Try
  pnlSearch.Visible = False
  pnlResults.Visible = True
  _Review = New CReview
  If bSpoken = False Then
    'The user just typed in their query
    ds = _Review.QueryCourses(txtTitle.Text, _
     cboDept.SelectedValue.ToString, _
     cboInstructor.SelectedValue.ToString, _
     cboDays.SelectedValue.ToString, _
     cboStartTime.SelectedValue.ToString)
  Else
    'The user spoke their query
    Dim strDays As String
    strDays = txtDay1.Text + txtDay2.Text + txtDay3.Text
    ds = _Review.QueryCourses(txtTitle.Text, _
     cboDept.SelectedValue.ToString, _
     txtInstTitle.Text, txtInstFName.Text, _
     txtInstLName.Text, strDays, txtOperator.Text, _
     txtHour.Text, txtMinute.Text)
    If ds.Tables(1).Rows.Count > 0 Then
       DataTableNavigator1.DataSource = ds.Tables(1)
       DataTableNavigator1.DataBind()
    End If
```

```
      End If
      grdResults.DataSource = ds.Tables(0)
      grdResults.DataKeyField = "courseid"
      grdResults.DataBind()
      If ds.Tables(0).Rows.Count = 0 Then
        lblError2.Text = "No records were found matching "
        lblError2.Text = lblError2.Text + "the search criteria."
      End If
Catch ex As Exception
      ExceptionManager.Publish(ex)
      pnlSearch.Visible = True
      pnlResults.Visible = False
      lblError1.Text = "Were sorry, but we were unable to "
      lblError1.Text = lblError1.Text + "complete the search. "
      lblError1.Text = lblError1.Text + "Please contact the "
      lblError1.Text = lblError1.Text + "Registration Office."
Finally
      ds = Nothing
      _Review = Nothing
End Try
```

The overloaded version of the QueryCourses method (used to handle a spoken query) will first build a string based on values passed in as parameters. The resulting string will then be passed to the QueryCourses stored procedure and will represent the WHERE clause used to query the database. The code to build the WHERE string is seen as follows:

```
Dim sWhere As String = ""
' Create a where clause that will be passed to the
' QueryCourses stored procedure
If Title <> "" Then
  sWhere = " and c.title LIKE ''%" + Title + "%''"
End If
If DeptID <> "" Then
  sWhere = sWhere + " and d.deptid = " + DeptID
End If
If InstTitle <> "" Then
  sWhere = sWhere + " and i.title = ''" + InstTitle + "''"
End If
If InstFName <> "" Then
  sWhere = sWhere + " and i.firstname = ''" + InstFName + "''"
End If
If InstLName <> "" Then
```

```
  sWhere = sWhere + " and i.lastname = ''" + InstLName + "''"
End If
If Days <> "" Then
  sWhere = sWhere + " and dy.daysabbr = ''" + Days + "''"
End If
If Operator <> "" Then
  If Operator = "gt;" Then
    sWhere = sWhere + " and c.starttime >= ''" + _
    Hour + ":" + Minute + "''"
  ElseIf Operator = "lt;" Then
    sWhere = sWhere + " and c.starttime <= ''" + _
    Hour + ":" + Minute + "''"
  End If
End If
```

Formatting the Results

The results of the data query will then be used to populate both the DataTableNavigator speech control and a standard DataGrid Web control. This is done because the results of the search will be spoken to the user as well as displayed on the Web page. Each control will require different data fields, so in the following code we create two different data tables:

```
'Define the first table
Dim dTable1 As New DataTable
Dim colSubject As DataColumn = New DataColumn("subject", _
  System.Type.GetType("System.String"))
dTable1.Columns.Add(colSubject)
Dim colTitle As DataColumn = New DataColumn("title", _
  System.Type.GetType("System.String"))
dTable1.Columns.Add(colTitle)
Dim colCourseID1 As DataColumn = New DataColumn("courseid", _
  System.Type.GetType("System.Int32"))
dTable1.Columns.Add(colCourseID1)

'Define the second table
Dim dTable2 As New DataTable
Dim colCourseID2 As DataColumn = New DataColumn("courseid", _
  System.Type.GetType("System.Int32"))
dTable2.Columns.Add(colCourseID2)
Dim colCourseDesc As DataColumn = New DataColumn("coursedesc", _
  System.Type.GetType("System.String"))
dTable2.Columns.Add(colCourseDesc)
```

```
'Populate the tables
Dim rowTable1 As DataRow
Dim rowTable2 As DataRow
For Each row As DataRow In ds.Tables(0).Rows
 rowTable1 = dTable1.NewRow
 rowTable1("subject") = Convert.ToString(row("subject"))
 rowTable1("title") = Convert.ToString(row("title"))
 rowTable1("courseid") = Convert.ToString(row("courseid"))
 dTable1.Rows.Add(rowTable1)

 rowTable2 = dTable2.NewRow
 rowTable2("courseid") = row("courseid")
 Dim strDesc As String
 strDesc = "Course Number " + Convert.ToString(row("courseid"))
 strDesc = strDesc + " " + Convert.ToString(row("title")) + " in the "
 strDesc = strDesc + Convert.ToString(row("department")) + " taught by "
 strDesc = strDesc + Convert.ToString(row("insttitle")) + " "
 strDesc = strDesc + Convert.ToString(row("firstname")) + " "
 strDesc = strDesc + Convert.ToString(row("lastname")) + " on "
 strDesc = strDesc + Convert.ToString(row("days")) + " for "
 strDesc = strDesc + Convert.ToString(row("credits")) + " credits"
 rowTable2("coursedesc") = strDesc
 dTable2.Rows.Add(rowTable2)
Next
Dim ds2 As New DataSet
ds2.Tables.Add(dTable1)
ds2.Tables.Add(dTable2)
```

The data in the first data table will be used to populate the standard data grid control. The second data table will be used to populate the DataTableNavigator speech control. The second data table will contain a field named coursedesc. This field will contain a string value that represents an entire phrase spoken to the user. For instance, one course would result in the following output phrase, "Course Number 1, Financial Accounting 1 in the Business department, taught by Doctor Jan Davis on Tuesday and Thursday for 3 credits."

As opposed to the DataTableNavigator control used in the last chapter, this one does not depend on user commands for navigation. Instead, the entire detail string is spoken to the user in a continuous list. This is accomplished by setting the **ShortInitialTimeout** property to a value greater than zero. When the speech control reaches the last record, the phrase "Select a course from the list to review the course information" is spoken.

The course titles will still be displayed on the Review.aspx page, but since the detail of each course is recited, students have the option to only drill down on the exact course they are interested in.

Students who select a course from the list will be directed to the CourseDetail.aspx page which provides information for that course. From here, if the class is available, they can select the **Add to my schedule** button. If the current class size exceeds the student limit, the **Add to waiting list** button is available instead.

The Manifest File

The Manifest.xml file contains a reference to the start page used for the application along with a listing of resources that can be preloaded by Speech Engine Services (SES). When you create a new speech project, it automatically includes entries for the default project grammars. If new grammars are added, make sure a reference to them is added to this file in order to take advantage of the preloading ability. The manifest for this chapter is seen as follows:

```xml
<manifest>
  <application frontpage="Default.aspx">
    <resourceset type="MultimodalRecognizer">
      <resource src="Grammars/Library.grxml"/>
      <resource src="Grammars/Days.grxml"/>
      <resource src="Grammars/Departments.grxml"/>
      <resource src="Grammars/Instructors.grxml"/>
      <resource src="Grammars/QueryPostamble.grxml"/>
      <resource src="Grammars/QueryPreamble.grxml"/>
      <resource src="Grammars/SpeakQuery.grxml"/>
      <resource src="Grammars/StartTimes.grxml"/>
      <resource src="Grammars/Title.grxml"/>
    </resourceset>
  </application>
</manifest>
```

The manifest file contains a resourceset node with a type attribute. This value specifies the type of engine to use when loading a resource. For voice-only applications it should be valued as "TelephonyRecognizer." For the multimodal application in this chapter, it is valued as "Multimodalrecognizer."

Running the Application on PocketPC

In order to access the sample application from a PocketPC device, you must first install the speech add-in for Internet Explorer on the device. The files for this install are found on the installation CD for Microsoft Speech Server. They can be found in the Redistributable Installers\Speech Add-in for Pocket Internet Explorer directory.

To install the files, ensure that the PocketPC device is connected to your PC using ActiveSync. You will then browse to the setup directory on your PC and execute setup.exe. The setup will install the necessary files and notify you if any additional steps are necessary.

To allow PocketPC devices to access the application, you must set the MIME type for all .aspx pages. This ensures that the Speech Add-in is able to instantiate SALT objects. To set the MIME type, add the following to the Page_load routine for all pages:

```
Response.ContentType = "text/salt+html"
```

TIP: The application can include code that checks the HTTP header for the correct value. If it is not set correctly, the user should be notified.

Application Tuning

The SASDK offers several options for debugging and tuning your speech application. When testing and deploying an application used by the general public, it is vital to maintain a log of all recognitions. These log files can be used to later identify problems with the grammar files.

Speech Debugging Console Logging

Speech Debugging Console allows you to enable logging which is helpful during the development and debugging process.

To enable logging, execute the following steps:

1. Go to Start and Microsoft Speech Application SDK 1.0.
2. Click **Debugging Tools** and **Speech Debugging Console Configuration**.
3. Select **Record Log Files** and specify an existing log files base path. This is the location where log files will be stored. It might be

helpful to specify an application folder within your Inetpub directory (i.e., C:\Inetpub\wwwroot\SpeechLogs\).

4. Click OK to exit the Speech Debugging Console Configuration application. From here on, every time a recognition event occurs, whether it results in success or failure, a new XML flog file will be created.

Refer to Figure 4.7 to see what a log file resulting in a non-recognition exception looks like. In this case, the user entered the phrase "list all financial accounting 1" and would have received an error stating that the phrase was not recognized. Non-recognition exceptions are those resulting in a Type value of "NoReco."

```
- <GrammarList NumGrammars="1">
    - <GrammarInfo>
        <GrammarName>Listen1_Grammar1</GrammarName>
        <LangID>en-us</LangID>
        <MimeType />
        <GrammarURI>http://localhost/Chapter3/Grammars/SpeakQuery.grxml#TopLevel</GrammarURI>
        <XMLNameSpace />
        <InlineGrammar />
        <IsInlineGrammar>false</IsInlineGrammar>
      </GrammarInfo>
    </GrammarList>
  </ListenInitialized>
</IncomingNotification>
- <IncomingNotification>
  - <ListenStarted>
      <IsClientUsingSpeech>false</IsClientUsingSpeech>
    </ListenStarted>
  </IncomingNotification>
- <IncomingNotification>
  - <ClientReady>
      <ClientReadyState>ListenStarted</ClientReadyState>
    </ClientReady>
  </IncomingNotification>
- <OutgoingNotification>
  - <EmulateListenText>
      <EmulateText>list all financial accounting 1</EmulateText>
      <Confidence>1.000000</Confidence>
    </EmulateListenText>
  </OutgoingNotification>
- <IncomingNotification>
  - <ListenException>
      <Type>NoReco</Type>
      <Status>-13</Status>
      <Reason />
    </ListenException>
  </IncomingNotification>
</ReplayLog>
```

Figure 4.7 Portion of an application log file in which the recognition was unsuccessful. In this case the user entered the phrase "list all financial accounting 1." This phrase was not recognized prior to a change in the grammar and would have resulted in an error. The non-recognition exception is indicated with a Type value of "NoReco."

TIP: You do not want to leave logging enabled indefinitely because it adds overhead to the speech process. However, the log files can be invaluable during a period in which you are identifying application grammar errors.

Examining Log Files from MSS

Trace log files, produced on the Speech Server, can also be used to debug a speech application. The SASDK provides three methods for extracting data from trace log files. In order to retrieve this data you must first enable trace logging on the Microsoft Speech Server by creating a log trace session. This is typically done by an Administrator using the logman utility provided with Windows XP. The session is defined from a command prompt and an output path is specified. Starting a trace session results in the creation of a file with an .etl extension

It is not necessary for developers to install MSS in order to access logging functionality. Instead, developers can ask the Administrator of the Microsoft Speech Server to send them the resulting .etl file. This text-based file can then be analyzed using any of three tools available with the SASDK installation:

1. **MSSLogToText** creates a log file containing event categories you may be interested in. These categories include such events as operational messages, audio streams, detailed analysis messages, and debug trace messages. The resulting text file contains a row for each event captured.
2. The **MSSUsageReport** analysis tool is used to create a text file containing events within a certain date range or from a certain URL. The resulting file contains different sections with detailed analysis about the restricted events. Sections included are a summary section, tasks report, latency report, and speech recognition report. This is useful for getting the big picture of how your application is performing.
3. **MSSContentExtract** is a tool used in combination with the MSSLogToText tool to identify certain suspect recognition events. The log tool is then used to recreate a wave file containing the incoming audio content for these events.

The three logging tools available with the SDSDK can be accessed by browsing to **Microsoft Speech Application SDK 1.0**, **Debugging**

Tools, and **Microsoft Speech Application SDK Command Prompt**. This will open a command-prompt window that points to the location of the logging tools. Instructions on which command parameters to use can be accessed by typing the tool name followed by "/?".

Call Viewer

Chapter 2 introduced the Call Viewer Utility as a method for analyzing MSS .etl files. This is a great visual tool for developers to use while debugging an application. The utility is not installed by default, but is available with the SASDK. To install the tools, execute the following steps:

1. From the setup directory used to install the SASDK, browse to the ..\Redistributable Installers\Microsoft Speech Application Log Analysis Tools\ directory.
2. Execute **Setup.exe** and follow the wizard to install the tools.
3. Access the Call Viewer application by browsing to **Microsoft Speech Application SDK 1.0** and **Log Analysis Tools**.

Once Call Viewer is installed, you will need to import the log data to a Microsoft SQL Server Database. The import can be done with a **DTS (Data Transformation Services)** package or with the **MSSLogToDatabase** command line tool. To import the log files with a DTS package, refer to the help file for the Log Analysis Tools. The help file, named **LogAnalysis.chm** is available in the ..\Redistributable Installers\Microsoft Speech Application Log Analysis Tools\Program Files\Microsoft Speech Application SDK 1.0\SDKTools\LogAnalysis\ directory.

Summary

- To be competitive in today's business environment, companies must design unique and functional applications. The Microsoft .NET Speech SDK offers an easy way to add speech capabilities to ASP.NET applications. Multimodal applications offer the user a choice of input mechanisms. In today's environment of smaller mobile devices, the use of speech can be a much-needed benefit.

- When designing multi-modal applications, it is not enough to speech-enable every input. Since the user has a choice not to use speech, intuitive and additional functionality must be added to entice the user.
- The Query grammar for the sample application is more complex than the one presented in Chapter 3. It involves a hierarchy of rules combined with the use of list elements and rule refs.
- Optional Preamble and Postamble rules are used to account for additional words in a spoken phrase. For instance, it is not necessary to capture "List all classes" from the phrase "List all classes for Doctor Davis." Instead, the first three words are part of an optional subphrase. The grammar would still be considered valid if the subphrase was included, but the subphrase itself would not be captured as a semantic item.
- Query results are displayed to the user visually through a standard data grid. In addition, the detail for each course is spoken in a continuous fashion so the student is not forced to drill down into each course to get all the information. This functionality is accomplished by setting the ShortInitialTimeout property to a value greater than zero.
- The manifest.xml file is used to preload resources, such as grammar files, used by Speech Services.
- When running a multimodal application on a PocketPC device, you must first install the speech add-in for Internet Explorer on the device. Applications designed for the PocketPC must also set the MIME type to ensure that the Speech-Addin can instantiate SALT objects.
- The Microsoft .NET Speech SDK offers several options for application tuning. One option allows you to enable Speech Debugging Console Logging for each successful or unsuccessful recognition. SML will be captured to an XML-based file, which can be very helpful for testing an application and during the initial rollout phase. Developers can also analyze trace session files created on the Speech Server using one of three log utilities provided with the SASDK.

CHAPTER 5

Data-Mining Predictions

Improving human-to-computer interaction through speech processing is just one area of computing that can benefit from enhanced computing. On the other side of the interface is the backend, which usually ties in to a database. It is here that enhanced computing can help users get the most from their data.

Over the past ten years, there has been a dramatic increase in computer usage—and in the number of home users. Electronic commerce has resulted in the collection of vast amounts of customer and order information. In addition, most businesses have automated their processes and converted legacy data into electronic formats. Businesses large and small are now struggling with the question of what to do with all the electronic data they have collected.

Data warehousing is a multi-billion-dollar industry that involves the collection, organization, and storage of large amounts of data. Data cubes—structures comprising one or more tables in a relational database—are built so that data can be examined through multiple dimensions. This allows databases containing millions of records and hundreds of attributes to be explored instantly.

Data mining is the process of extracting meaningful information from large quantities of data. It involves uncovering patterns in the data and is often tied to data warehousing because it makes such large amounts of data usable. Data elements are grouped into distinct categories so that predictions can be made about other pieces of data. For example, a bank may wish to ascertain the characteristics that typify customers who pay back loans. Although this could be done with database queries, the bank would first have to know what customer attributes to query for. Data mining can be used to identify what those attributes are and then make predictions about future customer behavior.

Data mining is a technique that has been around for several years. Unfortunately, many of the original tools and techniques for mining data were complex and difficult for beginners to grasp. Microsoft and other software makers have responded by creating easier-to-use data-mining tools. A 2004 report titled "The Golden Vein" by the Economist.com states:

> As the cost of storing data plummets and the power of analytic tools improves, there is little likelihood that enthusiasm for data mining, in all its forms, will diminish.

This is the first of two chapters that will examine how a fictional retailer named Savings Mart was able to utilize Microsoft's **Analysis Services**, included with Microsoft SQL Server, to improve operational efficiencies and reduce costs. The present chapter will examine a stand-alone Windows program named LoadSampleData which is used to load values into a database and generate random purchases for several of the retailer's stores. A mining model will then be created based on shipments to each store. The mining model will be the first step toward revising the way Savings Mart procedurally handles product orders and shipments.

Chapter 6 will extend the predictions made in this chapter through the use of a Windows service designed to automate mining-model processing and the application of processing results. Finally, a modified version of the LoadSampleData program will be used to verify that Savings Mart was able to successfully lower its operating costs.

The chapter also includes a Microsoft case study which examines a real company that used Analysis Services to build a data-mining solution. In the case study, a leaser of technology equipment needed to predict when clients would return their leased equipment. By using Analysis Services, it was able to quickly build a data-mining solution that helped to reduce costs and more accurately predict the value of assets.

Introducing Data Mining with SQL Server

Although SQL Server 7.0 offered Online Analytical Processing (OLAP) as OLAP Services, it was not until the release of SQL Server 2000 that data-mining algorithms were included. Analysis Services comes bundled with SQL Server as a separate install. It allows developers to build complex

OLAP cubes and then utilize two popular data-mining algorithms to process data within the cubes.

Of course, it is not necessary to build OLAP cubes in order to utilize data-mining techniques. Analysis Services also allows mining models to be built against one or more tables from a relational database. This is a big departure from traditional data-mining methodologies. It means that users can access data-mining predictions without the need for OLAP services.

Data mining involves the gathering of knowledge to facilitate better decision-making. It is meant to empower organizations to learn from their experiences—or in this case their historical data—in order to form proactive and successful business strategies. It does not replace decision-makers, but instead provides them with a useful and important tool.

The introduction of data-mining algorithms with SQL Server represents an important step toward making data mining accessible to more companies. The built-in tools allow users to visually create mining models and then train those models with historical data from relational databases.

Data-Mining Algorithms

Data mining with Analysis Services is accomplished using one of two popular mining algorithms—decision trees and clustering. These algorithms are used to find meaningful patterns in a group of data and then make predictions about the data. Table 5.1 lists the key terms related to data mining with Analysis Services.

Decision Trees

Decision trees are useful for predicting exact outcomes. Applying the decision trees algorithm to a training dataset results in the formation of a tree that allows the user to map a path to a successful outcome. At every node along the tree, the user answers a question (or makes a "decision"), such as "years applicant has been at current job (0–1, 1–5, > 5 years)."

The decision trees algorithm would be useful for a bank that wants to ascertain the characteristics of good customers. In this case, the predicted outcome is whether or not the applicant represents a bad credit risk. The outcome of a decision tree may be a Yes/No result (applicant is/is not a bad credit risk) or a list of numeric values, with each value assigned a probability. We will see the latter form of outcome later in this chapter.

The training dataset consists of the historical data collected from past loans. Attributes that affect credit risk might include the customer's educational level, the number of kids the customer has, or the total household

Table 5.1 Key terms related to data mining with Analysis Services.

Term	Definition
Case	The data and relationships that represent a single object you wish to analyze. For example, a product and all its attributes, such as Product Name and Unit Price. It is not necessarily equivalent to a single row in a relational table, because attributes can span multiple related tables. The product case could include all the order detail records for a single product.
Case Set	Collection of related cases. This represents the way the data is viewed and not necessarily the data itself. One case set involving products could focus on the product, whereas another may focus on the purchase detail for the same product.
Clustering	One of two popular algorithms used by Analysis Services to mine data. Clustering involves the classification of data into distinct groups. As opposed to the other algorithm, decision trees, clustering does not require an outcome variable.
Cubes	Multidimensional data structures built from one or more tables in a relational database. Cubes can be the input for a data-mining model, but with Analysis Services the input could also be based on an actual relational table(s).
Decision Trees	One of two popular algorithms used by Analysis Services to mine data. Decision trees involves the creation of a tree that allows the user to map a path to a successful outcome.
Testing Dataset	A portion of historical data that can be used to validate the predictions of a trained mining model. The model will be trained using a training dataset that is representative of all historical data. By using a testing dataset, the developer can ensure that the mining model was designed correctly and can be trusted to make useful predictions.
Training Dataset	A portion of historical data that is representative of all input data. It is important that the training dataset represent input variables in a way that is proportional to occurrences in the entire dataset. In the case of Savings Mart, we would want the training dataset to include all the stores that were open during the same time period so that no bias is unintentionally introduced.

income. Each split on the tree represents a decision that influences the final predicted variable. For example, a customer who graduated from high school may be more likely to pay back the loan. The variable used in the first split is considered the most significant factor. So if educational level is in the first split, it is the factor that most influences credit risk.

Clustering

Clustering is different from decision trees in that it involves grouping data into meaningful clusters with no specific outcome. It goes through a looped process whereby it reevaluates each cluster against all the other clusters looking for patterns in the data. This algorithm is useful when a large database with hundreds of attributes is first evaluated. The clustering process may uncover a relationship between data items that was never suspected. In the case of the bank that wants to determine credit risk, clustering might be used to identify groups of similar customers. It could reveal that certain customer attributes are more meaningful than originally thought. The attributes identified in this process could then be used to build a mining model with decision trees.

OLE DB for Data-Mining Specification

Analysis Services is based on the **OLE DB for Data Mining** (OLE DB for DM) specification. OLE DB for DM, an extension of OLE DB, was developed by the Data Mining Group at Microsoft Research. It includes an Application Programming Interface (API) that exposes data-mining functionality. This allows third-party providers to implement their own data-mining algorithms. These algorithms can then be made available through the Analysis Services Manager application when building new mining models.

TIP: Readers interested in learning more about the OLE DB for Data Mining Specification can download documentation from the Microsoft Web site at http://www.microsoft.com/downloads/details.aspx?FamilyID=01005f92-dba1-4fa4-8ba0-af6a19d30217&displaylang=en.

Savings Mart

Savings Mart is a fictitious discount retailer operating in a single American state. It has been in business since 2001 and hopes to open new stores by achieving greater operational efficiencies. Since its inception, Savings

Mart has relied on a system of adjusting product inventory thresholds to determine when shipments will be made to stores. Every time a product is purchased, the quantity for that product and store is updated. When the quantity dips below the minimum threshold allowed for that product and store, an order is automatically generated and a shipment is made three days later.

Although this process seemed like a good way to ensure that the stores were well stocked, it resulted in shipments being made to each store almost every day. This resulted in high overhead costs for each store. Management now wishes to replace the order/shipment strategy with a system designed to predict shipment dates rather than rely on adjustable thresholds.

A sample application presented in this chapter allows the reader to create a training dataset for Savings Mart based on randomly generated purchases. The reader can then step through the process of creating a mining model based on the dataset.

Loading the Savings Mart Database

To execute the sample code with SQL Server, you will need to create a database using a script file available on the book's Web site. The installation steps are as follows:

1. Open SQL Server's **Query Analyzer** and connect to the server where you wish to install the database.
2. Click **File** and **Open**...
3. From the **Open Query File** dialog, browse to location of the **InstallDB.sql** file available on the book's Web site. Once selected, click **OK**.
4. Click **Query** and **Execute** or hit **F5**.
5. Once the script has completed executing, a new database named SavingsMart will be visible in the drop-down box on the toolbar.

Figure 5.1 is a diagram of the SavingsMart database. The Products table contains a record for every product available in the stores. Each product is associated with a certain vendor and assigned to a product type, such as beverage or medicine. A field named DiscontinuedDate will contain either a null, meaning it is not discontinued, or the date that it should no longer be available for order. Every product should have a UnitQuantity of one or greater, which indicates the number of items packaged with that product. The products UnitPrice represents the retail

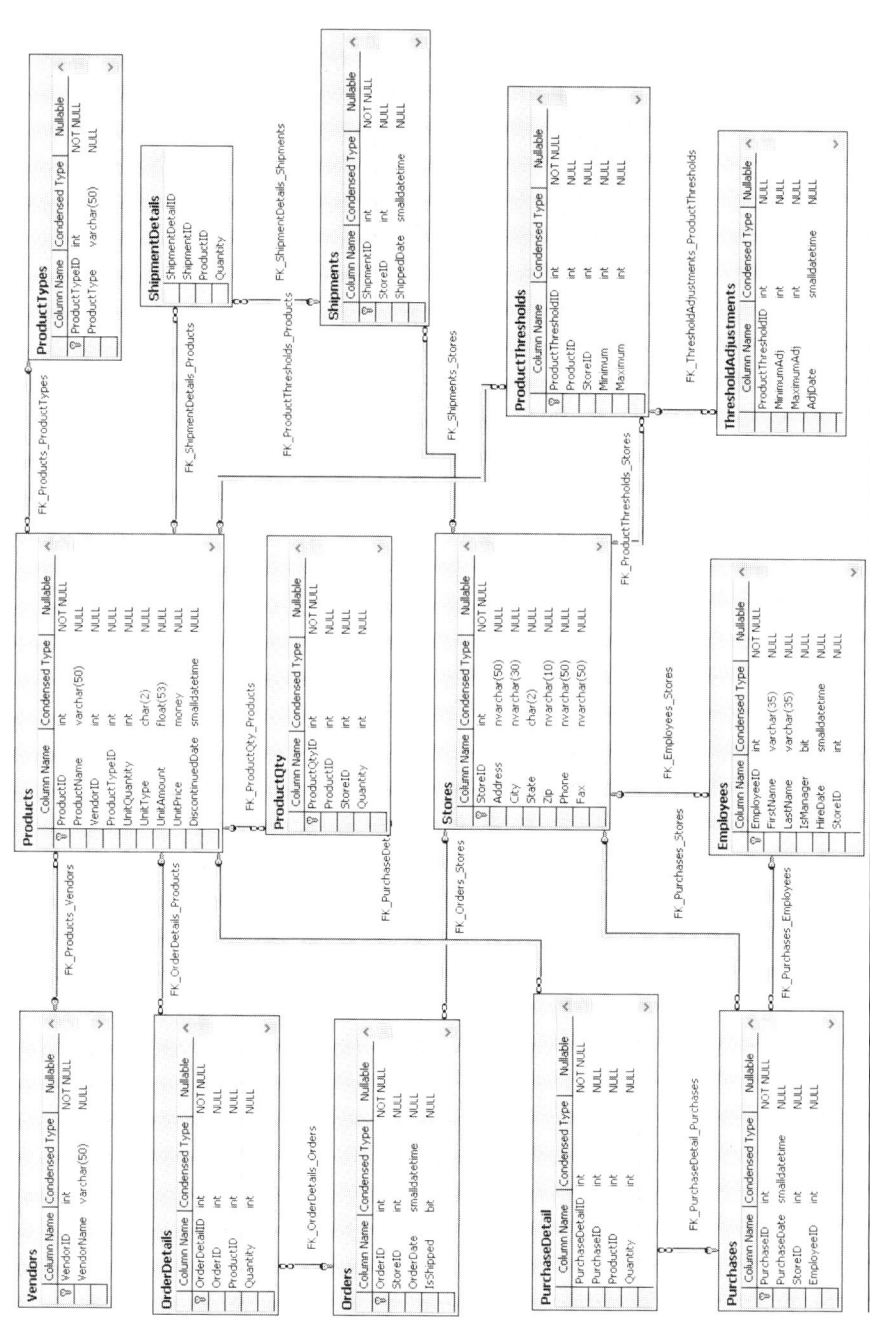

Figure 5.1 The SavingsMart database. The sample database contains five hundred products and five stores. Stores are stocked with all products according to threshold values contained in the ProductThresholds table. Each time a product is ordered and a shipment completed, the quantity field in ProductQty is updated.

price before any discounts are applied. The UnitType and UnitAmount fields may or may not contain values, depending on the product. For instance, a bottled water product will have a UnitType of "oz" and a UnitAmount of 16.4, indicating that it weighs 16.4 fluid ounces. It is not necessary to record the weight of a mop, so for this product these values would be null.

The Purchases table is written to every time a customer makes a single purchase. It records information common to all purchases, such as when the purchase took place, what store it was made in, and what employee rang up the purchase. Purchases are made for products available within a particular store. Availability is determined by examining the Quantity field in the table ProductQty. A purchase can include multiple products and more than one unit of each product. The ProductDetail table is a child of products, and it contains a record for each product associated with a single purchase. If the product purchased is on sale during the time of purchase, then the discount percentage, specified in the ProductDiscounts table is applied.

Once a product is sold beneath the minimum threshold allowed for the store, as indicated by the ProductThresholds table, an order is automatically placed. The quantity for the order is based on the maximum amount found in the ProductThresholds table. Each shipment is the direct result of an order and is typically completed three days after the order is placed.

Populating the Database

Once the SavingsMart database is created, the next step is to populate the database. Unlike the sample databases in Chapters 2 and 3, the SavingsMart database needs to be populated with a large quantity of data. To facilitate this process and provide a method for generating unique training datasets, a sample data-loading application is included on the book's Web site at http:// www.awprofessional.com/title/0321246268. The sample Windows application, named LoadSampleData, will allow you to simulate random purchases as well as to initiate orders and shipments needed to restock products.

Utilizing the LoadSampleData program ensures that you are dealing with a clean database. Very often, the most difficult and time-consuming part of successful data mining involves cleaning the historical database to remove or replace records holding invalid values. Refer to the next section, "Cleaning the Database," for more information about this.

The LoadSampleData program also gives you an opportunity to adjust factors affecting the mining model and therefore produce different results. For instance, the program allows you to select certain product types and vendor names that will be purchased more often.

The LoadSampleData application consists of one form, Form1.vb (see Figure 5.2). It utilizes the Microsoft Data Application block to handle data access and the Microsoft Exception Application block to handle writing exceptions to the event log. The **Load Data** button is used to populate tables with values from text files, available for download from the book's Web site. The following is a list of these text files along with a brief description of what they contain:

- Stores.txt—Data for a total of five stores.
- Employees.txt—Assigns three employees to each store.
- Vendors.txt—Data for a total of thirty-four vendors or product brands.
- ProductTypes.txt—A total of fourteen product types, including such items as Beverages and Kitchen Supplies.
- Products.txt—A total of five hundred products representing each of the product types and vendors.

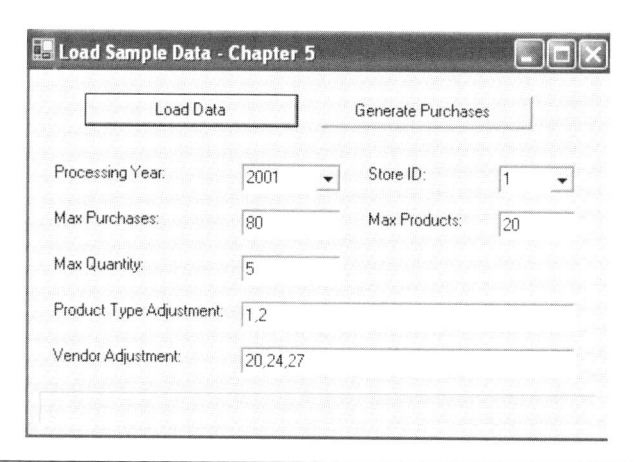

Figure 5.2 Screenshot of the main form used in the LoadSampleData program. This program will be used to load initial data values into the SavingsMart database. It will also allow the reader to simulate random customer purchases in order to populate a large historical dataset.

Chapter 5 Data Mining Predictions

The LoadData routine is also used to populate the ProductThresholds table with set values for minimum and maximum threshold amounts. The minimum field represents the minimum quantity of product that should be available in a certain store. The maximum field is the quantity that will be ordered for that store when the minimum threshold is broken. Initially, the minimum and maximum values will be set at ten and two hundred respectively. This will be the case for each product and each store, resulting in a total of twenty-five hundred records (500 products × 5 stores = 2500 records).

Finally, the LoadData routine will generate orders and shipments for each of the five stores. The initial orders will stock the stores with the maximum threshold for all five hundred products. The shipment date will occur three days after the order date to ensure that all stores are fully stocked on the first day of the year.

To begin loading data, execute the following steps:

1. Copy the contents of the LoadSampleData directory, available for download from the book's Web site, to a location accessible by your development machine. Note the location because it will be used to set the sPath variable in step 4.
2. Open the LoadSampleData project file with **Visual Studio .NET.**
3. From **Solution Explorer**, right-click Form1 and select **View Code**.
4. The top of the form contains two variables that will be unique to your installation. Ensure that the **sConn** and **sPath** variables are set correctly. sConn is a string variable containing the connection string used to connect to the SavingsMart database on SQL Server. sPath is a string variable containing the file path to the text files. The text files reside in a subdirectory name TextFiles. This subdirectory is located inside the LoadSampleData directory (created in step 1).
5. Execute the application by selecting **Start** from the **Debug** Menu. Figure 5.2 is a screenshot of form1.
6. To begin, click the **Load Data** button and ensure that the message box "Initial Data Load is complete" appears. Note that the form contains several combo and textboxes that will determine what and how data is loaded.

> **TIP:** If you do not wish to load the database utilizing the sample application provided, you can instead attach the database file supplied on the book's Web site. To attach the file, execute the following steps:
>
> 1. Copy the **SavingsMart.mdf** and **SavingsMart.ldf** files from the book's Web site to a local directory on the server where Microsoft SQL Server is installed.
> 2. Open SQL Server's **Enterprise Manager**.
> 3. Right-click the **Databases** node and click **All Tasks...** and **Attach Database**.
> 4. From the **Attach Database** dialog, browse to the directory where you copied the database files in step 1 and select the SavingsMart.mdf file. Click **OK**.
> 5. Click **OK** to attach the database.
> 6. To see the newly added database, you will need to click **Action** and **Refresh**.

The next step is to generate purchases for each of the five stores. Data mining is most effective in dealing with large datasets. Therefore, the GeneratePurchases routine, seen as follows, will insert approximately 100,000 records in the PurchaseDetail table for each store and calendar year. Purchases are generated for one store—one year at a time.

```
'Maximum # of purchases per day
Dim nMaxPurchases As Int16 = txtMaxPurchases.Text
'Maximum # of products per purchase
Dim nMaxProducts As Int16 = txtMaxProducts.Text
'Maximum value of quantity per product
Dim nMaxQuantity As Int16 = txtMaxQuantity.Text
Dim sYear As String = cboYear.Text
Dim nStoreID As Int16 = cboStoreID.Text

'These are the Product Types in which there is an
'increased chance of product selection
'The default of 1,2 represents snack foods and beverages
Dim sProductTypeAdj As String = txtProductTypeAdj.Text

'These are the Vendors in which there is an increased
'chance of product selection
'The default of 20,24,27 represents Kamp, Notch, and PNuts as Vendors
Dim sVendorAdj As String = txtVendorAdj.Text
```

```
ProgressBar1.Minimum = 1
ProgressBar1.Maximum = 366

Try
  Dim params(2) As SqlParameter
  params(0) = New _
   SqlParameter("@ID", SqlDbType.Int)
  params(1) = New _
   SqlParameter("@ProdTypeAdj", SqlDbType.VarChar, 50)
  params(2) = New _
   SqlParameter("@VendorAdj", SqlDbType.VarChar, 50)
 params(0).Value = nStoreID
 params(1).Value = sProductTypeAdj
 params(2).Value = sVendorAdj
 Dim ds As DataSet = _
 SqlHelper.ExecuteDataset(sConn, _
  CommandType.StoredProcedure, "GetProductIDS", params)
 Dim i As Int16 = 1
 Dim dtDate As DateTime
 dtDate = Convert.ToDateTime("01/01/" + sYear)
 'Loop through everyday of the year
 'We assume the store is open every day
 Randomize()
 Do Until i = 366
   'First thing is check to see if orders needs to
   'be fulfilled for this day and store
   'We assume that all orders are shipped 3 days
   'after the orderdate in one shipment
   Dim params1(1) As SqlParameter
   params1(0) = New _
      SqlParameter("@StoreID", SqlDbType.Int)
   params1(1) = New _
      SqlParameter("@Date", SqlDbType.SmallDateTime)
   params1(0).Value = nStoreID
   'order was placed 3 days ago
   params1(1).Value = dtDate.AddDays(-3)
   SqlHelper.ExecuteReader(sConn, _
     CommandType.StoredProcedure, "InsertShipment", params1)
   Dim x As Int16 = 1
   'This will be the total number of purchases for this day
   Dim nPurchases As Int16
   nPurchases = CInt(Int((nMaxPurchases * Rnd()) + 1))
   Do Until x = nPurchases + 1
```

```vb
Dim y As Int16 = 1
Dim nEmployeePos As Int16
nEmployeePos = CInt(Int((ds.Tables(1).Rows.Count * Rnd())))
Dim nEmployeeID As Integer = _
   Convert.ToInt32(ds.Tables(1).Rows(nEmployeePos).Item(0))
Dim params2(2) As SqlParameter
params2(0) = New SqlParameter("@ID1", SqlDbType.Int)
params2(1) = New _
  SqlParameter("@Date", SqlDbType.SmallDateTime)
params2(2) = New SqlParameter("@ID2", SqlDbType.Int)
params2(0).Value = nStoreID
params2(1).Value = dtDate
params2(2).Value = nEmployeeID
Dim nPurchaseID As Integer = _
  SqlHelper.ExecuteScalar(sConn, _
 CommandType.StoredProcedure, "InsertPurchase", params2)
'This is total number of products for this purchase
Dim nProducts As Int16 = _
  CInt(Int((nMaxProducts * Rnd()) + 1))
Do Until y = nProducts + 1
  'This is quantity for this purchase
  Dim nQty As Int16 = _
    CInt(Int((nMaxQuantity * Rnd()) + 1))
  'This is the product for this detail record
  Dim nProductPos As Int16 = _
    CInt(Int((ds.Tables(0).Rows.Count * Rnd())))
  Dim nProductID As Integer = _
   Convert.ToInt32(ds.Tables(0).Rows(nProductPos).Item(0))
  'Generate the detail record
  Dim params3(4) As SqlParameter
   params3(0) = New SqlParameter("@StoreID", SqlDbType.Int)
  params3(1) = New _
    SqlParameter("@ProductID", SqlDbType.Int)
  params3(2) = New _
    SqlParameter("@PurchaseID", SqlDbType.Int)
  params3(3) = New SqlParameter("@Qty", SqlDbType.Int)
  params3(4) = New _
    SqlParameter("@Date", SqlDbType.SmallDateTime)
  params3(0).Value = nStoreID
  params3(1).Value = nProductID
  params3(2).Value = nPurchaseID
  params3(3).Value = nQty
  params3(4).Value = dtDate
```

```
      SqlHelper.ExecuteScalar(sConn, _
        CommandType.StoredProcedure, _
        "InsertPurchaseDetail", params3)
      y += 1
    Loop
    x += 1
  Loop

  i += 1
  ProgressBar1.Value = i
  'Go to the next day
  dtDate = dtDate.AddDays(1)
  Loop
  MessageBox.Show("Purchases for store " _
    + Convert.ToString(cboStoreID.Text) + _
    " were generated successfully")
Catch ex As Exception
  MessageBox.Show(ex.Message)
  ExceptionManager.Publish(ex)
End Try
```

The amount of records is approximate because the routine utilizes a random number generator to determine the number of purchases per day along with the number of products per purchase. The number of records also varies depending on what input variables are chosen on form1.

The program utilizes default values specifying that purchases will be generated for Store 1 in the year 2001. The GeneratePurchases routine contains a main loop that will execute 365 times for each day of one calendar year. The variable max purchases defaults to 80 and is used to provide the maximum value for the random number generator when determining how many purchases will be generated for a single day.

The variable max products determines the number of distinct products that will be used for a single purchase. Max quantity is used to determine the quantity used in a single purchase detail record. By utilizing the random number generator and then adjusting these values for each store that is processed, we can simulate random purchase activity. In the section titled "Interpreting the Results," we will examine the results of one mining model. To ensure that your results are consistent with the explanations in this section, use the values in Table 5.2 when loading your database.

Table 5.2 Values to be used in the LoadSampleData application when generating purchases for all five stores.

Store	Field Caption	Value (only use the number values and not the literal values in parentheses)
1	Processing Year	2001
	Max Purchases	80
	Max Products	20
	Max Quantity	5
	Product Type Adjustment	1, 2 (Snack Foods and Beverages)
	Vendor Adjustment	20, 24, 27 (Kamp, Notch, and Pnuts)
2	Processing Year	2001
	Max Purchases	60
	Max Products	12
	Max Quantity	7
	Product Type Adjustment	2, 6 (Beverages and Baking Goods)
	Vendor Adjustment	13, 18 (Gombers and Joe's)
3	Processing Year	2001
	Max Purchases	70
	Max Products	12
	Max Quantity	7
	Product Type Adjustment	2 (Beverages)
	Vendor Adjustment	34 (Store Brand)
4	Processing Year	2001
	Max Purchases	100
	Max Products	5
	Max Quantity	2
	Product Type Adjustment	(leave blank)
	Vendor Adjustment	34, 18 (Store Brand and Joe's)
5	Processing Year	2001
	Max Purchases	50
	Max Products	15
	Max Quantity	8
	Product Type Adjustment	6 (Baking Goods)
	Vendor Adjustment	24, 27, 34 (Notch, Pnuts, and Store Brand)

Of course, since we are using a random number generator, the purchases generated will represent all products equally well over the long run. The Product Type Adjustment and Vendor Adjustment variables are introduced because equal distribution of product purchases is not realistic. These variables contain a comma-delimited list of ProductTypeID and VendorID values. The stored procedure **GetProductIDs** uses these values when returning the dataset of available ProductID's. If a ProductTypeID is specified, then every product that relates to that product type will be included in the list of available product id's more than once. This will increase the chances that the product will be selected for the PurchaseDetail record. The Vendor Adjustment works similarly in that for each VendorID specified, all products assigned to that vendor will appear in the available product list more than once.

If you do not alter the values on form1, the GeneratePurchases routine will take approximately twenty minutes to load data for each store and calendar year. A progress bar is used to indicate the status of the data load because the process is somewhat time-consuming.

TIP: Although it is not necessary to execute the GeneratePurchases routine for each store and all three years, make sure to load at least one store for one calendar year before continuing. This will provide you with enough data to use for processing.

Once the data has loaded, you should see a dialog with the message "Purchases were generated successfully."

If you do not receive the successful message and instead receive an error message, you will first need to resolve the error. Then you will need to delete the database from SQL Server Enterprise Manager and repeat the steps used to load data.

If you continue to receive an error, consider attaching the database per the instructions in the previous tip.

Case Study: ComputerFleet

ComputerFleet, (www.computerfleet.com.au), based in Sydney, Australia, leases technology equipment to companies in a number of different industries and to government agencies. Its wide range of clients includes small, medium, and large organizations.

Since it was necessary to store a large amount of data (twelve years worth), ComputerFleet was using a data warehouse built on top of Microsoft SQL Server 2000. The company was already using analysis tools like Microsoft Data Analyzer and Microsoft Excel to report on the data.

What ComputerFleet needed was a way to predict when its clients would return leased equipment. Unfortunately, this does not always occur on the agreed lease-end date. Having this information would allow ComputerFleet to better manage its equipment and save money. The company would also be in a better position to value its assets.

ComputerFleet asked a consulting company named Angry Koala (www.angrykoala.com.au) and Microsoft Consulting Services to help it obtain this information. Within a few weeks the consultants had built a data-mining solution with Microsoft Analysis Services.

The data-mining solution uses such attributes as the type of industry, type of equipment, and whether the client is new as input variables to the mining model. The predicted results are stored back in the data warehouse as the predicted asset-arrival time.

ComputerFleet was pleased not only because it was able to make valuable predictions, but because it did not have to purchase any extra proprietary software to do so. Also, it was easy to integrate the data-mining solution with the existing data warehouse in Microsoft SQL Server 2000.

This is a real example of a large company that was able to quickly take advantage of the built-in functionality of Microsoft SQL Server to decrease its operational costs. For more information about ComputerFleet and this Microsoft case study, go to www.microsoft.com/resources/casestudies/casestudy.asp?CaseStudyID=14375.

Cleaning the Database

Cleaning the database is one of the most important tasks in successful data mining. Databases to be mined are often constructed from multiple data sources. These data sources often involve data that is prone to a variety of errors that can destroy any chance you have of making useful predictions. Most everyone has heard or used the phrase "Garbage in, Garbage out." This phrase applies more than ever to data mining.

Possible errors include records with impossible values or values that fall outside the expected range. Also, records that include null values where nulls will negatively impact the decision-making process. Most of these errors could be prevented with database restrictions or application code, but this does not always happen. Since our sample database was artificially created, we can be reasonably sure that these errors do not exist.

The following is a list of the errors that could have occurred if our database existed in the real world:

- Store sale in which the ending data occurs before the starting date.
- A purchase handled by a store employee before their hire date or for a store they were not assigned to.
- An order made for a product that was discontinued before the order date.
- A shipment or order date that is invalid or outside the days of operation for the concerned store.
- A negative quantity in either PurchaseDetail, OrderDetail, ShipmentDetail, or ProductQty.
- A product not associated with a vendor or a purchase with no purchase date and quantity.
- A maximum amount that is greater than the minimum.

The methods used to clean a database can vary. Often, values can be corrected with a few update queries made in **Query Analyzer**. The hardest part is determining what the correct values should be. More than likely, outside help will be needed from people intimately familiar with the data, such as a store manager.

Creating Views

In order to ease the process of building a mining model, a special view will be created. The view, vw_Shipments, combines fields from five different tables and will be used in the next section to create the mining model. The view utilizes the function fn_GetLastShipmentDate to calculate the number of days between shipments. The Transact-SQL code (viewable from the User Defined Function tab in Enterprise Manager) for this function is as follows:

```
CREATE FUNCTION fn_GetLastShipmentDate
 (
 @ShipmentID int,
 @ProductID int
 )
RETURNS datetime
AS
BEGIN
```

```
DECLARE @ShippedDate smalldatetime, @TShipmentID int, @ret
smalldatetime
DECLARE cursor1 CURSOR SCROLL
FOR select shippeddate, s.shipmentid from shipments s
    left join shipmentdetails sd on s.shipmentid = sd.shipmentid
    where s.storeid IN (SELECT StoreID FROM Shipments
        WHERE shipmentid = @Shipmentid)
    AND sd.productid = @ProductID
    ORDER BY shippeddate
OPEN cursor1
FETCH NEXT FROM cursor1 INTO @ShippedDate, @TShipmentID

WHILE @@FETCH_STATUS = 0
BEGIN
    IF @ShipmentID = @TShipmentID
        BEGIN
        FETCH PRIOR FROM cursor1 INTO @ShippedDate, @TShipmentID
        SET @ret = @ShippedDate
        GOTO Close_Cursor
          END

    FETCH NEXT FROM cursor1 INTO @ShippedDate, @TShipmentID
END

Close_Cursor:
CLOSE cursor1
DEALLOCATE cursor1

RETURN(@ret)
END
```

The function accepts @ShipmentID and @ProductID as input variables. It then opens a scrollable cursor (similar to an ADO resultset) based on the following SQL statement:

```
SELECT shippeddate, s.shipmentid FROM shipments s
 LEFT JOIN shipmentdetails sd ON s.shipmentid = sd.shipmentid
 WHERE s.storeid IN (SELECT StoreID FROM Shipments
    WHERE shipmentid = @Shipmentid)
 AND sd.productid = @ProductID
 ORDER BY shippeddate
```

The function loops through the cursor results until it locates the ShipmentID supplied as an input variable. Once located, it moves to the preceding record and returns that shipment date. This shipment date is used as the first variable for the built-in SQL function DATEDIFF. The resulting variable, DaysSinceLastShipped, will be an important column for the Analyze Shipments mining model.

Working with Mining Models

Building a Mining Model

Now that the database has been created and populated, the next step is to create a mining model. Mining models can be created with the **Mining Model Editor** in **Analysis Manager** or programmatically with Decision Support Objects (DSO). Using DSO to create mining models is useful when you need to programmatically automate the mining-model process. For the most part, you will use Analysis Manager to create mining models.

Analysis Manager (see Figure 5.3) allows you to create and manage databases used by Analysis Services. A database node in Analysis Manager does not represent the physical storage of a large database. Instead, it represents the database that Analysis Services will use to hold the mining-model definitions and the results of processing these mining models. It will, however, reference a physical data source.

Each database in Analysis Manager is associated with one or more data sources. These data sources can be either relational databases or data warehouses. Data sources are created by right-clicking the **Data Sources** node and selecting **New Data Source**. From the **Data Link Properties** dialog, a data provider is selected along with the connection information. Analysis Services supports SQL Server, Access, and Oracle databases as data sources.

Mining models are the blueprint for how the data should be analyzed or processed. Each model represents a case set, or a set of cases (see Table 5.1). The mining-model object stores the information necessary to process the model—for instance, what queries are needed to get the data fields, what data fields are input columns or predictable columns, and what relationship each column has with other columns. Input columns are attributes whose values will be used to generate results for the predictable columns. In some cases, the attribute may serve both as an input column and a predictable column.

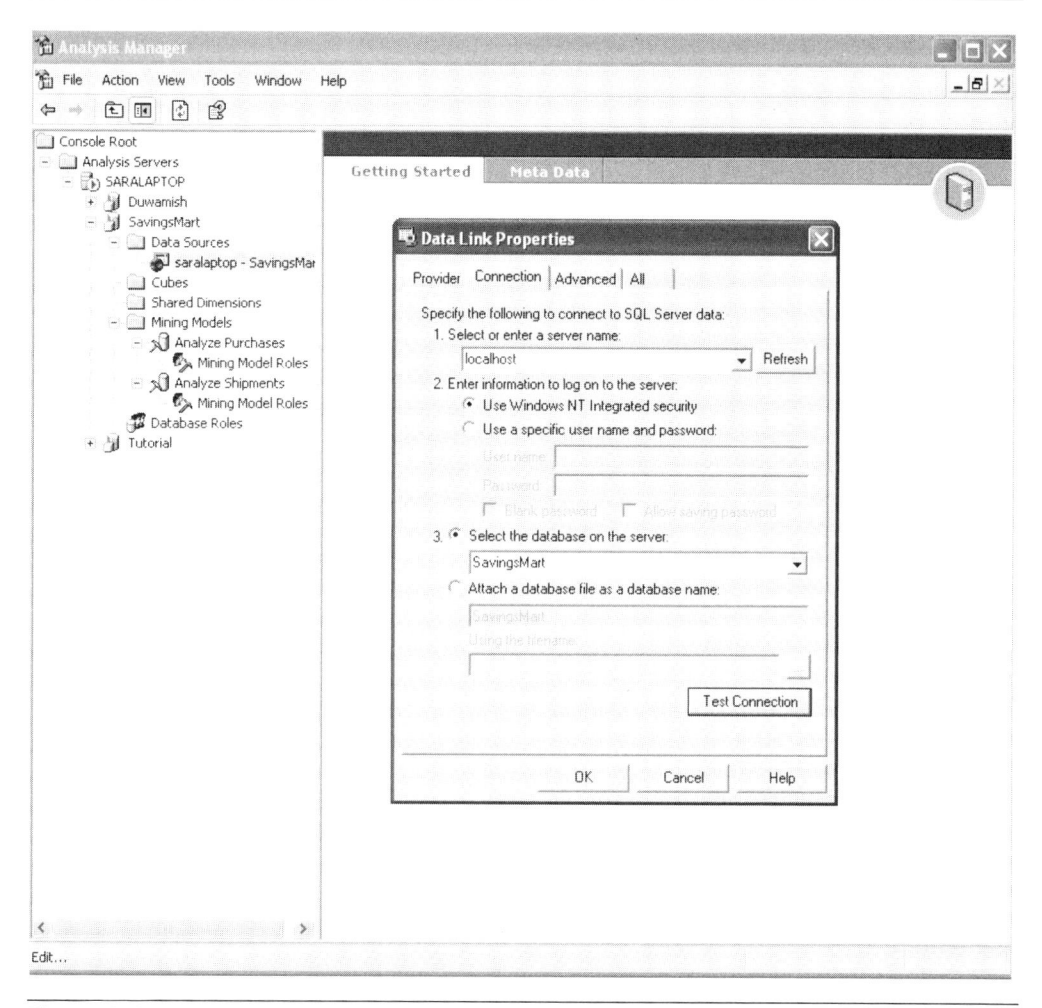

Figure 5.3 Screenshot of Analysis Manager, the utility used to create and manage mining models with Analysis Services. The Data Link Properties dialog box, used to specify the data source, is visible.

Once the model is processed, the data associated with the mining model represents what was learned from the data. The actual data from the training dataset is not stored in the Analysis Services database. The results of analyzing that data, however, are saved.

To quickly demonstrate the process of creating these models, we will walk through the process of creating a mining model using Analysis Manager.

> **TIP:** If you have not already done so, you will need to install Analysis Services. It is available as a separate install with the SQL Server 2000 setup. Make sure that you install the latest Service Pack release for SQL Server. Information about how to obtain the latest SQL Server service pack can be found at http://support.microsoft.com/default.aspx?kbid=290211.
>
> If you have problems connecting with Analysis Services, refer to the article by Alexander Chigrik titled, "Troubleshooting OLAP Problems" at http://databasejournal.com/features/mssql/article.php/1582491. This online article, featured in the Database Journal, is a troubleshooting checklist for solving common problems.

To begin, open **Analysis Manager** from the **Analysis Services** menu item. You will then need to create a new database and specify the data source by executing the following steps:

1. Right-click the server name in the left-hand pane and select **New Database...**
2. Specify 'SavingsMart' as the Database Name and click **OK**
3. Expand the newly added SavingsMart node, right-click Data Sources, and select **New Data Source...**
4. From the Data Link Properties dialog box, select Microsoft OLE DB Provider for SQL Server and click **Next**
5. Enter the SQL connection information for your SQL Server and test the connection before closing the Data Link Properties dialog

The next thing to do is create the mining model using the mining-model wizard. To do so, execute the following steps:

1. Right-click Mining Models in the left-hand pane and select **New Mining Model...**
2. Click **Next** on the Welcome Dialog
3. Click **Next** on the Select Source Dialog because we will be using Relational Data
4. Select the vw_Shipments view from the Available Tables list box in the Select Case Tables dialog and click **Next**. It would have been possible to select multiple tables, but utilizing the view allows access to a calculated field indicating the number of days between shipments.
5. Click **Next** to accept the default of Microsoft Decision Trees as the data-mining technique.
6. Click **Next** to accept ShipmentID as the default Case Key Column.

7. Select the **Finish the mining model in the editor** checkbox and click **Next**.
8. Name the model "Analyze Shipments" and click **Finish**.
9. From the Relational Mining Model Editor, as seen in Figure 5.4, click **Insert** and **Column...** and then select the column named DaysSinceLastShipped. Once added, change the usage to Input and Predictable (note that a diamond icon now appears next to the column). Then go to the **Advanced Properties** and enter DISCRETIZED(CLUSTERS) as the content type.

NOTE: Choosing discretized as the content type allows a continuous variable to be grouped discretely instead. Continuous variables are usually numeric-based values that have an infinite range of possibilities. Since we need predictable results, utilizing a discretization method allows for grouped results. DISCRETEIZED accepts two parameters, such as:

DISCRETIZED(<method>, <#buckets>)

where method could contain one of the following values:

EQUAL_AREAS—Divides into equal buckets
THRESHOLDS—Uses inflection points to estimate bucket boundaries
CLUSTERS—Uses a clustering algorithm to estimate buckets
AUTOMATIC (default)—Tries all algorithms and uses the first one that suggests number buckets

10. Click **Insert** and **Column...** and then select the column named StoreID. Once added, change the usage to Input and Predictable.
11. Click **Insert** and **Column...** and then select the column named Quantity. Once added, change the usage to Predictable, and from the Advanced Properties tab, enter DISCRETIZED(CLUSTERS) as the content type.
12. Click **Insert** and **Column...** and then select the column named VendorName.
13. Click **Insert** and **Column...** and then select the column named ProductType.
14. Click **Tools** and **Process Mining Model...** Click **OK** when asked to save the mining model. Then click OK to start a full process of the mining model. This process will take several minutes to run if you loaded data for all five stores. When complete, the message "Processing Complete" will appear in green text.

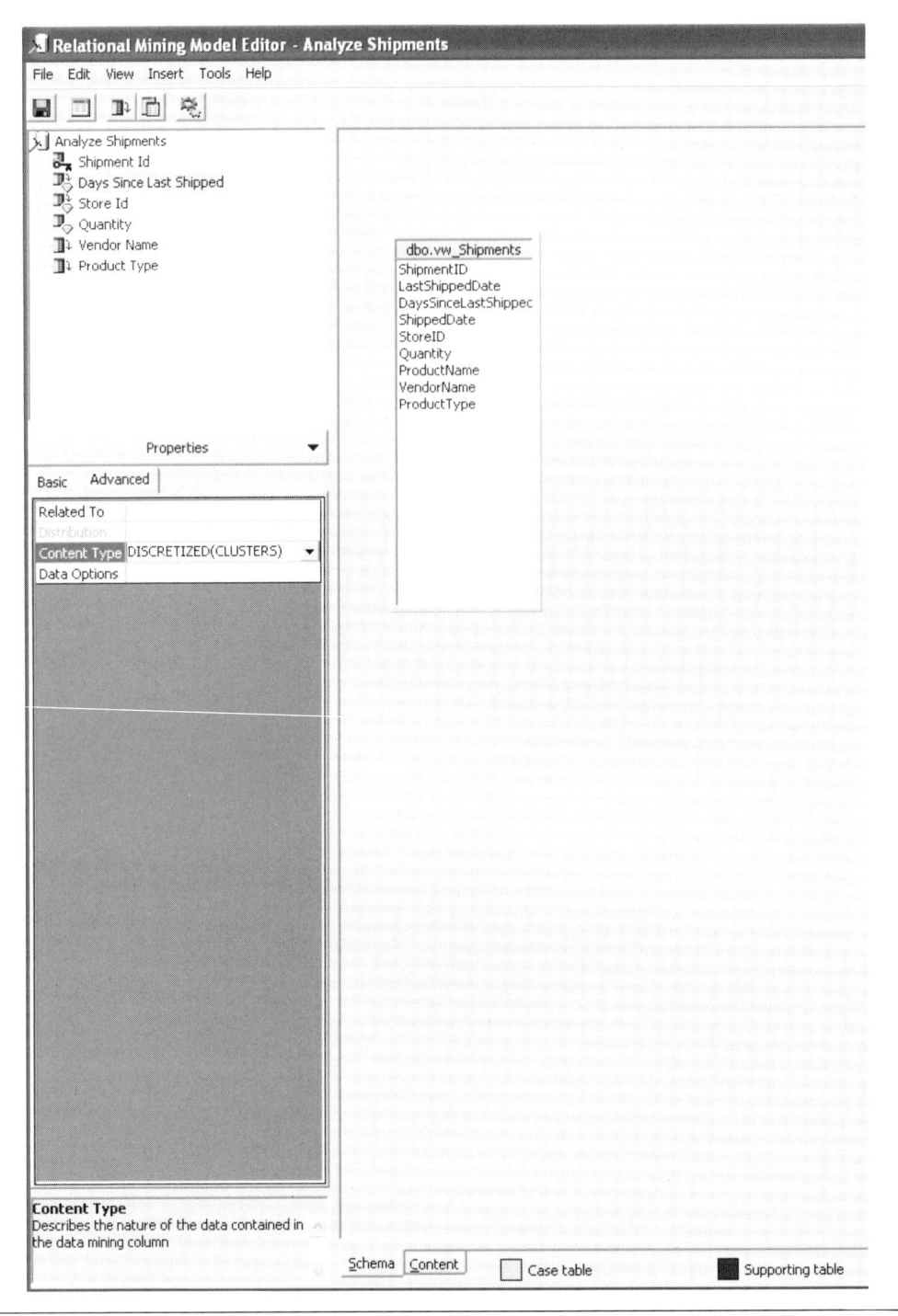

Figure 5.4 Screenshot of the Schema tab in the Relational Mining Model Editor after the columns have been added for the Analyze Shipments mining model.

Training the Mining Model

Training the mining model is accomplished by processing the results of a mining model using Analysis Manager. Alternatively, the same thing could be accomplished using a scripting language known as Data Definition Language (DDL) and a connection to the Analysis Server. We can see what DDL commands are used to train the model through the Process dialog box, as shown in Figure 5.5.

DDL is useful in cases when you want to programmatically process a mining model. The language can be executed through a connection to the Analysis Server. It is also useful for demonstrating how Analysis Manager processes a mining model.

A mining model is created using the CREATE MINING MODEL syntax. The syntax is similar to Transact SQL and should be instantly familiar to SQL developers. The CREATE statement for this mining model is as follows:

```
CREATE MINING MODEL [Analyze Shipments](
    [Shipment Id] LONG KEY,
    [Days Since Last Shipped] LONG DISCRETIZED(CLUSTERS) PREDICT,
    [Store Id] LONG DISCRETE,
    [Quantity] LONG DISCRETIZED(CLUSTERS) PREDICT_ONLY,
```

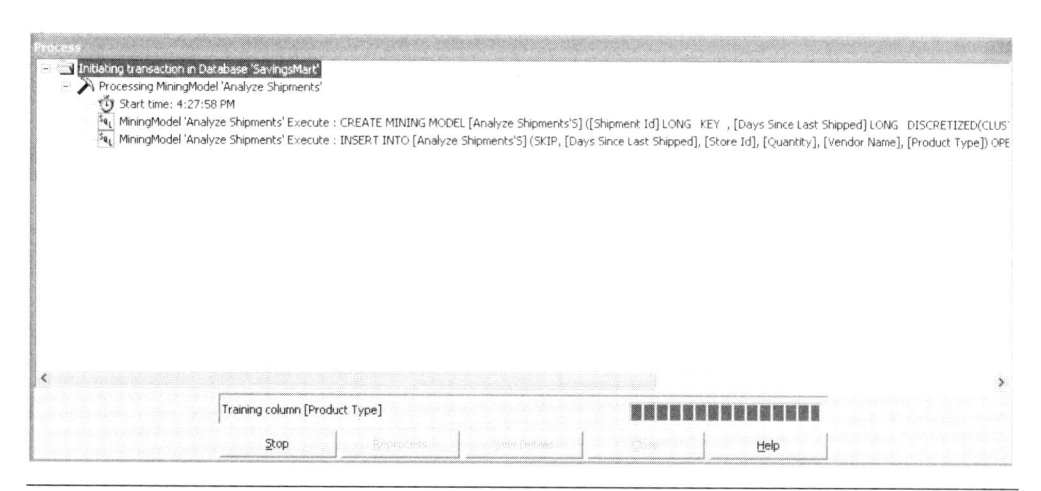

Figure 5.5 Screenshot of the dialog that appears when full process is initiated for a mining model. Note the DDL syntax used to create the model and then train it by populating it with historical data.

```
    [Vendor Name] TEXT DISCRETE,
    [Product Type] TEXT DISCRETE)
USING Microsoft_Decision_Trees
```

With the preceding statement, we are creating a new mining model named Analyze Shipments. The model utilizes Shipment ID as the case key. Days Since Last Shipped, and Quantity are each defined as predictable columns, but Days Since Last Shipped also functions as an input column. The remaining columns, Store ID, Vendor Name, and Product Type, are input columns only. Mining-model columns are defined as either input, predictable, or input and predictable.

The process of training a model involves the insertion of data into the mining model using the INSERT INTO syntax, as follows:

```
INSERT INTO [Analyze Shipments]
    (SKIP,[Days Since Last Shipped], [Store Id], [Quantity],
    [Vendor Name], [Product Type])
OPENROWSET('SQLOLEDB.1','Provider=SQLOLEDB.1;Integrated
    Security=SSPI;Persist Security Info=False;Initial
    Catalog=SavingsMart;Data Source=(local)',
    'SELECT DISTINCT "dbo"."vw_Shipments"."ShipmentID"
    AS "Shipment Id", "dbo"."vw_Shipments"."DaysSinceLastShipped"
    AS "Days Since Last Shipped", "dbo"."vw_Shipments"."StoreID"
    AS "Store Id", "dbo"."vw_Shipments"."Quantity" AS "Quantity",
    "dbo"."vw_Shipments"."VendorName" AS "Vendor Name",
    "dbo"."vw_Shipments"."ProductType" AS "Product Type"
    FROM "dbo"."vw_Shipments"')
```

The mining model will not store the actual data, but will store the prediction results instead once the mining algorithm is processed. In the preceding statement, the OPENROWSET keyword was used to specify the location of the physical data source.

Interpreting the Results

To examine the results from processing the model, select the **Content** tab. Figure 5.6 is a screenshot of the content detail when analyzing DaysSinceLastShipped. This screen indicates that VendorName was the most significant factor affecting DaysSinceLastShipped. We know this because it is the first split on the tree. For nodes that have additional branches, two lines will follow the node. To view the additional branches, double-click that node and the detail page will drill down to the next level.

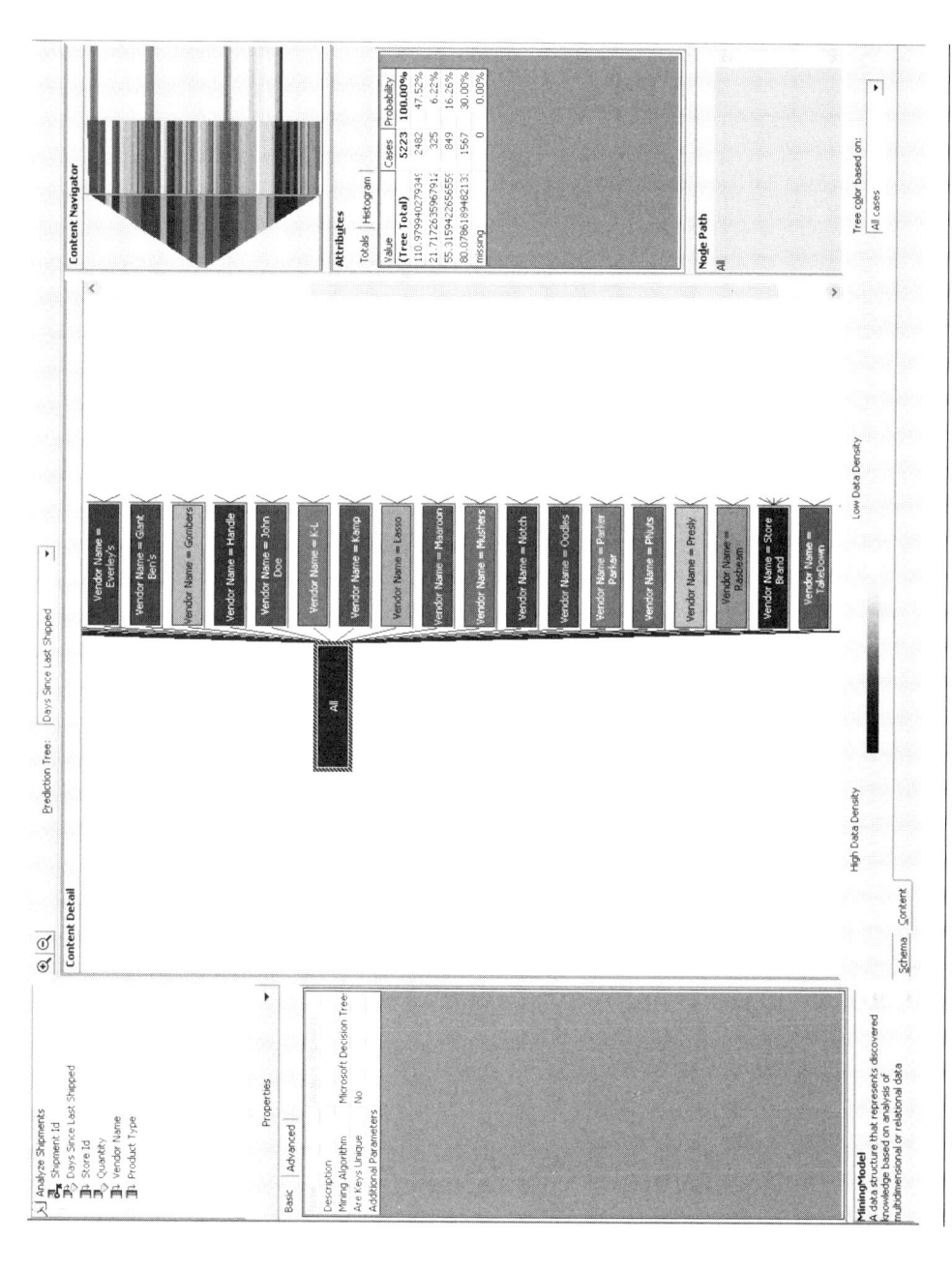

Figure 5.6 Screenshot of the content detail after processing the Analyze Shipments mining model. These results indicate the highest prediction level for the DaysSinceLastShipped column.

The **Content Navigator** box—seen in the top-right corner—offers an easy way to see all the mining-model results and drill down into a certain path. The **Attributes** box shows the totals associated with each node, grouped according to a clustering algorithm. In Figure 5.6, the cursor is selecting the outermost node labeled All. In this example, the attributes are shown for all the cases analyzed.

NOTE: If you did not attach the database file and instead loaded the data using the LoadSampleData program, you will encounter slightly different statistical results. The results presented in this section are specific to the database file available on the book's Web site.

If you attached your database using the file provided, your processing results should be the same as the ones we are about to interpret. The first thing to notice is that the darkest-shaded node is the one where the Vendor Name is Store Brand. Nodes that resulted in a higher data density, or more cases analyzed, will be shaded in a darker color. This result is not surprising, because 127 of the 500 products available, or 25 percent, are represented by the Store Brand. This can be confirmed in **Query Analyzer** with the following query:

```
SELECT v.VendorName,(COUNT(ProductID)/500.0) AS 'Percent'
FROM Products p
LEFT JOIN Vendors v ON p.VendorID = v.VendorID
GROUP BY v.VendorName
ORDER BY 'Percent' DESC
```

If the Store Brand node is double-clicked, the detail pane will show the next branching of the tree (see Figure 5.7). For the Store Brand Node, the first branching distinguishes between the different stores. If we click on the node Store ID = 2 and look at the attributes, the value with the highest probability is 119.33. This indicates that for all products where the Vendor name is Store Brand and the Store ID is 2, it is highly probable that there should be 119 days between shipments.

If we examine the attributes for the remaining nodes, we will see that predictions can be made for all the stores. For Store 1, there is one additional branching that distinguishes between a product type of Snack Foods versus all other product types. When the Store ID is 1, vendor name is Store Brand, and product type is snack foods, there is a 58 percent probability that there will be 60 days between shipments. When we examine the attributes

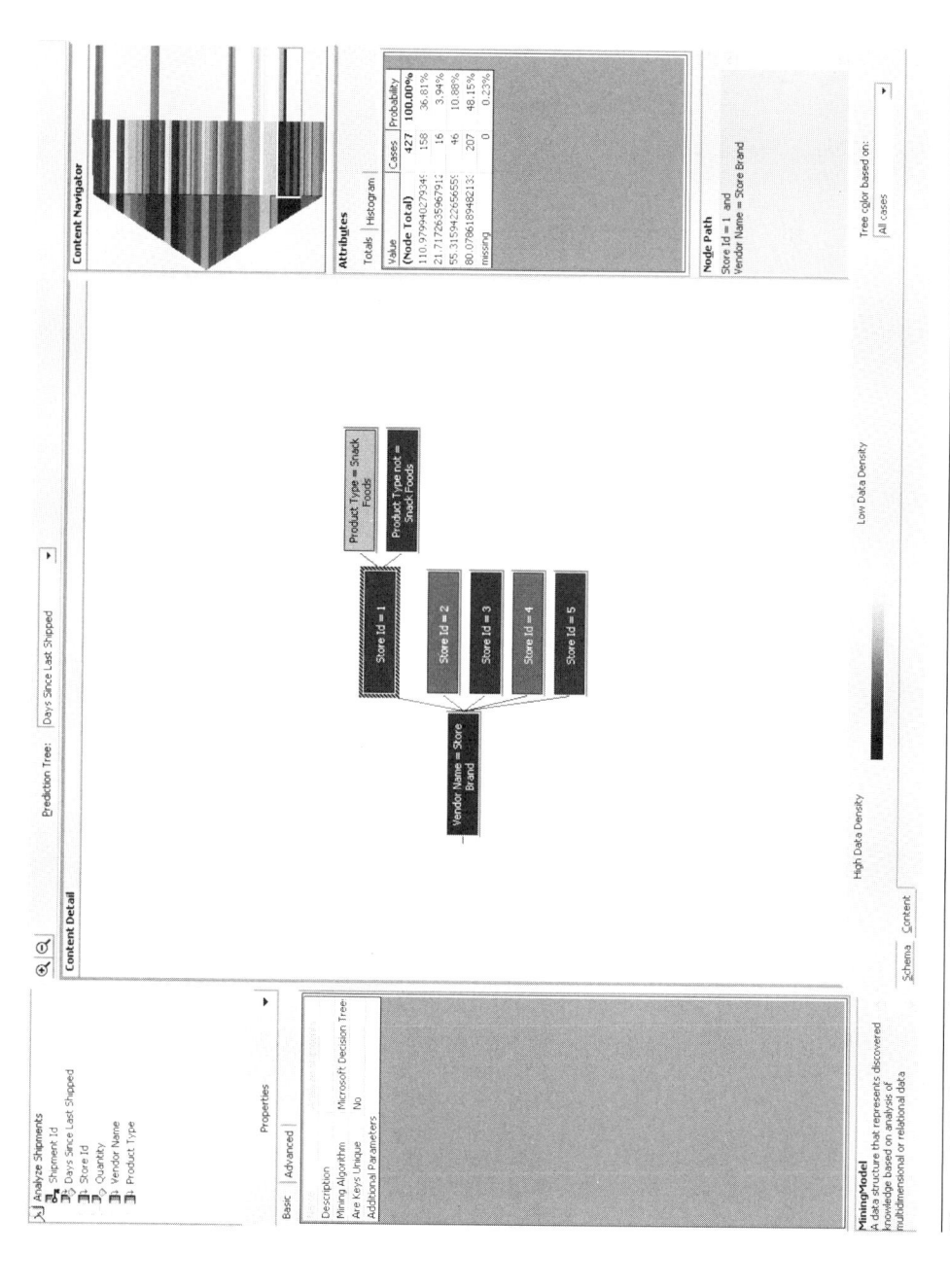

Figure 5.7 Screenshot of the Content Detail Editor as it displays the predictions for days since last shipped. In this example, the node path is where Store ID is 2 and the vendor name is Store Brand.

where product type is not snack foods, there is a 43 percent probability that there will be 119 days between shipments and a 53 percent probability that there will be 85 days between shipments. In this case, we could say that the 53 percent probability wins the toss, but that might not always be the best decision. This will be discussed further in the next chapter.

If you use the drop-down box above the Content Detail pane named **Prediction Tree** to select the quantity column, you will see that the main factor affecting quantity is the days since last shipped (see Figure 5.8).

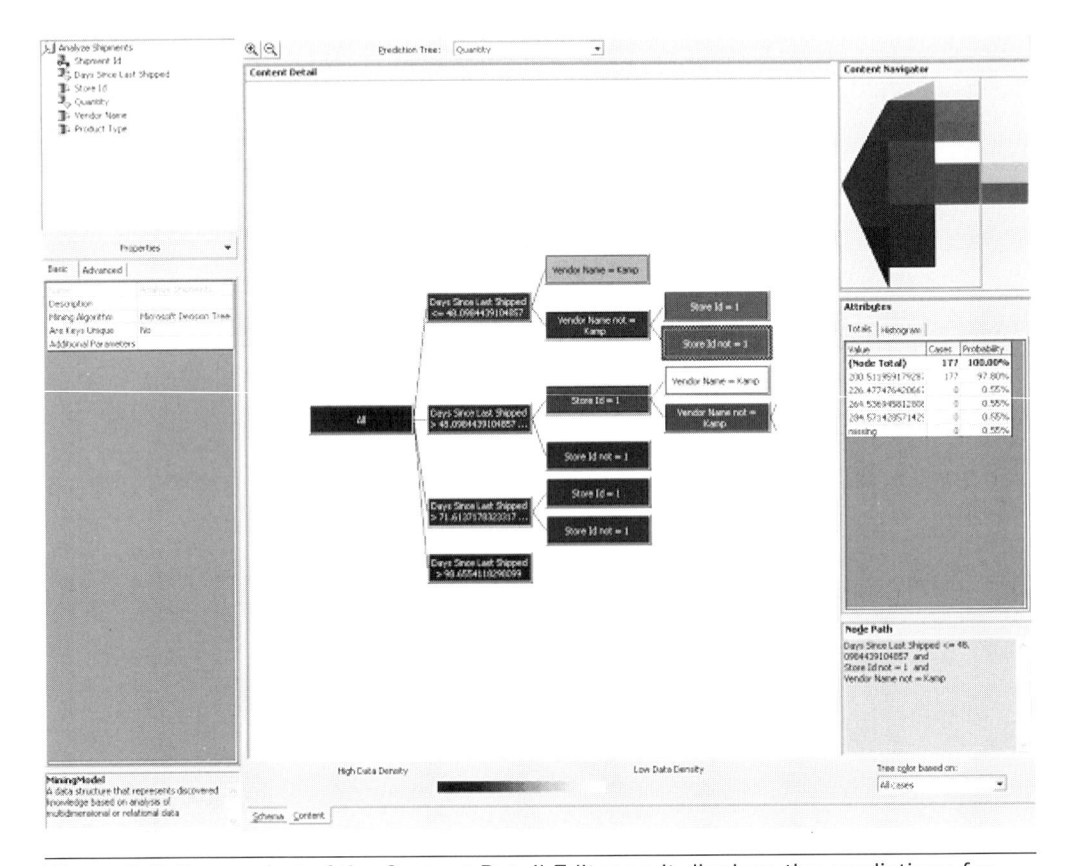

Figure 5.8 Screenshot of the Content Detail Editor as it displays the predictions for Quantity. In this example, the node path examined is where Days Since Last Shipped is less than or equal to 48 and Store ID is not equal to 1 and vendor name is not equal to Kamp.

This is possible because the column DaysSinceLastShipped was defined as an input and a predictable column.

The next factor affecting quantity is the vendor name. In the case where the vendor name is NOT Kamp, Store ID is an additional factor. In Figure 5.8 we can see that when the days since last shipped is less than or equal to 48 and the Store ID is NOT 1 and the vendor name is NOT Kamp, there is a 98 percent probability that the quantity should be 200. When the Store ID is equal to 1, the prediction drops to a 72 percent probability that the quantity will be 200.

The next chapter will involve interpreting the results from the mining model and then applying the predictions to a new shipment strategy. The goal of the new shipment strategy will be to reduce Savings Mart's operational costs by reducing the total number of shipments.

Summary

- The technology known as data warehousing has developed as a means of making use of the huge quantities of data available these days. In addition to storing all this data, data mining is needed to make useful predictions about it. Analysis Services, a separate install for SQL Server 2000, offers data-mining capabilities in an easy-to-use and scalable way.
- This chapter is one of two that examines the effort of a fictional discount retailer named Savings Mart to improve its operational efficiencies. A sample application named LoadSampleData, provided on the book's Web site, allows readers to generate a unique dataset for the data-mining model. Optionally, the reader can also attach a database file provided on the Web site.
- One of the biggest problems affecting successful data mining is invalid or incorrect data. Therefore, the process of cleaning a database is often the most time-consuming aspect of preparing a dataset.
- We step through the process of creating a mining model using Analysis Services. This involves creating a database, naming the data source, and using the mining-model wizard to create the actual model.
- Once a model is created, it can be trained with a training dataset to produce prediction results. The training dataset in this chapter represents one year's worth of purchases and shipments to all five stores. These results will be the basis for a Windows service created in the next chapter.

CHAPTER 6

Applying Data-Mining Predictions

In Chapter 5 we examined a data-mining model used by a fictional retailer named Savings Mart. This small retailer used the model to determine what factors most affected shipments to its stores. The model was designed to predict the number of days between shipments and the quantity for each store and vendor. The model was based on a decision tree algorithm. Processing the algorithm determined that Store ID, Vendor name, and Product type were the main factors determining what the number of days should be. Quantity was affected by the days since last shipped, Vendor name, and Store ID.

Now that the managers of Savings Mart are aware of the prediction results, they would like to redesign the way product orders and shipments are automatically generated. Their primary goal is to increase profits by reducing operational overhead. Previously, orders were generated based on minimum and maximum threshold quantities for each store and product. As purchases were made, the system would check to see whether the available quantity fell beneath the minimum threshold amount for that product. When this occurred, the system would automatically generate an order for that store with a quantity based on the maximum threshold amount.

The method for generating orders seemed like a good one when Savings Mart first began operating in 2001. Unfortunately, the company found that it resulted in the generation of shipments almost on a daily basis. The cost associated with shipments was high and thus reduced profitability for each store.

This chapter will examine code designed to generate new predictions and apply the results to a newly designed shipment methodology. The code is encased in a modified version of the LoadSampleData standalone

Windows program introduced in Chapter 5. The modified version will utilize a new table containing the results of the processed mining model.

The chapter also includes a case study about a data-mining solution used to predict Web usage. The solution was utilized by a Web site portal that organized content for its subscribers. The solution examined requested pages and used the prediction results to make suggestions about other pages the user might be interested in.

Working with the Sample Application

In order to execute the sample application included on the book's Web site at http:// www.awprofessional.com/title/0321246268, you will need to install files needed for communicating with Analysis Services. You will also need to apply certain database changes utilizing a SQL script, available for download from the book's Web site.

Communicating with Analysis Services

Old Method

Analysis Services, bundled with SQL Server 2000, was released prior to Visual Studio.NET and therefore is not natively supported by the .NET framework. Initially, communication with Analysis Services and .NET was done using COM integration and the Microsoft Active Data Objects Multidimensional (ADOMD) library. To do this, you had to add a COM reference to the ADOMD library. Unfortunately, this sometimes introduced problems and limitations to the process of communicating with Analysis Services. One such problem involved the use of C# with ADOMD. Since C# does not support omitting parameters, as Visual Basic does, you would be forced to set values for all parameters. If the potential values for these parameters changed during releases of ADOMD, this could cause your program to behave improperly.

New Method

The **ADOMD.NET SDK** was introduced as a means of consistently communicating with multidimensional sources of data like Analysis Services. It is a standard .NET data provider that utilizes interfaces from the System.Data and System.Data.Common namespaces. It offers an object model similar to the one used by ADO.NET. For instance, it uses a connection object to connect with the data source. It then has a command object for issuing commands and other objects to store the results of data queries.

> **TIP:** Readers interested in learning more about Analysis Services may want to refer to the following Web site, which is hosted by the development lead for the Microsoft Analysis Services engine, Mosha Pasumansky:
>
> http://www.mosha.com/msolap
>
> This site contains many links to technical information involving current and upcoming releases of SQL Server.

It communicates with standard data sources over the Web using the **XML for Analysis specification 1.1**. Multidimensional data can be queried and returned in an object similar to the ADO.NET DataReader. Connections are made using ADOMDConnection objects, and query parameters are passed using ADOMDCommand objects. ADOMD.NET also offers an object known as the CellSet that is similar to the ADO.NET dataset object. Refer to Table 6.1 for a listing of the main objects offered by ADOMD.NET. There are essentially three ways of retrieving data:

- The multidimensional CellSet object
- The read-only and forward-only DataReader object
- The XMLReader object

Of the three methods, the XMLReader, which returns raw XML, is the least resource intensive.

In order to reproduce results using the sample application for this chapter, you will need to install both the XML for Analysis specification 1.1 and the ADOMD.NET SDK. To do this, perform the following steps:

1. If you have not already installed the Microsoft XML Parser (MSXML) 4.0 or later, you must install it first by executing the msxml.msi file, available for download from the Microsoft Web site.
2. Initiate installation for the XML for Analysis specification 1.1 by executing the file named XMLASDK.exe, available for download from the Microsoft Web site.

Table 6.1 The topmost objects used in the ADOMD.NET SDK. This SDK was designed specifically for communicating with multidimensional data sources and Visual Studio.NET.

Object Name	Description
ADOMDConnection	Represents a connection to a multidimensional data source. This can include a data cube or a processed mining model. It will accept a connection string similar to the one used to connect to a SQL Server database. The difference is that ADOMD.NET uses the XML for Analysis specification which is optimized for the Web. A valid connection string used to communicate with the SavingsMart database defined on Analysis Server is, "Provider=MSOLAP;Data Source=http://localhost/xmla/msxisapi.dll;Initial Catalog=SavingsMart;"
ADOMDCommand	Used to specify an mdx statement or query to run against Analysis Services. It operates similarly to the command object used by ADO.NET and accepts parameters. It can be used to return CellSet, DataReader, or XMLReader objects. It can also be used to execute NonQuery and Scalar methods.
ADOMDDataReader	Just as with ADO.NET, the DataReader object is the fastest and most efficient way of returning data. It returns data using either the Execute or ExecuteReader method of the command object.
CellSet	A CellSet is a multidimensional result set that runs across more than one dimension or axis. This is necessary when returning data from a multidimensional (mdx) query of a data cube. A CellSet is disconnected and useful for caching purposes, but is also the most resource intensive.

3. Installing the ADOMD.NET SDK 8.0, the last step, is accomplished by executing the Setup.exe file, also available for download from the Microsoft Web site.

TIP: When installing the XML for Analysis SDK, make sure you check the **Enable HTTP Unsecure** checkbox. By default the XML for Analysis Service Provider will attempt to use a secure HTTPS connection with Secure Sockets Layer (SSL).

Applying Database Changes

In addition to installing the SDK, you will need to apply database changes in order to execute the sample code for this chapter. This is done by opening **Query Analyzer** and executing the SQL script named DBChanges.sql file, available for download from the book Web site. This script will add four new stored procedures and three new tables to the SavingsMart database. Refer to Table 6.2 for a listing of these changes.

NOTE: Readers who did not build the SavingsMart database in Chapter 5 must first attach a database file available for download from the book's Web site. The Version1database files are named SavingsMart.mdf and SavingsMart.ldf. This file contains data generated for all five stores in the year 2001.

1. Copy the **SavingsMart.mdf** and **SavingsMart.ldf** files from the book's Web site to a local directory on the server where Microsoft SQL Server is installed.
2. Open SQL Server's **Enterprise Manager**.
3. Right-click the **Databases** node and click **All Tasks...** and **Attach Database**.
4. From the **Attach Database** dialog, browse to the directory where you copied the database files in step 1 and select the SavingsMart.mdf file. Click **OK**.
5. Click **OK** to attach the database.
6. To see the newly added database, you will need to click **Action** and **Refresh**.

Generating New Shipment Schedules

The Mining-Model Results

In Chapter 5, Savings Mart used a system of minimum and maximum thresholds to indicate when shipments to stores should be generated. At the end of one year, management realized that 295 shipments were made for Store 1 alone. Thus, for every day of the year, there was an 81 percent probability (295/365 = .8082191) that a shipment would be made. Since each shipment involves substantial operating costs, management knew that a better system would have to be devised.

Table 6.2 Database changes included in the DBChanges.sql file available on the book's Web site. These changes will allow us to execute the code in the LoadSampleData project included with this chapter. Note that each time a database restore is performed, the DBChanges.sql script will also need to be executed.

Object Name	Description
ShipmentSchedules	Table that stores values attained from querying the mining model Analyze Shipments. This represents the predicted days between shipments and quantity for each vendor and store.
ProductAvailabilityTracking	Table written to during execution of the revised GeneratePurchases routine. A record will be written to it every time an attempt is made to purchase a product not available. This table will allow management to review the success of applying the mining-model predictions.
ServiceParms	Table used by the Windows service named WindowsSvc. Only one record will be stored in this table, and it will be used by the Windows service to identify when the mining model was last processed. It is possible to alter the code not to use this table and instead select a different method for scheduling the Windows service.
GetStoresAndVendors	Stored procedure that returns one result set containing all stores and another containing all vendors. This will be used to populate a data set used by the PopulateShipmentSchedulesTable routine.
InsertShipmentSchedule	Stored procedure used to insert records into the newly created ShipmentSchedules table.
CheckShipmentSchedule	Stored procedure executed by the revised GeneratePurchases routine. It is used to determine whether an order needs to be generated for the store and date being processed. It compares the value of DaysBetweenShipments in the ShipmentSchedules table against the last time an order was processed for each vendor of that store. If the number of days exceeds the predicted value, an order is generated for all products of that vendor.
InsertPurchaseDetailNew	Stored procedure similar to the InsertPurchaseDetail stored procedure used in the LoadSampleData project from Chapter 5. This new stored procedure is smaller because it does not need to check threshold values on every purchase. Instead it just checks to see if the product is available at that store and if it is not, it writes a record to the newly created ProductAvailabilityTracking table.

In Chapter 5, Analysis Services was used to build a mining model named "Analyze Shipments." This mining model attempted to predict the most influential factors affecting the days between shipments and the quantity to be shipped. When we examine the Content through the Relational Mining Model Editor, we can see that the most significant factor affecting days since last shipped is the vendor name.

If we drill down on the vendor named Ables (see Figure 6.1), we see that the next significant factor is the Store ID. The Store ID is used to distinguish predictions on two levels. The first split separates predictions for Store ID 1 from all the other stores. Beyond that, it also separates predictions for Store ID 3 from all the other stores—in this case Stores 2, 4, and 5. For the remaining stores, there is a 90 percent probability that there will be 111 days between shipments.

NOTE: Prediction results are dependent upon the data and will vary if you choose to run the LoadSampleData program in Chapter 5 with parameters different from the ones listed in the book. If you generated purchases just for Store 1 and not the others, the most significant factor will be product type and not vendor name.

For every vendor there are predictions of the time to ship products and what quantity should be shipped. The next step is to get the information into a useable format so that new shipping schedules can be estimated. This involves the ability to query the mining-model results for specific vendors and stores.

Refreshing the Mining Model

Once a mining model has been trained and tested, and you believe it will produce good results, you will need to set up a process that allows the mining model to be refreshed periodically. Refreshing a mining model involves retraining the mining model using new and/or updated data without recreating it. This can be done manually using Analysis Manager, or programmatically using Decision Support Objects (DSO).

The LoadSampleData project from Chapter 5 has been modified to include additional procedures for this chapter. The revised project LoadSampleData is available for download from the book's Web site. If you copy the files to your local machine, open the solution file, and expand the References node in **Solution Explorer**, you will see a reference for ADODB and DSO. The DSO reference is a COM-based reference to the Microsoft Decision Support Object library. This will

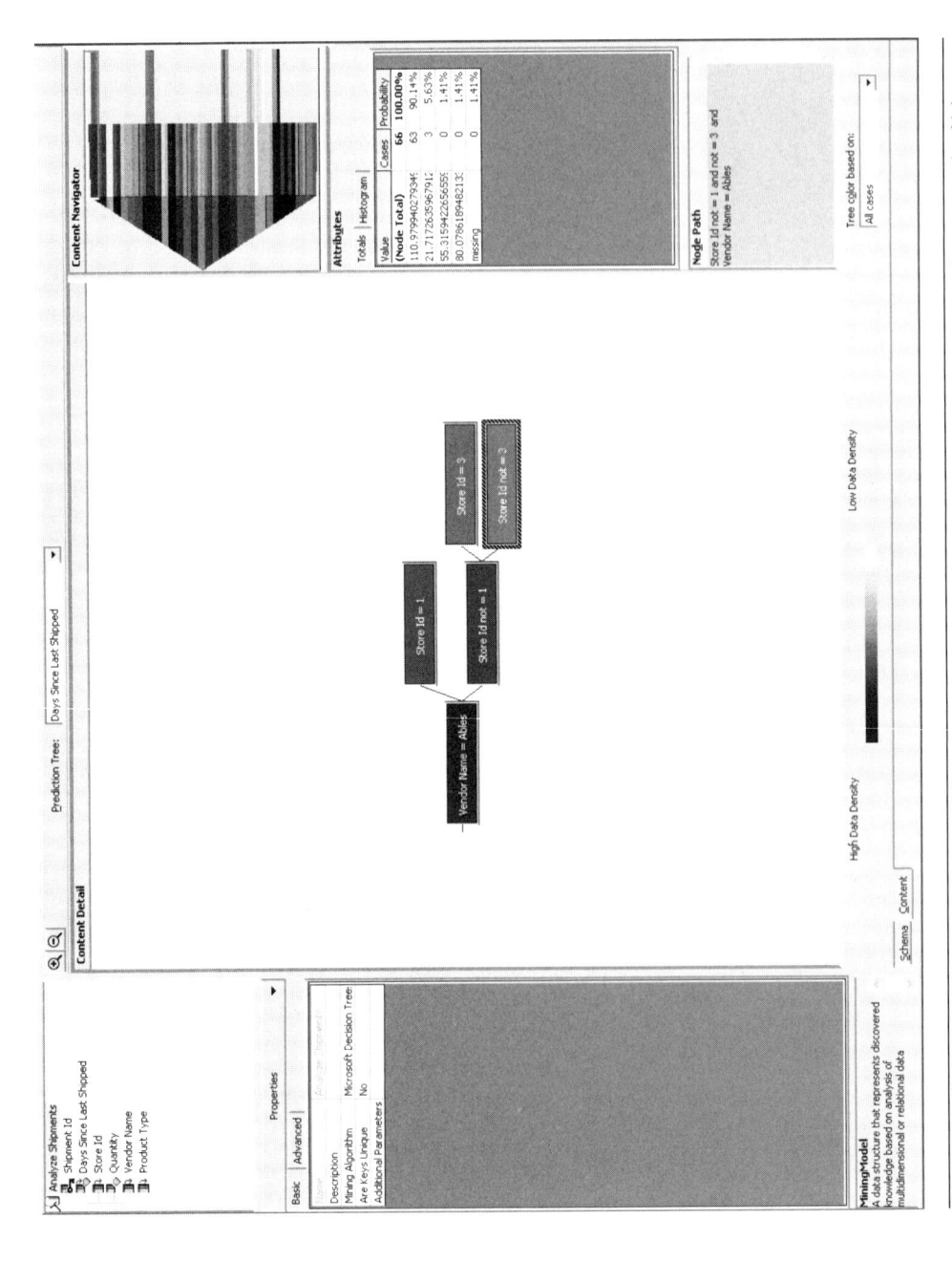

Figure 6.1 Screenshot of the Content Editor as it displays the node path where vendor name is Ables and the Store ID is not 1 and not 3.

Generating New Shipment Schedules

allow us to programmatically process the mining model. The third reference is a .NET reference to the ADOMD library namespace, **Microsoft.AnalysisServices.AdomdClient**. This will only be available after you have successfully installed the ADOMD.NET SDK.

Open the main form by double-clicking Form1.vb in **Solution Explorer**. You should see a new button titled **Apply Shipment Schedules** (see Figure 6.2). Clicking this button will execute two routines named ProcessMiningModel and PopulateShipmentSchedulesTable. Note that the input variables available in the last chapter were removed and hard-coded within the program to speed processing time.

Since the data is not stored with the mining model, the model will need to be reprocessed periodically. Processing a mining model is accomplished by right-clicking the model name from Analysis Manager and selecting **Process**. When a mining model is processed, the processing method is either a Full process or Refresh Data (see Figure 6.3). Refreshing the data involves retraining the model without completely recreating it. This is the faster option and the one that should be chosen if no changes are made to the structure of the model.

The ProcessMiningModel procedure programmatically accomplishes the same thing as clicking **Process...** from the Analysis Manager interface. It will reexamine the data using the mining model specified. It first opens a connection to the Analysis Server and sets a reference to the Analyze Shipments mining model (named oModel). It then initiates a refresh of the mining model by executing the following lines of code:

```
Try
  oModel.LockObject(OlapLockTypes.olapLockProcess, _
      "Training the Shipments mining model")
  oModel.Process(ProcessTypes.processRefreshData)
  oModel.UnlockObject()
Catch ex As Exception
  MessageBox.Show("Unable to refresh the mining model")
  Exit Sub
End Try
```

A lock is placed on the object before processing occurs in order to prevent conflicts and is released after the data is refreshed. At this point, what is refreshed are the predictions themselves. This is because Analysis Services does not store the raw data used as input, but instead stores the predictions made as a result of applying the data-mining algorithm.

Chapter 6 Applying Data-Mining Predictions

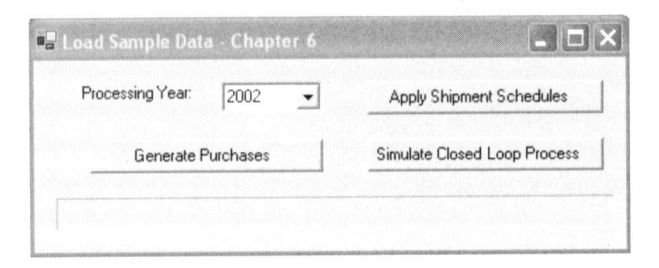

Figure 6.2 Screenshot of the main form used by the LoadSampleData project available with Chapter 6. This project is based on the same one in Chapter 5, but applies the predictions made by Analysis Services.

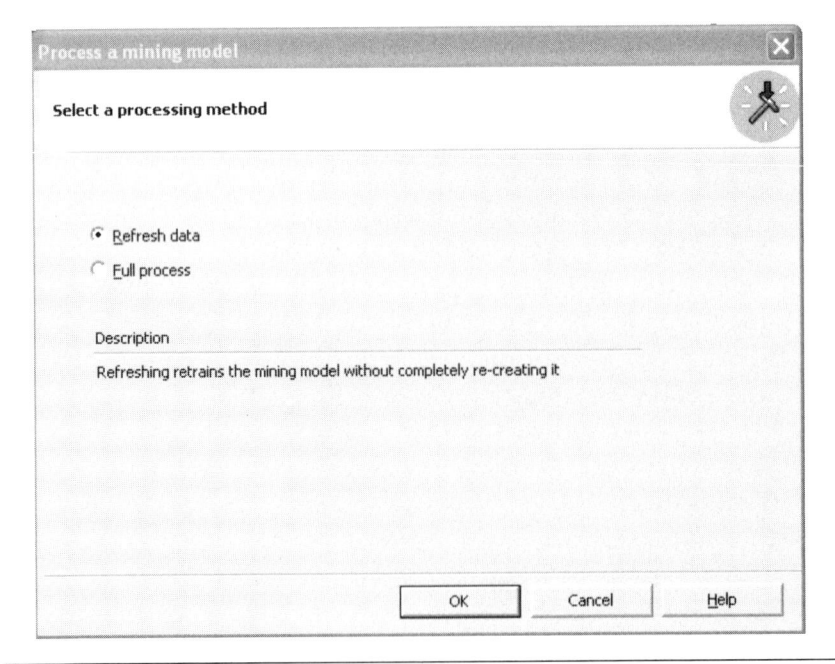

Figure 6.3 Screenshot of the wizard that appears when a mining model is processed from within Analysis Manager. Unless the structure of the model is changed, Refresh Data is the option that will be chosen here.

Querying the Mining Model

The PopulateShipmentSchedulesTable procedure, as follows, is where we will actually query the mining model for results.

```
' Open the connection to Analysis Services
AScn.ConnectionString = sASConn
AScn.Open()

' Get a list of vendors and stores from our SQL tables
Dim ds As DataSet = SqlHelper.ExecuteDataset(sConn, _
    CommandType.StoredProcedure, "GetStoresAndVendors")

' Now we will loop through the stores and vendors to get the
' predicted quantity and days between shipments.
' Results will be stored in the ShipmentSchedules table
Dim Vrow As DataRow
Dim nStoreID As Int16
Dim nVendorID As Int16
Dim sVendor As String, sType As String
For Each Vrow In ds.Tables(0).Rows()
    nVendorID = Vrow(0)
    sVendor = Convert.ToString(Vrow(1)).Replace("'", "''")
    sType = Convert.ToString(Vrow(2)).Replace("'", "''")
    Dim SRow As DataRow
    For Each SRow In ds.Tables(1).Rows()
        nStoreID = SRow(0)
        Dim cmd As New AdomdCommand
        cmd.Connection = AScn
        'Version 1
        Dim sSQL As String = "SELECT Predict("
        sSQL += " Days Since Last Shipped]), "
        sSQL += " Predict(Quantity)"
        sSQL += " FROM [Analyze Shipments] PREDICTION JOIN "
        sSQL += "(SELECT '" + sVendor + "' as VendorName, "
        sSQL += Convert.ToString(nStoreID) + " as StoreID) as t "
        sSQL += "ON [Analyze Shipments].[Vendor Name] = t.VendorName"
        sSQL += " AND [Analyze Shipments].[Store ID] = t.StoreID "

        'Version 2
        'Dim sSQL As String = "SELECT Predict("
        'sSQL += " Days Since Last Shipped]), "
```

Chapter 6 Applying Data-Mining Predictions

```
'sSQL += " Predict(Quantity)"
'sSQL += " FROM [Analyze Shipments] PREDICTION JOIN "
'sSQL += "(SELECT '" + sVendor + "' as VendorName, "
'sSQL += Convert.ToString(nStoreID) + " as StoreID, "
'sSQL += "'" + sType + "' as Type) as t "
'sSQL += "ON [Analyze Shipments].[Vendor Name] = t.VendorName "
'sSQL += "AND [Analyze Shipments].[Store ID] = t.StoreID "
'sSQL += "AND [Analyze Shipments].[Product Type] = t.Type "
cmd.CommandText = sSQL
Dim dr As AdomdDataReader = cmd.Execute()
dr.Read()
' Insert the results into the ShipmentSchedules table
If IsUpdate = False Then
   Dim params(3) As SqlParameter
   params(0) = New SqlParameter("@StoreID", SqlDbType.Int)
   params(1) = New SqlParameter("@VendorID", SqlDbType.Int)
   params(2) = New SqlParameter("@Days", SqlDbType.Int)
   params(3) = New SqlParameter("@Qty", SqlDbType.Int)
   params(0).Value = nStoreID
   params(1).Value = nVendorID
   params(2).Value = Convert.ToString(dr.Item(0))
   params(3).Value = Convert.ToString(dr.Item(1))
   Dim ret As Integer = SqlHelper.ExecuteScalar(sConn, _
     CommandType.StoredProcedure, "InsertShipmentSchedule", _
     params)
Else
   Dim params(3) As SqlParameter
   params(0) = New SqlParameter("@StoreID", SqlDbType.Int)
   params(1) = New SqlParameter("@VendorID", SqlDbType.Int)
   params(2) = New SqlParameter("@Days", SqlDbType.Int)
   params(3) = New SqlParameter("@Qty", SqlDbType.Int)
   params(0).Value = nStoreID
   params(1).Value = nVendorID
   params(2).Value = Convert.ToString(dr.Item(0))
   params(3).Value = Convert.ToString(dr.Item(1))
   Dim ret As Integer = SqlHelper.ExecuteScalar(sConn, _
     CommandType.StoredProcedure, "UpdateShipmentSchedule", _
     params)
  End If
  dr.Close()
 Next
Next
```

Generating New Shipment Schedules

The first line of code in this procedure creates a new AdomdConnection object. We then populate a regular ADO.NET dataset with a listing of all the vendors and stores. For each store we will loop through a listing of all the vendors and build the mining-model query. The code includes a commented version of the dynamic SQL statement. The commented version includes product type as a query variable. For now, product type is not included, since initial processing did not identify it as a factor affecting the outcome. This will change after further processing and will be discussed later. For now, Version 1 is the statement that will be executed.

Building a Prediction Query

The syntax for the query is very similar to a transact SQL statement executed against the SQL server. The string that follows is what one such query string looks like.

```
SELECT Predict([Days Since Last Shipped]),Predict(Quantity)
FROM [Analyze Shipments]
PREDICTION JOIN (SELECT 'Ables' as VendorName, 1 as StoreID) as t
ON [Analyze Shipments].[Vendor Name] = t.VendorName
AND [Analyze Shipments].[Store ID] = t.StoreID
```

In this query we select the two predicted outcome variables from the Analyze Shipments mining model. The PREDICTION JOIN keyword is used to specify that we want to return values for a specific vendor and store.

This particular query is known as a prediction query because it is used to retrieve results from an already trained model. The other type of query that Analysis Services supports is a content query. This type of query is used to browse the contents of a mining model and can be useful if you are programmatically trying to identify trends in the processed data.

TIP: If you would like to review the content of your mining model as raw XML, you can perform a query using Predictive Model Markup Language, or PMML. For instance, a query such as

SELECT * FROM [AnalyzeShipments].PMML

will return a result set in which item 5 contains the raw XML stream. The stream contains the actual statement used to create the mining model as well as a data dictionary that lists the categories and attributes involved. The global statistics section lists the data distribution or clustered segments for each attribute. Finally, the tree model contains the actual predictions made by the model's algorithm.

To view the raw XML associated with the Analyze Shipments model, refer to the pmml.xml file, available for download from the book's Web site.

Our prediction query is useful for extracting the top prediction result for each vendor and store. We knew to restrict the query to these values because they were identified as the top factors in predicting days between shipments. If you were to browse the contents of the Analyze Shipments mining model from the data-mining Model Browser in **Analysis Manager** (see Figure 6.4), you would be able to drill down into a specific node path. The prediction query built in the PopulateShipmentSchedulesTable routine returns the same results as using Analysis Manager.

Understanding the Query Results

For the Ables vendor and Store 1, Figure 6.4 lists the clustered node totals in the Attributes. Here we see that the case with the highest probability predicts that the days between shipments will be 55. This same result is returned if we execute the prediction query previously listed.

For all other stores we will ship 201 items every 111 days, except for store 3, which will ship 201 items every 80 days. Once the mining model is queried and the data is written to the ShipmentSchedules tables, we should see the following records listed first:

Shipment ScheduleID	VendorID	StoreID	DaysBetween Shipments	Quantity
1	1	1	55	225
2	1	2	111	201
3	1	3	80	201
4	1	4	111	201
5	1	5	111	201

If you were to run the following query in **Query Analyzer**, "SELECT DISTINCT DaysBetweenShipments FROM ShipmentSchedules," you should see these results: 22, 55, 80, and 111. This represents the clustered amounts predicted for days between shipments. The same query for quantity might reveal such values as 201, 225, and 283. The astute reader may

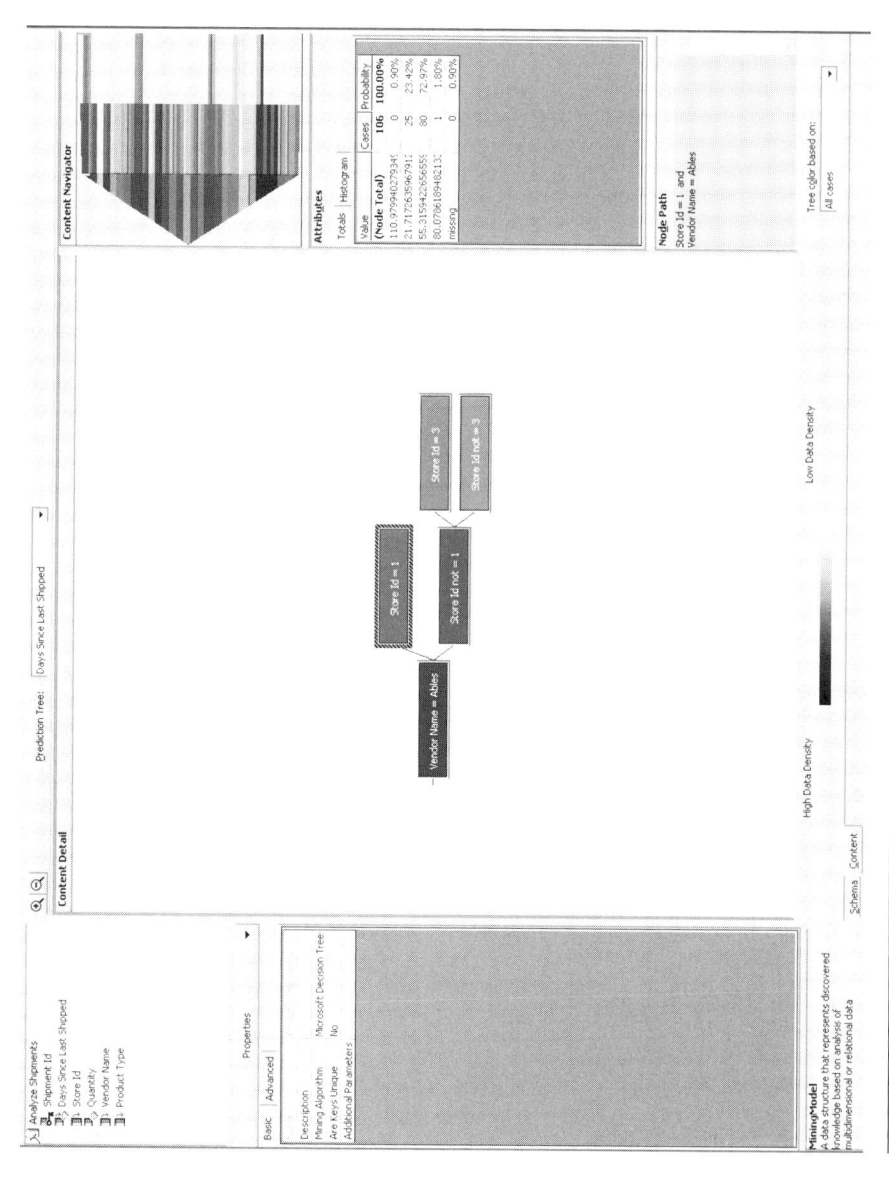

Figure 6.4 Screenshot of the data-mining model browser in Analysis Manager. This view is used to predict days between shipments for the node path where Store ID is 1 and the vendor name is Ables. The attributes section lists values for the four case sets along with their probability. The case with the highest probability (73%) has a value of 55, indicating that this is the predicted number of days between shipments.

notice that the four distinct days between shipments exactly match the same values in the global statistics section of the pmml.xml file.

The mining algorithms used by Analysis Services do not simply output averages of data values. They apply complex mathematical methods in an iterative fashion in order to cluster data into the most predictable groups. For a detailed explanation of the specifics of algorithms like decision trees, you can refer to the section in the latest **MSDN library** (available at msdn.microsoft.com) titled **Microsoft Decision Trees.**

Case Study: Web Usage Mining

Denis Susac, Webmaster and programmer for the AboutAI Web site (www.aboutai.net), used Microsoft SQL Server 2000 to add data-mining functionality to the Web site. AboutAI is a Web site dedicated to informing visitors and subscribing members about the different areas of AI. It acts as a portal and includes forums for connecting members.

The AboutAI Web site was built using Microsoft .NET and was based on the IBuySpy Portal application, available through MSDN. IBuySpy is a free ASP.NET Web development tool that Microsoft offers to give developers a head start on developing their own Web sites (www.ibuyspy.com).

Denis used Analysis Services to build mining models that examined data about Web usage. The usage data was stored in two specially created SQL Server tables named Hits and HitCount. A clustering algorithm was used to group users and Web pages into similar clusters. A decision tree algorithm was then used to make predictions about related pages that the user might like to visit. The results of the prediction were displayed to the user as suggestions.

The predictive capabilities of the system would take place each time a page was accessed on the Web site. The processing of the mining model, where historical data is fed into the mining algorithm, would take place at scheduled intervals.

I contacted Denis Susac in late 2004 to see if the Web usage mining engine was still useful to him. He informed me that the data-mining functionality was now being used inside another product, named the Mono .NET Portal Engine. The Mono .NET Portal Engine, available from http://www.mono-software.com/, is a customizable framework for building portal Web sites that is easy to use but offers a lot of functionality.

Denis feels that Analysis Services is a useful tool and had this to say about it:

> I like this utility very much—it requires some time to get everything organized, but when it finally starts processing usage log data, it seems almost like magic. Results were pretty good and I think it can be used in a variety of real-world scenarios, especially market basket analysis.
>
> For more information about how Denis created his data-mining solution, you can access a detailed article he wrote for ASP Today at www.asp-today.com/Content.aspx?id=1898

Measuring the Success of the New Shipment Method

In order to determine whether the new shipment method is a success, we will need to generate purchases for an entire year and examine the number of orders that are generated. To do this, we will need to utilize a revised copy of the GeneratePurchases routine introduced in the last chapter.

A Revised Copy of GeneratePurchases

In Chapter 5 we used the GeneratePurchases routine to simulate daily purchasing activity for each store on a yearly basis. Orders were generated when purchases brought the quantity levels at or below the minimum thresholds allowed. At the beginning of each day, the orders table was checked for unfilled orders and necessary shipments were generated.

The first overloaded GeneratePurchases routine in the LoadSample-Data program for Chapter 6 does something similar. The code for this routine is seen as follows:

```
'Maximum # of purchases per day
Dim nMaxPurchases As Int16
'Maximum # of products per purchase
Dim nMaxProducts As Int16
'Maximum value of quantity per product
Dim nMaxQuantity As Int16
Dim sYear As String = "2002"
Dim nStoreID As Int16
```

```vb
'These are the Product Types in which there
'is an increased chance of product selection
'The default of 1,2 represents snack foods
'and beverages
Dim sProductTypeAdj As String

'These are the Vendors in which there is an
'increased chance of product selection
'The default of 20,24,27 represents Kamp, Notch,
'and PNuts as Vendors
Dim sVendorAdj As String
Dim i As Int16
Try
  'Process for all 5 stores
  For i = 1 To 5
    nStoreID = i
    If i = 1 Then
      nMaxPurchases = 80
      nMaxProducts = 8
      nMaxQuantity = 5
      sProductTypeAdj = "1,2"
      sVendorAdj = "20,24,27"
    ElseIf i = 2 Then
      nMaxPurchases = 60
      nMaxProducts = 10
      nMaxQuantity = 3
      sProductTypeAdj = "2,6"
      sVendorAdj = "13,18"
    ElseIf i = 3 Then
      nMaxPurchases = 70
      nMaxProducts = 6
      nMaxQuantity = 4
      sProductTypeAdj = "2"
      sVendorAdj = "34"
    ElseIf i = 4 Then
      nMaxPurchases = 90
      nMaxProducts = 5
      nMaxQuantity = 2
      sProductTypeAdj = ""
      sVendorAdj = "34,18"
    ElseIf i = 5 Then
      nMaxPurchases = 50
      nMaxProducts = 12
      nMaxQuantity = 6
```

```
    sProductTypeAdj = "6"
    sVendorAdj = "24,27,34"
End If
Dim params(2) As SqlParameter
params(0) = New SqlParameter("@ID", SqlDbType.Int)
params(1) = New _
    SqlParameter("@ProdTypeAdj", SqlDbType.VarChar, 50)
params(2) = New _
    SqlParameter("@VendorAdj", SqlDbType.VarChar, 50)
params(0).Value = nStoreID
params(1).Value = sProductTypeAdj
params(2).Value = sVendorAdj
Dim ds As DataSet = _
 SqlHelper.ExecuteDataset(sConn, _
 CommandType.StoredProcedure, "GetProductIDS", params)
Dim j As Int16 = 1
Dim dtDate As DateTime = _
Convert.ToDateTime("01/01/" + sYear)
'Loop through everyday of the year
'we assume the store is open everyday
Randomize()
Do Until j = 182
   'First thing is check to see if orders
   'needs to be fulfilled for this day and store
   'We assume that all orders are shipped 3 days
   'after the orderdate in one shipment
    Dim params1(1) As SqlParameter
    params1(0) = New _
      SqlParameter("@StoreID", SqlDbType.Int)
    params1(1) = New _
     SqlParameter("@Date", SqlDbType.SmallDateTime)
    params1(0).Value = nStoreID
     'order was placed 3 days ago
    params1(1).Value = dtDate.AddDays(-3)
    SqlHelper.ExecuteReader(sConn, _
       CommandType.StoredProcedure, _
       "InsertShipment", params1)
    'We will also call a new stored procedure here
    'called CheckShipmentSchedules which will
    'be used to see if the store needs orders
    'generated for this day.
    Dim params1b(1) As SqlParameter
    params1b(0) = New _
      SqlParameter("@StoreID", SqlDbType.Int)
```

```
params1b(1) = New _
 SqlParameter("@Date", SqlDbType.SmallDateTime)
params1b(0).Value = nStoreID
params1b(1).Value = dtDate
 SqlHelper.ExecuteNonQuery(sConn, _
 CommandType.StoredProcedure, _
 "CheckShipmentSchedule", params1b)
Dim x As Int16 = 1
'This will be the total number of
'purchases for this day
Dim nPurchases As Int16 = _
  CInt(Int((nMaxPurchases * Rnd()) + 1))
Do Until x = nPurchases + 1
   Dim y As Int16 = 1
   Dim nEmployeePos As Int16 = _
    CInt(Int((ds.Tables(1).Rows.Count * Rnd())))
   Dim nEmployeeID As Integer = _
    Convert.ToInt32(ds.Tables(1).Rows(nEmployeePos).Item(0))
   Dim params2(2) As SqlParameter
   params2(0) = New _
     SqlParameter("@ID1", SqlDbType.Int)
   params2(1) = _
     New SqlParameter("@Date", SqlDbType.SmallDateTime)
   params2(2) = New SqlParameter("@ID2", SqlDbType.Int)
   params2(0).Value = nStoreID
   params2(1).Value = dtDate
   params2(2).Value = nEmployeeID
   Dim nPurchaseID As Integer = _
    SqlHelper.ExecuteScalar(sConn, _
    CommandType.StoredProcedure, _
    "InsertPurchase", params2)
   'This is total number of products for
   'this(purchase)
   Dim nProducts As Int16 = _
    CInt(Int((nMaxProducts * Rnd()) + 1))
   Do Until y = nProducts + 1
     'This is quantity for this purchase
     Dim nQty As Int16 = _
      CInt(Int((nMaxQuantity * Rnd()) + 1))
     'This is the product for this detail record
     Dim nProductPos As Int16 = _
       CInt(Int((ds.Tables(0).Rows.Count * Rnd())))
     Dim nProductID As Integer = _
```

```
                Convert.ToInt32(ds.Tables(0).Rows(nProductPos).Item(0))
                'Generate the detail record
                Dim params3(4) As SqlParameter
                params3(0) = New _
                  SqlParameter("@StoreID", SqlDbType.Int)
                params3(1) = New _
                  SqlParameter("@ProductID", SqlDbType.Int)
                params3(2) = New _
                  SqlParameter("@PurchaseID", SqlDbType.Int)
                params3(3) = New _
                  SqlParameter("@Qty", SqlDbType.Int)
                params3(4) = New _
                  SqlParameter("@Date", SqlDbType.SmallDateTime)
                params3(0).Value = nStoreID
                params3(1).Value = nProductID
                params3(2).Value = nPurchaseID
                params3(3).Value = nQty
                params3(4).Value = dtDate
                'Note that the stored procedure name being
                'called is different than the one from Chapter 4
                SqlHelper.ExecuteScalar(sConn, _
                CommandType.StoredProcedure, _
                "InsertPurchaseDetailNew", params3)
                y += 1
              Loop
              x += 1
            Loop
            j += 1
            ProgressBar1.Value = j
            dtDate = dtDate.AddDays(1)   'Go to the next day
        Loop
    Next
    MessageBox.Show("Purchases for all 5 stores were generated _
        successfully")
  Catch ex As Exception
      MessageBox.Show(ex.Message)
  End Try
```

It too will simulate random purchase generation for each store. The difference is that we now will use the ShipmentSchedules table to determine when products should be ordered. In addition, the time frame has been lowered to six months to shorten the amount of processing time necessary.

The newly created InsertPurchaseDetailNew stored procedure is used not only to generate purchase records, but also to verify that the product quantity requested is available. If the product quantity is not available, a record is written to the newly created ProductAvailabilityTracking table. Management can use this table to measure the success of the new shipment method. Each record indicates an attempt by a customer to purchase a product not available.

In a real-world situation it would be difficult to utilize such a table. After all, most customers will not announce or even know that they are trying to purchase a product not available. More than likely a store would utilize some other method of tracking product availability. This could involve store managers routinely checking the store aisles or an automated method of querying the database.

The important thing to note is that the application of predictions by data-mining algorithms should be continually measured and evaluated. It is not good enough to simply use Analysis Services to make predictions and then assume that everything will work fine.

For demonstration purposes, you can execute the GeneratePurchases routine by clicking the **Generate Purchases** button on Form1. The form does not contain input parameters like the ones used in the Chapter 5 application. Instead, the values are hard-coded within the routine itself.

After running the GeneratePurchases routine using the Version 1 database file, we see some interesting results. If you were to perform the following query in **Query Analyzer**, SELECT COUNT(ShipmentID) FROM Shipments WHERE StoreID = 1 and ShippedDate > '01/01/2002', you might get a return value of 53. So for six months in 2002, only 53 shipments were made to Store 1. This number is significantly less than the 295 shipments made the entire year before. It would be very easy to consider these numbers alone indicative of success, but we must consider something else.

For this chapter, a new table named ProductAvailabilityTracking was created. This table is written to every time a randomly generated purchase is attempted and the product is not available. For Store 1, 1232 records were written to this table. This indicates that in the year 2002 more than 1200 customers were displeased to find that the product they wanted was not available. Any business major will tell you that missed sales opportunities and negative customer impressions can outweigh the benefits of reducing operational costs. In the next section we will examine another method of applying predictions that may lead to better results.

Tuning the Mining Model

Even though the initial run of our Generate Purchases scenario indicated success in that shipments were reduced, further analysis uncovered a flaw. It was discovered that using the mining model would result in a large number of customers not being able to purchase the products they needed.

The biggest factor is the data itself. You will train the mining model based on a set of data that was preselected. For real-world applications this will be a subset of the data that has been scrutinized or cleaned (as was discussed in Chapter 5). Chapter 5 relied on simulated data generated for all five stores in one year. The simulation was based on parameters supplied to the GeneratePurchases routine. Depending on the parameters selected, a varied number of records would be generated.

Utilizing a Version 2 Database File

To demonstrate the significance of the training data utilized, another database file has been provided. The Version 2 database files are also available for download from the book's Web site. This database version was the result of modifying the parameters used to generate purchases in Chapter 5. Table 6.3 lists the parameters along with the values used to build the Version 1 and Version 2 database files.

Version 1 is a snapshot of the data as it would look if the steps in Chapter 5 were followed. Version 2 is an alternative version of the database utilizing different input parameters. The input parameters introduced in Chapter 5 have been lowered to introduce more variability and speed up the processing time.

At this time you should attach the Version 2 file by performing the following steps:

1. Open SQL Server's **Enterprise Manager**.
2. Right-click the SavingsMart database node and click **All Tasks...** and **Detach Database**. You may have to clear any connections currently open.
3. Copy the **SavingsMart.mdf** and **SavingsMart.ldf** files from the book's Web site to the local directory where Version 1 was located. Click **OK** to replace the files.
4. Right-click the **Database** node and click **All Tasks...** and **Attach Database**.

Table 6.3 Comparison of the input parameters used to generate purchases for Version 1 and Version 2 backups. The values that are different are bolded in the Version 2 values column.

Store	Field Caption	Version 1 Values	Version 2 Values
1	Processing Year	2001	2001
	Max Purchases	80	80
	Max Products	20	**8**
	Max Quantity	5	5
	Product Type Adjustment	1, 2	1, 2
	Vendor Adjustment	20, 24, 27	20, 24, 27
2	Processing Year	2001	2001
	Max Purchases	60	60
	Max Products	12	**10**
	Max Quantity	7	**3**
	Product Type Adjustment	2, 6	2, 6
	Vendor Adjustment	13, 18	13, 18
3	Processing Year	2001	2001
	Max Purchases	70	70
	Max Products	12	**6**
	Max Quantity	7	**4**
	Product Type Adjustment	2	2
	Vendor Adjustment	34	34
4	Processing Year	2001	2001
	Max Purchases	100	**90**
	Max Products	5	5
	Max Quantity	2	2
	Product Type Adjustment		
	Vendor Adjustment	34, 18	34, 18
5	Processing Year	2001	2001
	Max Purchases	50	50
	Max Products	15	**12**
	Max Quantity	8	**6**
	Product Type Adjustment	6	6
	Vendor Adjustment	24, 27, 34	24, 27 ,34

5. From the **Attach Database** dialog, browse to the directory where you copied the database files in step 3 and select the Savings-Mart.mdf file. Click **OK**.
6. Click **OK** to attach the database.

Once the files are attached, you will need to click the **Apply Shipment Schedules** button so that the mining model is refreshed and new values are written to the ShipmentSchedules table. After the routine completes successfully, open up **Analysis Manager** and expand the Savings-Mart database. Right-click the Analyze Shipments mining model and click **Browse.** You should instantly see that the model content is significantly different. The tree contains more branches and involves product type. The first factor affecting days between shipments is Store ID as opposed to vendor name. If you double-click the Store ID = 1 node, you will drill down farther into the tree. Figure 6.5 is a screenshot of what this view would look like.

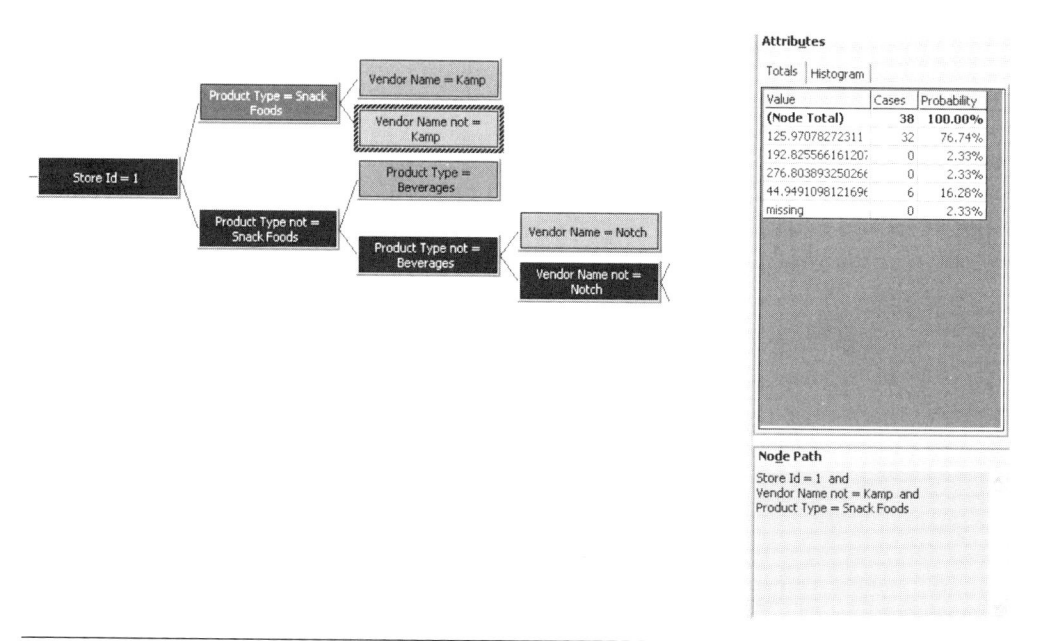

Figure 6.5 Screenshot of the Content Detail in Analysis Manager once the model has been refreshed with data from the Version 2 backup file. The next split is based on product type and finally vendor name. This is in stark contrast to the results seen when utilizing the Version 1 backup file.

Since product type is now considered a factor when determining days between shipments, we will have to modify the query used to retrieve predictions from the mining model. The PopulateShipmentSchedulesTable procedure contains the code used to generate this query; this is the commented code that was discussed earlier. The string shown below is an example of what the new query string would look like.

```
SELECT Predict([Days Since Last Shipped]),Predict(Quantity)
FROM [Analyze Shipments]
PREDICTION JOIN (SELECT 'Ables' as VendorName, 1 as StoreID,
    'Beverages' as Type) as t
ON [Analyze Shipments].[Vendor Name] = t.VendorName
AND [Analyze Shipments].[Product Type] = t.Type
AND [Analyze Shipments].[Store ID] = t.StoreID
```

Note that the query now includes product type as a filter. It also joins the mining model based on product type so that more granularity is achieved.

If you were to execute the GeneratePurchases routine by clicking **Generate Purchases**, you would attain different results. For instance, the query, SELECT COUNT(ShipmentID) FROM Shipments WHERE StoreID = 1 and ShippedDate > '01/01/2002', might return a result of 4. This result is a definite improvement over the amount of 53 attained when processing the Version 1 database file. The best part is that the entries to the ProductAvailabilityTracking table have also been reduced. They went from 1232 for Store 1 to 118. Thus we have not only reduced the number of shipments, but we have also ensured greater product availability.

Tuning Parameters

Other factors that can affect the predictions of a mining model are based on the number of splits that occur within the decision tree. Some of these factors can be controlled through the use of parameters assigned to the model. Table 6.4 lists two parameters available with the decision trees mining model.

Closed Loop Processing

Successful data-mining involves testing the predictions against additional datasets. It can also involve evaluating the success of predictions through various means. A table named ProductAvailabilityTracking is utilized for our simulation of purchases made at SavingsMart. This table indicates

Table 6.4 The two mining-model parameters available with the decision trees algorithm. These parameters are set in the Additional Parameters property using the Relational Mining Model Editor.

Parameter Name	Type	Range	Description
COMPLEXITY_PENALTY	Float	0–1	Used to restrict the growth of the tree. The decision tree algorithm produces splits that result in the creation of multiple branches. A low value for COMPEXITY_PENALTY indicates that splits will occur more frequently, and a high value that splits will occur less frequently. The default value varies depending on the number of attributes specified for the mining model.
MINIMUM_LEAF_CASES	Integer	0–2,147,483,647	Similar to the COMPLEXITY_PENALTY in that it controls the number of splits that occur. This parameter, though, is based on the number of leaf nodes present in the tree; a low value indicates that splits will occur more frequently, and a high value that they will occur less frequently. The default value is 10.

missed sales opportunities for each store. Initially we attempted to apply the predictions made by the mining model once and then utilize the same predictions for the next six months.

Closed loop processing involves an iterative process of reevaluation in which the mining model is refreshed with new data and therefore new predictions may be made. The new predictions are then written back to the database in an effort to attain better results.

The LoadSampleData project for Chapter 6 has a button named Simulate Closed Loop Process. This button initiates the SimulateDailyProcessing routine, as follows:

```vb
' We will loop through a process for a half a year,
' but will only refresh the mining model and apply the
' results once every 14 days instead of once a day
' since refreshing the data takes a long time.
Dim i As Int16, j As Int16 = 0
Dim dDate As DateTime = "01/01/2002"
For i = 0 To 182
   GeneratePurchases(dDate)
   dDate = dDate.AddDays(1)
   j += 1
   If j = 13 Then
      j = 0
      ProcessMiningModel(dDate)
      PopulateShipmentSchedulesTable(True)
      ApplyShipmentSchedules()
   End If
Next
```

The closed loop process generates purchases for fourteen days and then initiates a refresh of the Analyze Shipments mining model. Refreshing the Analyze Shipment model is accomplished by calling the ProcessMiningModel routine and may result in the prediction of new values for the ShipmentSchedules table. The code for this routine is as follows:

```vb
Dim oServer As New DSO.Server
Dim oDatabase As New DSO.Database
Dim oModels As DSO.OlapCollection
Dim oModel As DSO.MiningModel

'Connect to the Analysis Server
Try
  oServer.Name = sAS
  oServer.Connect()
Catch ex As Exception
  MessageBox.Show("Connection to the Analysis Server failed")
  Exit Sub
End Try

'Open the database and set reference to the mining model
Try
  oDatabase = oServer.MDStores.Item(sASDB)
  oModels = oDatabase.MiningModels()
  oModel = oModels.Item(sModel)
```

```
Catch ex As Exception
  MessageBox.Show("Unable to open the database and mining
model")
  Exit Sub
End Try

'Update the mining model
Try
  oModel.LastUpdated = sDate
  oModel.Update()
Catch ex As Exception
  MessageBox.Show("Unable to update the mining model")
  Exit Sub
End Try

'Refresh the mining model
Try
  oModel.LockObject(OlapLockTypes.olapLockProcess, "Training _
      the Shipments mining model")
  oModel.Process(ProcessTypes.processRefreshData)
  oModel.UnlockObject()
Catch ex As Exception
  MessageBox.Show("Unable to refresh the mining model")
  Exit Sub
End Try
```

Closed loop processing is the best method for dealing with real-world situations. After all, many factors go into customer buying habits. What was true at the beginning of the year, may not hold true at the end. Closed loop processing allows you to continually reevaluate the data to ensure that predictions have not changed.

Summary

- Chapter 5 introduced the fictional retailer SavingsMart and used Analysis Services to build a mining model that predicted days between shipments and quantity. This chapter expands on the results obtained from the mining model to create a new shipment method.
- Communicating with Analysis Server is accomplished using the Microsoft Active Data Objects Multidimensional (ADOMD) library. It also

involves the installation of XML for Analysis specification 1.1 and the latest version of the MSXML parser.
- A modified version of the LoadSampleData program used in Chapter 5 was used to apply prediction results and generate new purchases for 2002. Using database files available for download from the book's Web site, the reader simulated results with the new shipment method. Initial observations indicate that although the total shipments will be reduced, customers will be less likely to find the products they need.
- Since mining-model results are highly dependent on the training datasets utilized, an alternative database file is provided. Reprocessing the mining model using this new database file results in more branches and the inclusion of an additional factor. After utilizing the new predictions, total shipments are reduced even further, as are missed sales opportunities.
- Closed loop processing involves the continual reprocessing of mining models and the reapplication of their predictions. This ensures that mining-model predictions remain as accurate as possible when conditions change. The LoadSampleData program provides an example of how this can be done.

CHAPTER 7

An Evolving Database

Every day we use formal and informal rules to control our actions. We know that a hot flame will burn our skin and will hurt. Therefore, we know not to touch the flame. Automobile drivers know that if they drive too fast, they may get a speeding ticket.

Businesses also utilize rules to control the actions they take. Business rules encapsulate the logic and procedures used by businesses to handle certain situations. Such rules can exist formally in policy manuals or informally as the experiences of employees. An example of a business rule involving a small widget retailer would be, "If the quantity of widgets falls below 200, then order 500 more widgets."

Rule-based systems seek to capitalize on the knowledge of experts by defining a set of rules used to represent a particular area. In the case of the widget retailer, the experts would be store managers, buyers, or stock clerks. These employees all understand the particular facets of their jobs. They would therefore be the most knowledgeable when it comes to defining how their jobs should be done.

The set of rules used by these employees can overlap and may vary depending on slight differences. For instance, the rule about ordering more widgets may change if it is November because widgets do not sell well in that month.

Every rule is associated with actions, and once a rule is defined, it is applied to a set of inputs. The inputs are such factors as the quantity of widgets or the current month. The end result or action applied depends on how the rules are applied to the inputs.

In the financial industry, rule-based systems have been very helpful in decision-making about stock performance or creditworthiness. These systems can be used either to enhance a human's deductive capabilities or, in some cases, to replace them. In today's 24/7 world of instant accessibility, it is sometimes vital for companies to be able to make decisions involving customers as quickly as possible. Rule-based systems allow companies to "bottle" their employees' decision-making capabilities so they will be available for quick and efficient use.

This chapter will examine a rule-based system used by a fictional financial lender named Zoom Lending. The ASP.NET application is used by employees to create and manage borrower surveys. The program contains a simplified rule engine used to determine when new survey questions should be added as new fields in the database.

Rule-based systems can involve just about any situation in which an automated response requires that a decision be made. The rules are dynamic, and different ones come into play depending on the input. The application in this chapter is a simple rule-based system in which the expert is the database administrator (DBA). Since decisions involve the addition of fields to the database, the DBA is the person most knowledgeable of how those fields should be defined.

The chapter also contains profile boxes featuring two Microsoft products that utilize rule-based systems. The Microsoft Outlook rules wizard, part of the Microsoft Outlook product family, can automatically manage messages using user-defined rules. BizTalk Server 2004, now in its third major release, features a way to create and modify business rules through a graphical interface that can be used even by those who are not developers.

Understanding Rule-based Systems

Rule-based systems vary greatly in complexity. Rules are usually stored in some repository, such as a database. The total collection of rules is known as the rule base or knowledge base. Simple rule-based systems typically utilize an IF…THEN format to store rules. Each rule lists a condition (the if part) that must be met for the rule to be true. The rule also specifies what action or result (the then part) must take place.

There is no set standard for forming rules, but they should be based on meaningful and clear ideas. Since the rules need to be formalized in written language that dictates programmatic action, it may take some time to create a useful rule base.

The sample application in this chapter will parse human language and then use rules to determine how data should be stored in a database.

NOTE: The sample application in this chapter will parse a sentence and use rules to determine how the data should be stored in a database. The portion of code that examines the sentence is *not* the same as natural language processing (NLP). NLP is a complex process that attempts to understand human language. It is discussed further in Chapter 9.

The Phases of Rule-based Systems

Applications that use rules may apply them in a four-phase process. The phases are as follows:

1. The **Condition Matching phase** involves looping through all the rules and determining which ones have true conditions. Depending on the input data, several rules may be true. In some cases the actions associated with these rules may conflict.
2. A **Priority Evaluation phase** is necessary in order to determine which rules should be applied. A priority value is assigned to each rule. This phase may indicate the order in which the rules should be applied or may eliminate conflicting rules.
3. The third phase, the **Application of Results phase**, involves the execution of the rules identified in the second phase.
4. Since the application may execute an inappropriate action, there is usually an **Adjustment phase**. This final phase requires that a human expert review the decisions made by the application. If a wrong decision was made, the expert will either add, delete, or change some of the rules.

The final phase is the most critical one. It is not realistic to expect that rules will never have to be changed once they are defined. Just as a human employee must be trained and then retrained, so too does a successful rule-based system.

BizTalk Server 2004

BizTalk Server 2004 is a development tool that can be used by developers and non-developers to automate certain business processes. The main purpose of the tool is to facilitate communication between applications. The applications can exist on a single network or across networks for different companies.

(continued)

The 2004 version of BizTalk Server is built around the .NET framework, and solutions can be created inside Visual Studio.NET. It utilizes XML files and Web Services to connect different applications. You can connect applications of many kinds, ranging from those running on a mainframe to those running on a Windows-based network.

The Business Rule Composer, new with this version of BizTalk Server, is a tool that allows users to create new rules and modify existing ones. The rules are then processed by the Business Rule Engine.

Users can start by creating a vocabulary that maps friendly, nontechnical names to the variables used to build rules. Terms can be associated with fields in a database table or an XML document. They can also be associated with the results of complex database queries. A vocabulary is useful for situations in which people who are not developers use the composer to build rules. Terms in the vocabulary are more meaningful than the items they are associated with. A vocabulary is not required to build rules, but it can be helpful.

Rules are defined in an If...Then format. If certain conditions evaluate to true, a corresponding action is initiated. The conditions operate on facts that apply to terms defined in the vocabulary. Multiple facts can be combined with operators like "AND," "OR," or "NOT." The actions are invoked by calling methods, setting properties, or manipulating documents or database tables.

Once the rules are defined, they are grouped together to form policies. In most cases, every application will have its own policy. Once tested, all the rules can be published together through the policy as a policy version. A policy can be deployed independently of the associated application so that the code does not have to be recompiled when the policy is changed.

The Business Rule Engine is encapsulated within a .NET namespace, and its functions can be invoked by other .NET applications. You can write custom .NET applications that utilize the Rules Engine without using BizTalk Server 2004.

The main benefit of using the Business Rule Engine in BizTalk Server is that rules can be created by the people who are most familiar with the actual business policies even if they are not developers. In addition, rules can be changed without any need for a code recompile.

BizTalk Server is not a magic bullet and is by no means the optimal development solution for all business applications. But it can be a great time saver for applications that need to easily automate business processes and facilitate communication between applications. It can also be the best way to tap into a company's expertise through the knowledge of its employees.

Zoom Lending

Zoom Lending is a fictional finance company that specializes in refinancing and second mortgages. It has more than two hundred offices nationwide, situated in areas of diverse socioeconomic levels. Each office is responsible for soliciting business from past customers. To do this, it often collects information about borrowers that goes beyond the data on their loan applications. Since the offices are located in different socioeconomic areas, the questions asked of borrowers can be quite different.

Initially, the company created one form that contained every possible question, and the employees were expected to only enter data that was applicable. It was soon found that they were not using the form. There were several reasons for this. First, the form was too long and time-consuming to utilize. In addition, branches were often interested in collecting data that was not available on the form.

A Web-based application was developed to build separate surveys for the various branches. The branch manager would select questions applicable to the branch. If employees wanted to add a new question, they would send an e-mail to the DBA. The DBA would add the question as a field in the database and then notify the employee. This process usually took one or two days, and sometimes, as a result, data was not collected.

To increase application efficiency, rule-based functionality was added to the application. If an employee wanted to add a new question, the application would first search the database for a match. If none was found, it would apply rules to determine where and how the field should be added. For instance, if a question contained the phrase "How many," the field would be defined as an integer. If the question contained the word "vehicle," it would be added to the ResponseAutos table.

Log files are written to every time an employee tries to enter a new question. Periodically, the DBA examines the log files to evaluate the application's success. If a field was added incorrectly, the DBA may need to make adjustments to the rules. This chapter will examine the code used to implement the rule-based functionality.

Loading the Zoom Lending Database

Zoom Lending utilizes a SQL Server database named ZoomLending. To execute the sample code available for download from the book's Web site at http://www.awprofessional.com/title/0321246268, you will first need to attach a database file to your instance of SQL Server. To do this, execute the following steps:

1. Copy the ZoomLending_Data.mdf and ZoomLending_Log.ldf files from the book's Web site to a local directory on the server where Microsoft SQL Server is installed.
2. Open **Microsoft Enterprise Manager.**
3. Right-click the **Databases** node and click **All Tasks…** and **Attach Database…**
4. From the **Attach Database** dialog, browse to the directory where you copied the database files in step 1 and select the ZoomLending_Data.mdf file. Click **OK**.
5. Click **OK** to attach the database.
6. To see the newly added database, you will need to click **Action** and **Refresh**.

Since Zoom Lending is a finance company, there are several tables designed to collect borrower data. The data in these tables consists of information collected on a loan application. The tables utilized by the rule-based functionality are displayed in Figure 7.1.

The **RuleType** table is used to group rules according to generalized conditions and results. The IF…THEN part of the rule is contained in the ConditionText and ResultText fields. It also contains placeholders for parameters. The **Rule** table is a child of the RuleType table. Values for the parameters used in the RuleType table are stored in the ConditionValue and ResultValue fields. We will cover defining rules in the section titled "Rule Maintenance."

The **Response** tables are written to each time a borrower responds to a survey. For each record in the **Questions** table there is an associated field in one of the Response tables. The application relates the question text to the response tables through the ResponseField and ResponseTable fields.

Building a Rule-based Application

Loading the Sample Application

Table 7.1 contains a listing of the single project that comprises the sample application. To execute the sample code available for download from the book's Web site, you will need to execute the following steps:

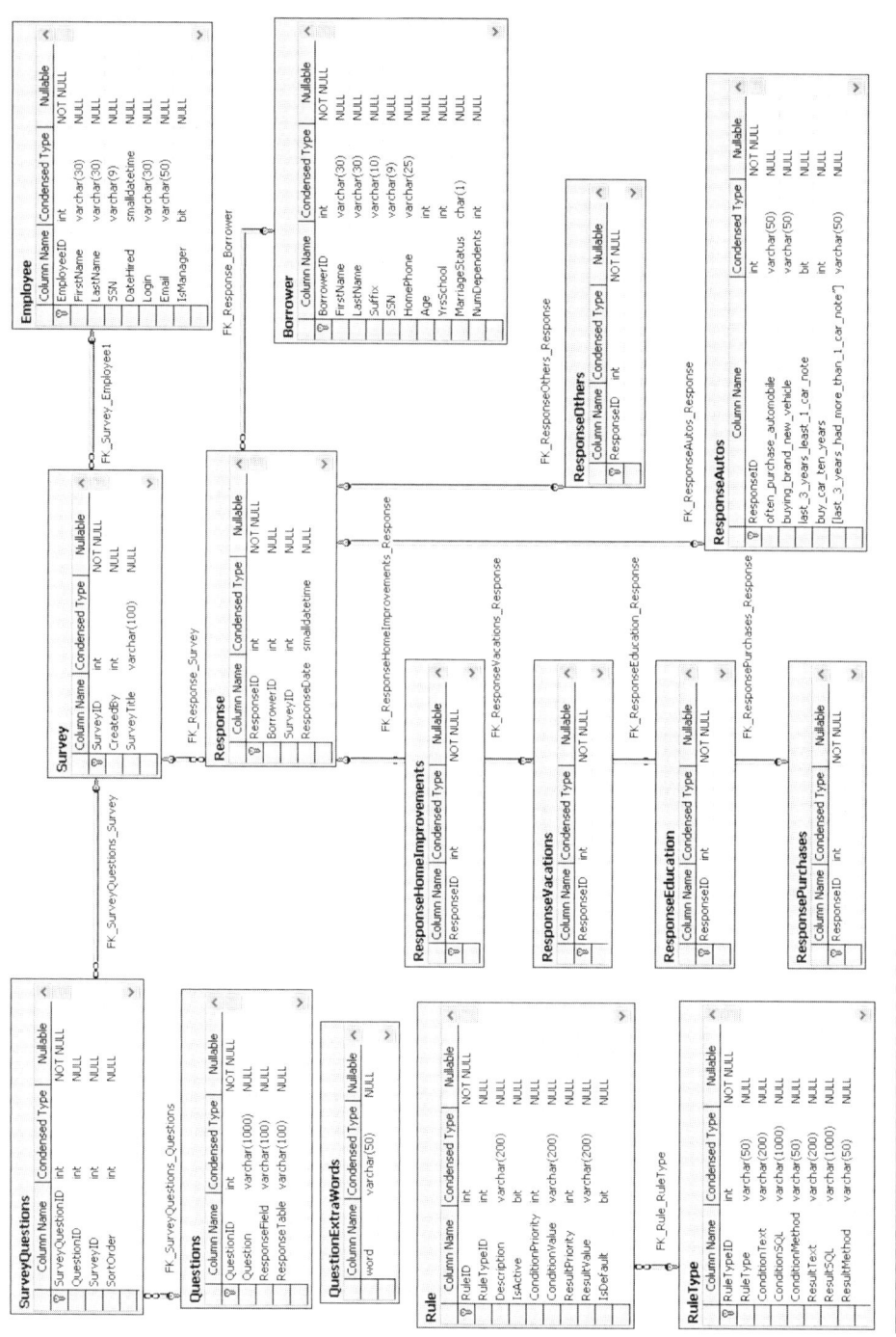

Figure 7.1 Tables from the ZoomLending database. These tables are the ones central to the rule-based functionality discussed in this chapter. The Response tables contain borrower data collected from branch surveys. They will be expanded as new questions are added to the database.

Table 7.1 Code listing for the Chapter 7 project. The files can be accessed by opening the Chapter7.sln file.

Project	File Name	Description
Chapter7	Chapter7.sln	Solution file
	Components/Rule.vb	Contains server-side Visual Basic code used to add and update rules, evaluate rules, and execute actions.
	Components/Survey.vb	Contains server-side Visual Basic code used to process surveys and evaluate whether the questions are already represented in database.
	Banner.ascx	User control included at the top of each Web page; contains the left-hand menu for the application.
	EditRule.aspx	Web page used to add new rules and edit existing ones.
	EditRuleType.aspx	Web page used to add new rule types and edit existing ones.
	NewQuestion.aspx	Web page used to enter new survey questions. Executes code to evaluate whether the question is new and will initiate the four rule phases.
	Rules.aspx	Web page used to view existing rules and rule types. Can also be used to navigate to the EditRule.aspx and EditRuleType.aspx pages.

1. If IIS has already been installed on your machine, then you will have by default a directory named C:\Inetpub\wwwroot. Create a new folder in this directory named Chapter7 and copy the contents of the code directory (available for download from the book's Web site) to this location.
2. You will then need to open the Internet Information Services Manager and browse to the **Default Web Site** node. Right-click the Chapter7 folder and click **Properties**. From the Directory tab, click the **Create** button. When finished, click **OK** and exit Internet Information Services Manager.

3. If Visual Studio .NET has already been installed on your machine, you can open the code sample by double-clicking the solution file named Chapter7.sln from the C:\Inetpub\wwwroot\Chapter7 directory using Microsoft Windows Explorer.
4. After opening the solution file, you will need to set the start page. This is done by right-clicking the start page, **Rules.aspx**, from Solution Explorer and clicking **Set as Start Page**.

Rule Maintenance

The application lists four main functions in the left-hand menu. The first, Rule Maintenance (see Figure 7.2), is functionality that would only be available to an administrator. It is from here that rules and rule types will be defined.

NOTE: The sample application provided with this chapter only includes functionality related to the processing of rules. Therefore, only two of the items listed in the main menu (New Question and Rule Maintenance) are included.

The application also does not include a proper method for user authentication. The Banner.ascx user control does contain code to capture the identity of the current user, but this will only be useful if security has been enabled for the IIS virtual directory.

An actual production system would include an authentication method of some sort (such as forms or windows authentication). Based on the identity of the authenticated user, only administrators would be granted access to the Rule Maintenance menu item.

Defining Rule Types

As stated earlier, rule types are used to group rules together. They act as a template for the rules. To view the rule types already defined in the database, open the solution file for Chapter 7 (refer to Table 7.1), right-click Rules.aspx from **Solution Explorer**, and click **Set as Start Page**. You can then execute the application by hitting **F5**.

If you click the Rule Types drop-down box, you should see a list of four rule types. Select **DataType** and click **Edit Rule Type**. Figure 7.3 is a screenshot of the Rule Type Web page. Note that the Condition Text and Result Text fields utilize a value named "param1." Param1 is a placeholder

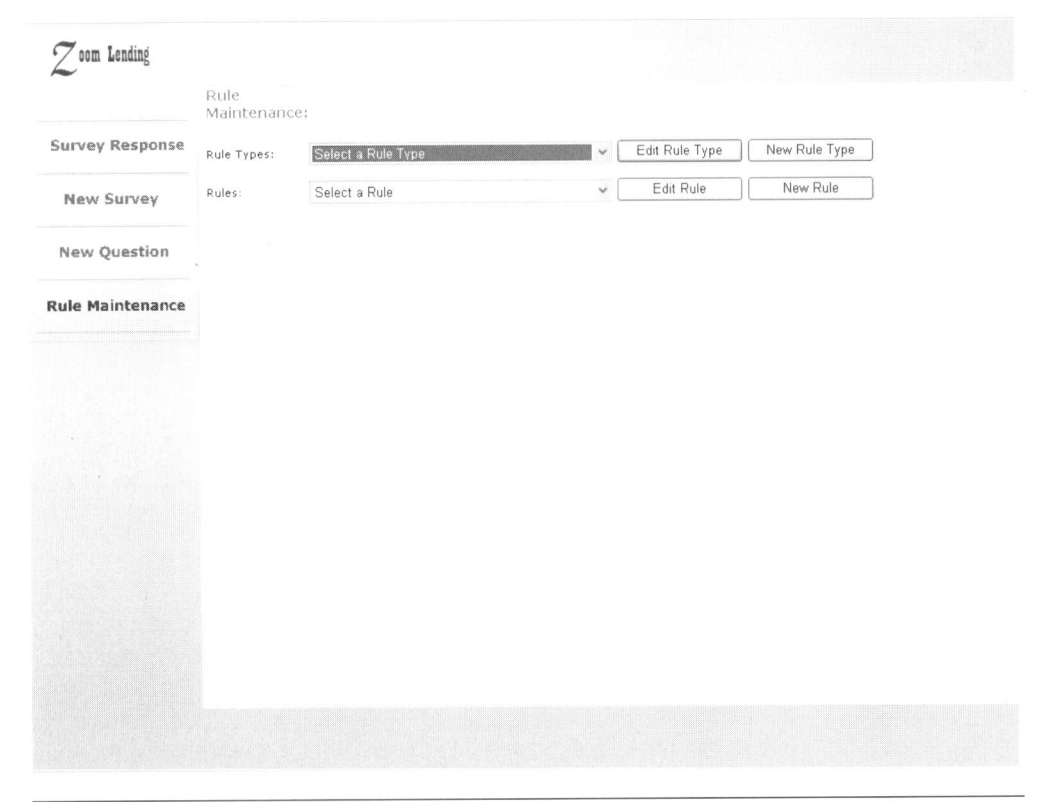

Figure 7.2 Screenshot of the Administrative Web page, Rule Maintenance. From here, administrators can add new rules and rule types or edit existing ones.

used to indicate where condition and result values will be placed. Each rule definition contains values that will replace param1 when the rule is executed.

For this rule type the Condition SQL textbox is blank. The Result SQL textbox, however, contains the following valid SQL statement, SELECT name as id, name as param1 from systypes. The Systypes table is a system table used by SQL Server to store information about data types. The data returned by this SQL statement will be used later to populate a drop-down box on the Edit Rule page. The SQL statement is therefore used to restrict the possible values entered as rules are defined.

The Condition Method and Result Method textboxes are used to specify compiled method names. These method names will be called dynamically during the Condition Matching and Application of Results phases. For each rule type, the combined values in these textboxes should be unique. This is because each rule type represents a distinct condition

Figure 7.3 Screenshot of the Edit Rule Type Web page. This page is used to add or edit rule types used by the application.

that must occur and the resulting action that will take place. A unique index defined in SQL Server ensures that this will be the case.

NOTE: When setting up a rule base, the most time-consuming process will involve deciding how to define the rule types and which ones to include. The rule type defines the distinct combination of a specific condition that must be met in order for an action to be executed.

Defining Rules

Click **Cancel** to return to the Rules.aspx page. Select **integer** from the Rules drop-down box and click **Edit Rule**. Figure 7.4 is a screenshot of the Edit Rule Web page. Note that the labels above Condition Value and

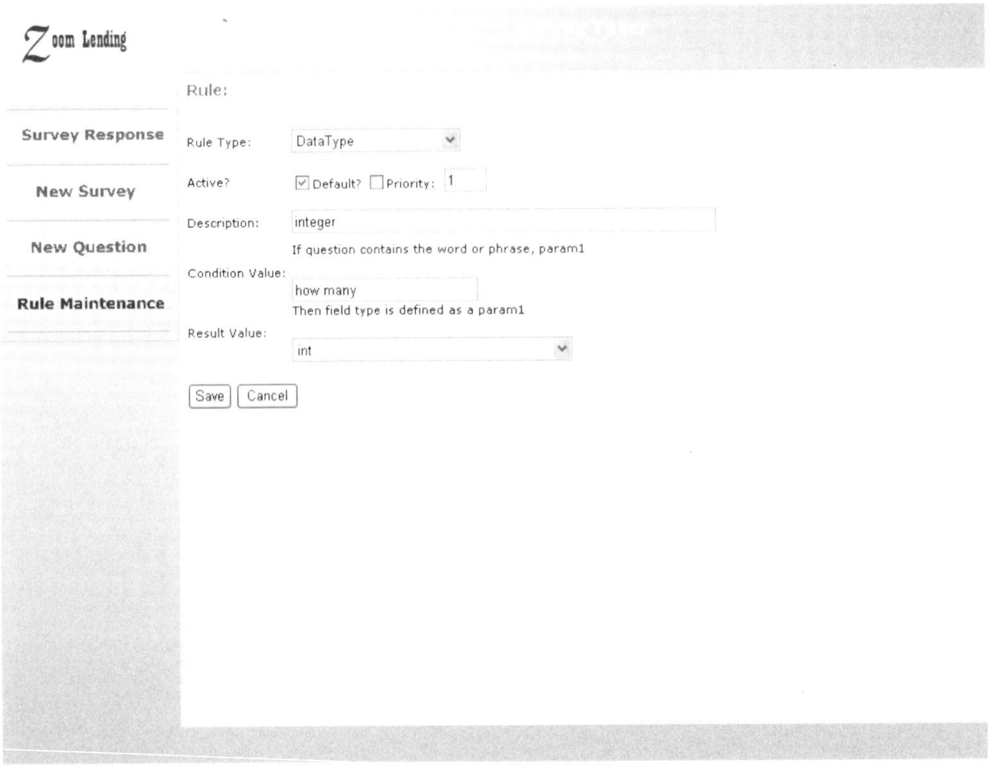

Figure 7.4 Screenshot of the Edit Rule Web page named EditRule.aspx. This page is used to add or edit rule definitions. Rules are based on template values defined for the associated rule type.

Result Value were defined when setting up the DataType rule type. They are repeated here to assist the user when defining the Condition Value and Result Value textboxes. Thus when this rule is evaluated in the Condition Matching phase, it will look to see if the question contains the word or phrase "how many." If this condition is true, the integer rule will be considered valid.

NOTE: For the sample application, rules are applied only when a new question is entered. Therefore, the rule base for the sample application is small and simple in scope. This was done intentionally for demonstration purposes. Keep in mind however, that an actual rule-based system would consist of a much larger rule base. The rules may involve several different aspects of the application and perform a wide array of actions.

Using a Threshold Value

The first thing to do, when entering a new question, is to attempt to match it with fields already in the database. Sometimes a proposed question is similar to one already entered. To rate the similarity, the application utilizes an adjustable threshold percentage value. If the question is considered too similar to an existing question, it is not added and the user is notified. This threshold value is stored as an application setting in the Web.config file and is named **ThresholdPercent** with a default value of 70. Details about how this threshold enters into the similarity comparison are given below.

A new question is entered on the NewQuestion.aspx page when an employee types in the entire question and clicks **Next**. Most of the code we will examine is spawned from this event. To review this code, right-click the NewQuestion.aspx page from Solution Explorer and click **View Code**.

The ApplyRules method will execute a series of functions from the Rule and Survey class files, located in the Components folder. The first function from the Survey class file, seen as follows, is named StripQuestion.

```
'First replace common chars with word equivalents
'or just remove entirely
Dim strQuestion As String = Question
strQuestion = strQuestion.Replace("%", " percent")
strQuestion = strQuestion.Replace("&", "and")
strQuestion = strQuestion.Replace("@", "at")
strQuestion = strQuestion.Replace("+", "plus")
strQuestion = strQuestion.Replace("=", "equals")
strQuestion = strQuestion.Replace("-", "minus")
strQuestion = strQuestion.Replace("'", "")
strQuestion = strQuestion.Replace("""", "")
strQuestion = strQuestion.Replace(",", "")
strQuestion = strQuestion.Replace("~", "")
strQuestion = strQuestion.Replace("`", "")
strQuestion = strQuestion.Replace("?", "")
strQuestion = strQuestion.Replace(";", "")
strQuestion = strQuestion.Replace(":", "")
strQuestion = strQuestion.Replace("/", "")
strQuestion = strQuestion.Replace("\", "")
strQuestion = strQuestion.Replace("|", "")
strQuestion = strQuestion.Replace("{", "")
strQuestion = strQuestion.Replace("}", "")
strQuestion = strQuestion.Replace("[", "")
strQuestion = strQuestion.Replace("]", "")
```

```vb
strQuestion = strQuestion.Replace("!", "")
strQuestion = strQuestion.Replace("#", "")
strQuestion = strQuestion.Replace("^", "")
strQuestion = strQuestion.Replace("*", "")

Dim arrIn As String()
Dim strT As String
Dim strSql As String = "SELECT word FROM QuestionExtraWords _
          WHERE word IN ("
arrIn = strQuestion.Split(" ")
Dim i As Int16 = 0
For Each strT In arrIn
  'Check to see if the word is in the ExtraWords table
  'by building one query statement
  If i = 0 Then
    strSql += "'" + strT + "'"
  Else
    strSql += ",'" + strT + "'"
  End If
  i += 1
Next
strSql += ")"

'Execute the newly created query statement
Dim dr As SqlDataReader = _
  SqlHelper.ExecuteReader(AppSettings("Chapter7.Connection"), _
  CommandType.Text, strSql)
Dim arrExtra As New ArrayList
'Copy the Extra words into an array list
Do While dr.Read
   arrExtra.Add(Convert.ToString(dr.Item(0)).ToLower)
Loop

'We will loop through our two arrays and compare
' the results. A temporary array list will be built
' with those words not found in the extra words
' table and returned as OutArray
Dim arrOut As New ArrayList
Dim blnFound As Boolean = False
Dim strE As String
For Each strT In arrIn
  For Each strE In arrExtra
    blnFound = False
    If strT.ToLower = strE Then
```

```
          blnFound = True
          Exit For
        End If
      Next
      If blnFound = False Then
        arrOut.Add(strT)
      End If
    Next
    OutArray = arrOut
    Return True
```

Most of the words in a sentence are not meaningful and could be considered filler words. For example, words such as "the," "a," and "this." These words will be removed from the incoming question.

The StripQuestion function will also remove any extra characters, such as "*", "!", and "^". Some characters are converted to their English word equivalents. For example, the character "%" is changed to the word "percent." Once the question has been stripped, it is split and each word is stored in an ArrayList object. This ArrayList will be used as an incoming parameter for the next executed function, ApplyThreshold.

Responses are grouped into broad categories, and the corresponding table reflects the category name. For example, the table that contains question responses about automobiles is named ResponseAutos. Data for any similar question will be stored in one of the Response tables seen in Figure 7.1.

ApplyThreshold is viewable by right-clicking the Survey.vb file in Solution Explorer and clicking View Code. Select **ApplyThreshold** from the right-hand drop-down box. The ApplyThreshold function, seen as follows, will first execute a SQL query that returns all the fields from any of the tables that have a name starting with the word "Response."

```
'First get all the fields in the database that are dedicated
'to question responses. This list represents the potential
'field names that our incoming question may match to.
Dim strSQL = "SELECT sc.name as fieldname, so.name as tablename "
strSQL += "FROM syscolumns sc "
strSQL += "LEFT JOIN sysobjects so ON sc.id = so.id "
strSQL += "where sc.id IN "
strSQL += "(select id from sysobjects where xtype = 'U' "
strSQL += "and substring(name, 1, 8) = 'Response' "
strSQL += "and name <> 'Response') "
strSQL += "AND sc.name <> 'Responseid'"
```

```vb
Dim blnMatchFound As Boolean = False
Dim arrFieldName As Array
Dim strField As String
Dim intNumMatchingWords As Int16 = 0
Dim arrMatches As New ArrayList
Dim dblThreshold As Double = _
Convert.ToInt16(ConfigurationSettings.AppSettings("ThresholdPercent")) _
             * 0.01
dr = SqlHelper.ExecuteReader(AppSettings("Chapter7.Connection"), _
   CommandType.Text, strSQL)
Do While dr.Read
  arrFieldName = Convert.ToString(dr.Item("fieldname")).Split("_")
  intNumMatchingWords = 0
  'Now, see how many words in our incoming array
  'match with the words in the field name
  objWord = New Microsoft.Office.Interop.Word.ApplicationClass
  objWord.Visible = False
  For Each strField In arrFieldName
    If CheckSynonyms(InArray, strField.ToLower) = True Then
       intNumMatchingWords += 1
    End If
  Next
  objWord.Visible = True
  objWord.Quit()
  objWord = Nothing
  'If the number of matching words divided by the number
  'of available words exceeds the threshold percentage
  'specified, then we consider a match to be found
  If intNumMatchingWords / _
    (arrFieldName.GetUpperBound(0) + 1) > dblThreshold Then
    blnMatchFound = True
    'Lookup the question so we can return it to the user
    strSQL = "SELECT question FROM Questions WHERE ResponseTable = '"
    strSQL += dr.Item("tablename") + "' AND ResponseField = '"
    strSQL += dr.Item("fieldname") + "'"
    dr2 = SqlHelper.ExecuteReader(AppSettings("Chapter7.Connection"), _
       CommandType.Text, strSQL)
    Do While dr2.Read
      CSurvey.ResultLogDetailEntry(LogID, "QM", 0, _
         dr2.Item("question"))
      arrMatches.Add(Convert.ToString(dr2.Item("question")))
    Loop
    dr2.Close()
  End If
```

```
Loop
dr.Close()
Dim strMatch As String
If arrMatches.Count > 0 Then
 'We have at least one potential match, so we need to format the
 'return message for the user
   RetMsg = "The following questions have been found as potential "
   RetMsg += "matches in the database. <br> If you wish for the "
   RetMsg += "question to still be considered, then click "
   RetMsg += "'Consider Question'. <p>"
   For Each strMatch In arrMatches
      RetMsg += strMatch + "<br>"
   Next
End If
Return blnMatchFound
```

The ApplyThreshold function reads the threshold percent value from Web.config and proceeds to loop through all the potential field names. Individual words in the field names are separated with an underscore character (e.g., often_purchase_automobile). Therefore, the field name is split into an array of individual words. This array is looped through to compare each word in the field name against each word in the incoming question.

Since most words have several meanings, it is necessary for the application to check each word against a thesaurus. The CheckSynonyms function executes routines from the Microsoft Word API. It first looks to see if the word matches exactly. If it does, it just exits the routine. Otherwise, it will create an instance of a Word document.

NOTE: To execute the code in this chapter you will need to install the Microsoft Office XP Primary Interop Assembly. The install file is available for download on MSDN. Once downloaded, you will need to execute the oxppia.exe file to install the XP Interop.

Since the Word API is COM-based, the XP Interop allows unmanaged code to be called from a managed environment (.NET). There are assemblies available for each application in Microsoft Office. Refer to the Readme.htm file available with the Interop install for instructions on installing the Word interop assembly.

The text contained in the new document is the incoming field name. A SynonymInfo object is populated with the results of the SynonymInfo property.

Chapter 7 An Evolving Database

```
Dim objSyn As SynonymInfo = objDoc.Range.SynonymInfo
```

The newly created object, objSyn, now contains all the possible meanings. If the MeaningCount property is greater than zero, we will use the SynonymList property to return an array of these meanings. We will then loop through that array looking for a match, such as:

```
Dim arrList As Array = objSyn.SynonymList(1)
For i = 1 To UBound(arrList)
    If InArray.Contains(arrList(i)) Then
        blnFound = True
        Exit For
    End If
Next i
```

The CheckSynonyms function will return a true value if the field name exactly matches a word in the question or a synonym for one of the words. The variable intNumMatchingWords will be incremented each time this function returns a true value. We will then divide the variable by the total number of words in our field name array, such as:

```
intNumMatchingWords/arrFieldName.GetUpperBound(0)+ 1) > dblThreshold
```

If the number of matching words divided by the number of available words exceeds the threshold percentage specified, we consider a match to be made. In this case, the value of dblThreshold is .70. So if at least 70 percent of the meaningful words match an existing field, we retrieve the question text for that field and populate an outgoing array list.

To demonstrate the Threshold matching functionality, execute the application by hitting **F5** and click **New Question** from the left-hand menu. Type the question "How often do you buy a car?" and click **Next**.

NOTE: Readers familiar with Microsoft tools may wonder why Microsoft's English Query was not used to interpret the English questions. English Query is a tool available with SQL Server 2000. It allows database administrators to build an XML-based domain file using a front end based in Visual Studio 6.0. The domain file contains rules for applying language to specific fields in a database. Once defined, the file can be used by Web pages and Windows applications to query a database with natural language queries.

The main reason it was not used in this chapter is that it only generates a query statement and cannot be used as a language interpreter. There is also no .NET interface or support available for this tool.

The database file, available for download, has four fields defined in the ResponseAutos table. In this case, the ApplyThreshold function will find that the field named often_purchase_automobile is a potential match (see Figure 7.4). It considers the match to be 100 percent because three matching words were found. Buy is a synonym for purchase, and car is a synonym for automobile.

If the question was changed to "How many times do you buy a car?" the ApplyThreshold function would not consider the question a match. In that

Figure 7.5 Screenshot of the new survey question page. In this case the question entered matches with an existing field in the database. The user is notified about the match and given the option to still have the question considered.

case, the number of matching words would be two. When you divide this value by three, or the number of potential matches, the result is 0.6667.

> **NOTE:** The threshold percentage value is easily modifiable by editing the Web.config file. It is not necessary to recompile the application every time this value is changed. It could also be fed from a database table. It may be necessary to either raise or lower the threshold value in order to attain better results.

Condition Matching Phase

Once it is determined that no match exists, the decision is made to add the new question to the database. The system still must determine where in the database to place the question and what kinds of fields will be required. This is where the rule-based process comes into play. The first phase of the process is the Condition Matching phase. This involves examining all the rules and determining whether the condition is satisfied. If it is, then the rule will be added to an array list and passed to the next phase as a parameter.

The function that performs this phase is located in the Rule.vb file and is named ConditionMatchPhase. It utilizes functions and types from the System.Reflection namespace to programmatically invoke the condition method for each rule. In essence, this function utilizes .NET's reflection capabilities to translate text descriptions into references of methods and parameters.

The first thing this function does is check to see whether the rule is a default. Default rules are rules that are executed if no other matching rule has the same result method. If the rule is a default rule, it is added to the outgoing array list. Otherwise, the condition method name for the rule will be invoked. The code to accomplish this is as follows:

```
Dim objType As Type = objAssembly.GetType("Chapter7.BLL.CRule")
Dim Method As MethodInfo = objType.GetMethod(dr.Item("ConditionMethod"))
Dim Obj As Object = objAssembly.CreateInstance(objType.FullName)
Dim MethodParameters(2) As Object
If Not Method Is Nothing Then
   MethodParameters(0) = CType(dr.Item("ConditionValue"), String)
   MethodParameters(1) = CType(Question, String)
   MethodParameters(2) = CType(Login, String)
   Dim blnMatch As Boolean = Method.Invoke(Obj, MethodParameters)
   If blnMatch = True Then
      OutArray.Add(dr.Item("RuleID"))
   End If
End If
```

This code will create a type object to store a portion of the compiled assembly for this chapter. The path "Chapter7.BLL.CRule" is included to restrict which group of methods is returned to objType. It then populates a MethodInfo object with the results of the GetMethod method.

TIP: To be consistent, each method is passed three parameters, ConditionValue, Question, and Login. Since the Login parameter is used only by a particular condition method, it is not necessary to pass it to all the invoked routines. The code could be modified to programmatically determine which parameters should be passed to the invoked routine.

The CRule class contains two condition methods named QuestionContains and EmployeeEntered. QuestionContains determines whether the incoming question contains one of the words or phrases specified in the rules condition value. Since there may be more than one value specified, it uses the Split function to move all the words or phrases into an array. It then loops through this array, and if anything matches, it returns a true value. The EmployeeEntered function returns a true value if the user's login matches the employee specified in the rule.

To step through the code for this function, set a breakpoint at the start of the function by setting the cursor on a line of code and hitting **F9**. Type in the question "How many times do you buy a car in 10 years?" and click **Next**. Hit F10 or F11 as you step through the code and examine the variable values. Before exiting the function, type "? Outarray" from the **Command Window** and hit **enter.** You should get the following result:

```
{Length=7}
    (0): 1 {Integer}
    (1): 4 {Integer}
    (2): 5 {Integer}
    (3): 10 {Integer}
    (4): 17 {Integer}
    (5): 2 {Integer}
    (6): 12 {Integer}
```

The OutArray variable contains the RuleID value for all the rules where the condition method returned a true value. Note that in this case, six rules were found as matches. Table 7.2 lists the conditions associated with each of these rules.

Table 7.2 Conditions for rules found as matches when the question "How many times do you buy a car in 10 years?" was entered.

Rule ID	Rule Description	Condition	Is Default?
1	Integer	If question contains the word or phrase "how many."	No
4	Linda Notify	If question was entered by the following employee, Linda Wright.	No
5	Default Data Type	No condition specified because this is a default rule.	Yes
10	Linda Table	If question was entered by the following employee, Linda Wright.	No
17	Default Table	No condition specified because this is a default rule.	Yes
2	Auto Table	If question contains the word or phrase "car," "auto," "automobile," "vehicle," "sedan," "van," or "truck."	No
12	Purchase Table	If question contains the word or phrase "purchases," "purchase," "buy," "finance," "financing," or "assets."	No

Two of the six rules returned by the Condition Matching Phase are defaults. The other four were found because the condition method returned a true value. The condition methods supplied with the sample application are simple. Keep in mind that a production rule-based system may involve longer and more complex routines.

Handling E-mails with Rules

Rule-based applications can be very effective when it comes to automatically managing messages. Microsoft Outlook includes its own rule-based system in the form of the Outlook rules wizard. This wizard allows users to define the rules and actions used to handle all incoming e-mails. Rules can be applied at either the client or the server level.

A wide variety of third-party tools provide general message-processing capabilities. Some of them can be used to eliminate junk e-mail, create custom replies, move message text into databases, or just archive old e-mails. There are also tools that provide specific functionality, such as creating contacts for people you send e-mails to or automatically saving attachments to folders based on different rules.

For companies that want to create their own custom rules, Microsoft Outlook 2000 and above allow you to create your own custom rules using Visual Basic for Applications.

If you are a Microsoft .NET developer, then there is a good chance you already have access to Microsoft Outlook. To access the rule wizard from a Outlook 2003 client, go to **Tools** and **Rules and Alerts**. The tab labeled E-mail Rules shows the rules that will be applied to your messages in the order they are shown. New rules can be created using a template, or you can start with a blank rule. Rules created from templates allow you to do predefined things, such as move messages to a certain folder if they are from a particular person or contain certain words in the subject.

To create blank rules, the wizard walks you through a series of steps in which you specify the condition for the rule to be applied along with the action it will take. You then name the rule something meaningful to you and choose to apply it to all existing messages or just those going forward.

The Outlook rules wizard is specific in that it is used to handle a limited number of conditions and actions. It is restricted to handling messages for Microsoft Outlook only. In this case, the expert is the individual Outlook user and the domain of expertise is Outlook messaging.

The rules wizard is a good example of how a rule-based system can work. If you have never used the rules functionality in Outlook, you might want to look at it before developing your own rule-based system. It may give you some ideas about how to create an easy-to-use interface with which users can create and apply rules.

Priority Evaluation Phase

Typically, the Condition Matching phase will return several matching rules. Since the actions of these rules may override each other, it is necessary to resolve any conflicts. The administrator is able to assign numeric priority values to the rules as they are defined in Rule Maintenance. These priority values will be used to rank rules according to which are most important.

The numeric value can be any positive value from 1 on up. If a rule is so important that it is always to be executed when the condition is true, it should be assigned a value of 1. Other rules that execute the same result method should be assigned a higher priority value.

TIP: The Rule Maintenance page provided with the sample application is very simple. It would be helpful if the administrator had a page that displayed the priority hierarchy for rules associated with a specific result. You may want to consider this if you design your own rule-based system.

In the last section, six rules had matching conditions. Table 7.3 lists these rules along with the priorities and result method names assigned to each.

Table 7.3 The six rules identified in the last section along with the priority and result method names assigned.

Rule ID	Rule Description	Condition	Priority	Result Method	Is Default?
1	Integer	If question contains the word or phrase "how many."	1	FieldType	No
4	Linda Notify	If question was entered by the following employee, Linda Wright.	1	E-mail Notify	No
5	Default Data Type	No condition specified because this is a default rule.	1	FieldType	Yes
10	Linda Table	If question was entered by the following employee, Linda Wright.	1	Question Category	No
17	Default Table	No condition specified because this is a default rule.	1	Question Category	Yes
2	Auto Table	If question contains the word or phrase "car," "auto," "automobile," "vehicle," "sedan," "van," or "truck."	2	Question Category	No

Rule ID	Rule Description	Condition	Priority	Result Method	Is Default?
12	Purchase Table	If question contains the word or phrase "purchases," "purchase," "buy," "finance," "financing," or "assets."	3	Question Category	No

Note that the result method named QuestionCategory appears four times in the table. Since the result method performs a distinct action, having three rules execute the same result method could cause a conflict.

The code for this phase exists in the CRule class and is named PriorityEvaluationPhase. The function executes a SQL statement that queries the rule base and orders the results according to how they should be evaluated. If executed, the function would build the following SQL statement to process the six rules listed in Table 7.3.

```
SELECT ruleid, resultmethod
FROM [rule] r
LEFT JOIN ruletype rt on r.ruletypeid = rt.ruletypeid
WHERE ruleid in (1,4,5,10,17,2,12)
ORDER BY resultmethod, isdefault, conditionpriority
```

The SQL statement would return the results seen in Table 7.4.

Table 7.4 Query results obtained when the SQL statement that queries the rule base and orders the results according to how they should be evaluated is executed.

Rule ID	Result Method
4	E-mail Notify
1	FieldType
5	FieldType
10	QuestionCategory
2	QuestionCategory
12	QuestionCategory
17	QuestionCategory

As the results are read, the program will add the first rule with a distinct result method to the outgoing array. So the function will return rules 4, 1, and 10. It will ignore rules 2 and 12 because they have a higher priority value. Rules 5 and 17 will be ignored because they are default rules. The default rule is only applicable when no other rule with the same result method is found.

Adjustment Phase

The final phase, the Adjustment phase, is the most important. It involves the evaluation of decisions made by the application. Decisions are based on the definition of rules and rule types. If the administrator determines that a field was added incorrectly, it may be necessary to adjust a priority or to add a new rule.

The ResultLog and ResultLogDetail tables are used to record decisions made during the first three phases. A record is inserted into the ResultLog table immediately following the StripQuestion function. Child records are inserted into the ResultLogDetail table every time a decision is made or an error is encountered.

The ResultLog table contains the question text along with the id of the employee who entered it. It also contains a date/time stamp and the name of the new field created. If an error is encountered, a new child record is inserted into the ResultLogDetail table along with the error message. Whenever a question is entered and the application determines that a question already matches it, a record is inserted with the value "QM" (Question Matched) in the Result field.

For each rule that is found to have a matching condition, another record is inserted into ResultLogDetail. These types of records are indicated with the value "CM" (Condition Matched) in the Result field. For each rule in which the result method is invoked, another record is inserted with a value "RA" (Result Applied) in the Result field.

TIP: Although not included with the sample application, it would be helpful for administrators to have access to a report style interface for the Result log. You may want to consider creating such an interface if you are designing your own rule-based system.

Administrators can periodically review the records in these tables to determine how the application arrived at certain decisions. Queries like the one that follows can be issued using SQL Server's **Query Analyzer**.

```
SELECT rl.resultlogid, rl.question AS [Question Entered],
e.firstname + ' ' + e.lastname AS [Entered By],
entereddate, rld.question AS [Question Matched]
FROM resultlog rl
LEFT JOIN resultlogdetail rld ON rl.resultlogid = rld.resultlogid
LEFT JOIN employee e ON rl.enteredby = e.employeeid
WHERE result = 'QM'
```

The preceding query returns all the log entries where the question entered matched a question already in the database. Table 7.5 lists the query results obtained if you execute the program and enter the question "How often do you buy a car?"

In the last example, the application made an appropriate decision and no adjustment is necessary. Consider, however, the following question, "In the last 3 years have you had **at least** 1 car note?" If the question "In the last 3 years have you had **more than** 1 car note?" already exists in the database, the application will consider the two questions to be a match. In this case, the questions are similar but will collect entirely different answers from survey respondents.

Administrators who wish to restrict the number of fields in the database would be pleased that the application made the preceding decision. If, however, the administrator prefers to allow the alternative question, then an adjustment of the Threshold percentage is necessary. If the value is changed from 70 to 90 and the question reentered, a different result will be obtained. In the case of a 90 percent threshold percentage, an existing

Table 7.5 Query results obtained when the program is executed and the question "How often do you buy a car?" is entered. In this case the question "How often do you purchase an automobile?" already exists in the database and is seen as a matching question.

Result Log ID	Question Entered by User	Employee That Entered Question	Entered Date	Matching Question Already in Database
48	How often do you buy a car?	Linda Wright	2004-05-04 09:45:00	How often do you purchase an automobile?

match will not be found and the question will be added to the ResponseAutos table.

The number of adjustments will depend on the expectations of the experts controlling it. Initially, one should expect quite a few adjustments. The number of adjustments will decline as the application is utilized and input variances are identified.

Summary

- Rule-based systems capitalize on the knowledge of experts by encapsulating it into a set of rules that can be programmatically evaluated against a set of inputs. This chapter examines a simple rule-based system used by a fictional financial lender named Zoom Lending. The application uses rules to determine how and where new fields will be added to the database.
- Rules are typically stored in a database and consist of two parts: the condition, or if part, and the result, or then part. Four phases are used to apply all potential rules: condition matching, priority evaluation, application of results, and adjustment phases.
- The Rule Maintenance pages allow the administrator to add or edit rules and rule types. Rule types are templates used to define similar rules. They specify distinct combinations of condition and result methods that will be called programmatically. Rules are ranked according to condition and result priorities. Rules marked as default will always be selected during the Condition Matching phase. The default rule applies if no other rules with the same result method are selected.
- The sample application applies a threshold percentage to determine whether the question entered already exists in the database. The percentage value is stored in the Web.config file and can be altered without recompiling the application. The Microsoft Word API is used to check words against matching synonyms and thereby increases the likelihood that a match will be found.
- The Condition Matching phase identifies all the rules for which the condition method returns a true value. The function associated with this phase utilizes the System.Reflection namespace to programmatically invoke condition methods.
- The Priority Evaluation phase orders the rules identified in the first phase according to the result method name, default flag, and condition

priority value. It will then accept the first rule with a distinct result method and pass the results to the next phase.
- The Application of Results phase orders the rules to be executed according to the value of the result priority field. It then utilizes the invoke method of the System.Reflection namespace to execute each result method. Once successfully executed, it logs a detailed entry record indicating that the rule was applied.
- The Adjustment phase involves the ongoing analysis of records in the ResultLog and ResultLogDetail tables. These tables will record every time the application determines that a matching question exists, finds a matching condition, invokes a result method, or encounters an error. Adjustments to the threshold percentage or to the rules and rule types may be deemed necessary.

CHAPTER 8

Building an Agent

The primary reason for creating software agents is to empower the user. Software agents can often help the user to do more with less effort. That is why they are part of enhanced computing.

Unfortunately, there are many definitions and interpretations of what exactly a software agent is. It gets even more confusing when an agent is considered to be "intelligent." After all, most people have trouble measuring the intelligence of humans, let alone the intelligence of software.

A strategy white paper written for IBM offered the following definition of intelligent software agents:

> Intelligent agents are software entities that carry out some set of operations on behalf of a user or another program with some degree of independence or autonomy, and in so doing, employ some knowledge or representation of the user's goals or desires.

A more general definition would state that agents are software that represents users in the same way the users would represent themselves. Just as a sports agent acts in the best interest of an athlete, a software agent should act in the best interest of its client—the user. It should be able to identify a specific need that the user has and act on that need.

This chapter will examine some software agents designed to assist remote users in maintaining a local repository of company files available from the corporate Web server. Visual Studio.NET is an idea development tool for the solution in this chapter. The agents are able to utilize built-in functionality to easily automate many of their tasks.

Understanding Agents

Characteristics of Agents

Software agents have many different characteristics. Table 8.1 lists some characteristics commonly associated with agents. In the author's opinion, software should possess at least three of these characteristics if it is to be considered an agent but may assume all of them.

Readers may observe that the characteristics associated with agents are common to some modern-day software programs. Chapter 1 described

Table 8.1 Characteristics common to software agents. Although an agent need not possess all these characteristics, it will generally possess the first three.

Characteristic	Description
Function independently	Able to function alone with little or no user intervention required.
Able to communicate	Can communicate with the user or with other agents. Communication with the user usually involves the notification of desired outcomes or events. Communication with other agents allows the agents to retrieve additional information or to distribute processing of specialized tasks.
Reactive to its environment	In addition to operating independently, agents should be able to react to events without the need for specific instructions from their users.
Personalized	Tailored to fit the specific needs to their users. This usually involves the use of configuration files or personal information stored in a database. Personalization can also involve agents with human-friendly interfaces, such as those that utilize a speaking character.
Able to learn	This characteristic is generally associated with agents that possess intelligent capabilities. Agents that are able to learn from their users and therefore adapt their behaviors are the most complex and useful.

a phenomenon known as the "AI effect." This is an effect that occurs once a technology becomes widely accepted and from then on is no longer considered AI. In much the same way, the ideas behind software agents have been absorbed into modern-day programming. Therefore, many programs not labeled as agents may assume many, if not all, of the characteristics listed in Table 8.1.

In order to work properly, it is necessary for most agents to be autonomous and able to function independently. They must also be able to react to the environment so that they can quickly act in the best interest of their user. And they will usually need to communicate with the user or another program. The Internet not only allows for greater access to data, but provides a vehicle for communication with other agents. Because of this, many software agents exist as tools and resources on the World Wide Web. Multiple agents, or those that communicate with other agents, are especially useful because they can often perform complex tasks.

Perhaps the most debated characteristic associated with agents is the ability to learn. This is also the characteristic that can give software its greatest value and is generally used to identify those that are "intelligent." An intelligent agent can learn from the user's behavior and modify its own behavior accordingly. For instance, consider an agent used to browse the Internet. Such an agent can be particularly effective if it is able to modify the content returned to the user based on pages the user has previously visited. Imagine a user who is a computer programmer and frequently browses Web pages from software companies. If this user initiated a Web search for the word "Agent," it is very likely that the preferred results would be from computer-related Web sites rather than from online travel agencies.

Commercially Available Agents

Today, most commercially available agents perform very specific tasks. They are quite limited in their domains of knowledge and ability. Most agents deal with automating redundant tasks or making Web surfing more efficient. Table 8.2 lists functions that many of these agents perform.

The increased usage of the Internet has contributed greatly to the popularity of agents. Many Web users are overwhelmed by the vast amounts of information available on the Internet. They need better ways to find and organize this information.

Copernic Agent Professional (www.copernic.com/en/products/agent/professional.html) is a tool that allows users to search for information on the Internet. The primary difference between this tool and other search

Table 8.2 Categories that some commercially available software agents fall into. The description gives specific examples of how these categories can be implemented.

Agent Category	Description
Efficient Web surfing	Many products, ranging from those that remove spyware to those that speed up your connection, allow users to get more from the Internet.
Observation tools	Inconspicuous agents can be used to monitor a remote computer and take control of it if necessary. These agents can watch for a specific activity to occur and are sometimes used by parents to monitor their children's Web surfing.
Process automation	Agents can be very useful at automating redundant tasks and making business processes more efficient.
Network Management	Managing a large number of computers on a network is a perfect task for agents. They can automate many of the maintenance and monitoring tasks involved in managing multiple servers.
E-commerce tools	Every year, the amount of products sold and bought over the Internet increases. To help users make the most of their online shopping experience, e-commerce agents can be configured to search for specific deals or products that the user desires.
Friendly interfaces	Some agents are designed to provide entertainment or companionship rather than perform a specific task. These agents usually communicate with the user through an animated character and natural language.
Information access	Agents that help users retrieve specific information and filter out unwanted information are perhaps the most popular—for instance, agents that filter a user's e-mail to remove spam.

engines is that it combines search results from thousands of search engines. It also allows you to keep track of changes made to certain Web pages and notifies you via e-mail when changes have been made.

One of the most annoying drawbacks to using the Internet today is the proliferation of spyware or adware. Spyware is software intended to reside on a user's computer for the purpose of collecting information about the user or redirecting the user to certain Web sites. Adware can be used to initiate popup boxes displaying advertisements. Both spyware and adware can result in a user's computer slowing down and/or in the user's suddenly receiving unwanted advertisements. There are now a variety of products, such as Ad-Aware Plus, version 6.0 (www.lavasoftusa.com) that can safely remove these sometimes unwanted intruders. Ad-Aware includes a real-time monitoring system that can watch for the installation of new spyware/adware and alert you to when an intrusion is detected.

The paradox here is that many of the programs considered to be spyware and adware could also qualify as agents. They are programs intended to act in the best interest of the advertiser or marketer by collecting useful information for them. They act independently and are able to communicate with both the targeted computers and their original users. They are also able to propagate themselves without specific instructions and in many cases mask their identities to avoid detection.

Some companies offer software-development toolkits designed to build agents. These kits allow developers with very little knowledge of software agents to develop them quickly. Of course, it is not necessary to utilize an agent toolkit when building agents. Essentially, any programming language can be used.

An Example of Using Multiple Agents

This chapter will examine multiple software agents designed to assist remote users in maintaining a local repository of company files available from the corporate Web server. The Agent solution file (available for download from the book's Web site at http://www.awprofessional.com/title/0321246268) contains two Windows service projects. One of the Windows services executes independently on the remote user's laptop and utilizes a "pull method" to retrieve information. This allows it to assume the first characteristic listed in Table 8.1—function independently. The files will be pulled asynchronously from a remote server utilizing Microsoft's Background Intelligent Transfer Service (BITS).

The other Windows service project is designed to execute on a central server and is responsible for independently publishing data used by the client-based agents. Utilizing Microsoft's **File System Watcher** functionality, it will watch for changes to published files and directories. Finally, there is a Web service project that exposes two methods. The Web service will be used by the remote agent and is used to determine when updates have occurred.

The agent solution presented in this chapter is one example of how multiple agents can work together to achieve a common goal. In this case, the goal is simple: keep the user up to date. Agents can be especially effective in more complex systems because each agent can assume a specific task. Breaking up the tasks into manageable items allows each agent to specialize in a specific task. It also distributes the processing among multiple sources, thereby giving the entire system more power. In today's distributed work environments, these types of solutions will become increasingly more important.

Building a Multiple Agent Solution

A Remote Access Problem

Chapter 3 introduced a fictional company named Slugger Sports. The company produces a wide variety of sports equipment for T-ball and youth baseball games. It employs dozens of regional sales representatives who work almost entirely on the road. These salespeople utilize laptops and mobile phones to communicate with the central office about sales opportunities. Because they are remote, they do not always have consistent and reliable Internet access.

Marketing people and sales managers located at the central office often produce documents that may be useful to the sales representatives. The remote reps need a reliable way of accessing all this changing information as quickly as possible. In addition, new or updated sales opportunities are constantly being added to the central database. The sales representative needs a way of being notified when a change has occurred.

Loading the Sales Scheduling Database

To run the code accompanying this chapter, you will need to create a database in **Microsoft SQL Server** named **SalesScheduling**. You may have already done this if you ran the code for Chapter 3. This chapter will utilize the same database used in that chapter, and the SalesScheduling.mdf file can be downloaded from the book's Web site.
To attach the SQL database, execute the following steps:

1. Copy the SalesScheduling.mdf and SalesScheduling.ldf files from the book's Web site to a local directory on the server where Microsoft SQL Server is installed.
2. Open **Microsoft Enterprise Manager**

3. Right-click the **Databases** node and click **All Tasks…** and **Attach Database…**
4. From the **Attach Database** dialog, browse to the directory where you copied the database files in step 1 and select the SalesScheduling.mdf file. Click **OK**.
5. Click **OK** to attach the database.
6. To see the newly added database, you will need to click **Action** and **Refresh**.

Loading the Sample Application

Figure 8.1 is a diagram representing the remote access solution presented in this chapter. The solution consists of a remote agent and a server agent. Table 8.3 is a listing of the different projects that make up the solution. To execute the sample code available for download from the book's Web site, you will need to execute the following steps:

1. If IIS has already been installed on the machine, then you will have by default a directory named C:\Inetpub\wwwroot. Create a new folder in this directory named Chapter8 and copy the contents of the code directory (from the book's Web site) to this location.
2. You will then need to open the Internet Information Services Manager and browse to the **Default Web Site** node. Right-click the AgentWebService directory (within the Chapter8) folder and click **Properties**. From the Directory tab, click the **Create** button. When finished, click **OK** and exit Internet Information Services Manager.
3. If Visual Studio .NET has already been installed on your machine, you can open the code sample by double-clicking the solution file named Agent.sln from the C:\Inetpub\wwwroot\Chapter8\Agent directory using Microsoft Windows Explorer.

The remote agent is responsible for pulling files and database updates from the central server. The sales representatives will all execute the same remote agent code on their local machines. The application will behave differently depending on the values stored in the user configuration file. The server agent is responsible for producing an XML file used by each remote agent to determine which files it needs to pull. The Web service is the method by which the remote agent will access information from the central server. It is essentially the interface to the data.

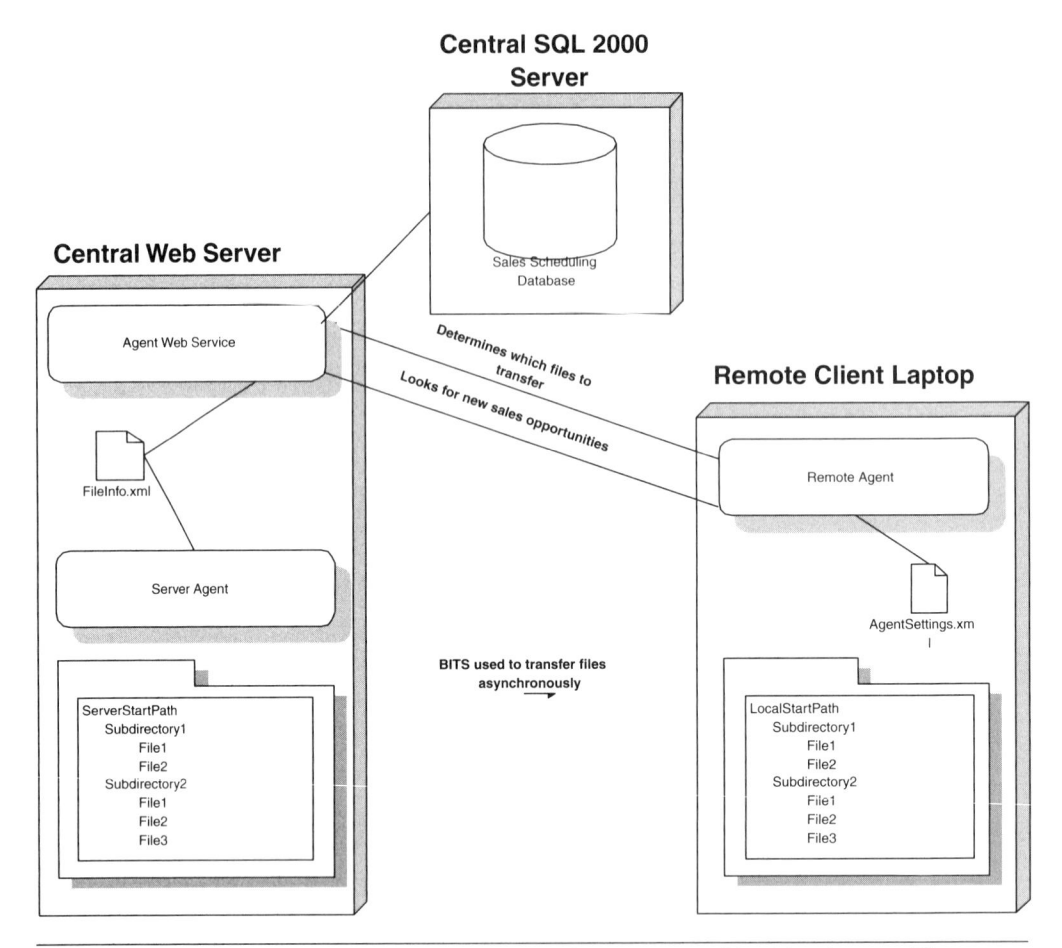

Figure 8.1 Diagram of the remote access solution presented in this chapter. The server agent is responsible for publishing information about changing files and directories on the central server. The remote agent is responsible for retrieving desired changes from a Web service when an Internet connection is available. Files are transferred asynchronously using Microsoft's Background Intelligent Transfer Service (BITS).

Remote Agent

The remote agent (represented by the project named **Agent**) will execute continuously as a Windows service and thus can operate independently. If it encounters errors, it will log them in the Windows Event Log and continue processing. Because it is a Windows service, it can be configured to start automatically so that the user is not responsible for executing it specifically.

Table 8.3 Code Listing for the Chapter 8 project. The files can be accessed by opening the Agent.sln file, located in the Agent subdirectory. There are four different projects associated with this solution. One represents the remote agent (Agent), one represents the Web service (AgentWebService), one represents the C++ code needed to set the credentials for BITS (BITSCredentials), and the last one represents the server agent (ServerAgent).

Project	File Name	Description
Agent	Agent.sln	Solution file
	Components/Background Copy.vb	Contains Visual Basic code used to create and manage file downloads using BITS.
	Components/Database.vb	Contains Visual Basic code used to get new opportunities from the database using a call to a Web service.
	Components/File Monitor.vb	Contains Visual Basic code used to monitor files being copied manually to the local start path or files that are created new in the start path.
	Components/Inet Connection.vb	Contains Visual Basic code used to check for the existence of an Internet connection on the client.
	Components/Settings.vb	Contains Visual Basic code used to read values from and write values to the AgentSettings.xml file.
	AgentSample.vb	Contains Visual Basic code and represents the main code file for the project. Using a timer control it will poll for a connection every two minutes and if found will execute methods from the other code files in the components folder.
AgentWeb Service	AgentWebService.asmx	Main file used by the Web Service. Contains Visual Basic code used to retrieve the contents of the FileInfo.xml file and new sales opportunities form the database.
BITS Credentials	Source Files/BITS Credentials.cpp	Main code file used by BITS to set the credentials of the client when initiating a new transfer job. Contains C++ code.

(continued)

Project	File Name	Description
Server Agent	Header Files/BITS Credentials.h	Header file that corresponds to the BITSCredentials.cpp code file.
	Components/File Monitor.vb	Contains Visual Basic code used to monitor files being added or updated on the central server. Changes will be written to the FileInfo.xml file.
	ServerAgentSample.vb	Contains Visual Basic code and represents the main code file for the project. It will call methods from the FileMonitor code file.

The agent will periodically check to see if the laptop is connected to the Internet. The InternetGetConnectedState function is used because we do not want the sales representative to be prompted to provide connection details every time the agent polls for a connection. This function is exposed by the **Windows Internet (WinInet) API**. The code that uses this function to poll for a connection is encapsulated inside the InetConnection class file and is seen as follows:

```
Public Shared Function CheckInetConnection() As Boolean
    Dim lngFlags As Long

    If InternetGetConnectedState(lngFlags, 0) Then
       Return True
    Else
       Return False
    End If
End Function
```

If CheckInetConnection returns a true value, it will begin the process of checking for updates. If it determines that specific files the user is interested in have been updated or new files added, it will initiate a BITS job. The BITS job is responsible for asynchronously transferring files over a network despite network interruptions or bandwidth restrictions. BITS is covered in more detail in the section titled "Background Intelligent Transfer Service (BITS)."

The agent is customized for each sales representative through the use of an XML-based configuration file (see Figure 8.2). The configuration file, named **AgentSettings.xml**, should be located in the application data directory for all users. Typically, this path is C:\Documents and Settings\All Users\Application Data\Agent.

This file contains information about which documents the user is interested in. The remote agent determines which files the user wants based on certain predetermined file attributes, such as extension, author, and keywords. Thus, if the configuration file contains a node for an author named Mark Peters, the remote agent will pull all the files in which Mark Peters is the author.

The sales representative is required to select an existing directory on the local hard drive in which to store all transferred documents. This value is stored in the node named LocalStartPath. This path may contain as many nested subdirectories as necessary.

The configuration file will be modified by the remote agent every time the sales representative copies a new file into the local directory. This is because the agent will assume that the representative is interested in knowing about future updates to the file. A sample configuration file is shown as follows:

```xml
<?xml version="1.0" encoding="utf-8" ?>
<UserSettings>
 <LocationSettings>
    <ServerName>CentralServer</ServerName>
    <ServerStartPath>AgentServerPath</ServerStartPath>
    <LocalStartPath>C:\AgentLocalPath</LocalStartPath>
 </LocationSettings>
 <FileSettings>
    <Authors>
       <Author>mark peters</Author>
       <Author>lauren jones</Author>
    </Authors>
    <FileTypes>
       <FileType>.xls</FileType>
       <FileType>.doc</FileType>
    </FileTypes>
    <Keywords>
       <Keyword>2003</Keyword>
       <Keyword>budget</Keyword>
       <Keyword>spalding</Keyword>
       <Keyword>t-balls</Keyword>
    </Keywords>
 </FileSettings>
</UserSettings>
```

Chapter 8 Building an Agent

For the sample file shown, the local start path is C:\AgentLocalPath. The configuration file also specifies that the user is interested in all files with an .xls or .doc extension.

Using the Windows FileSystemWatcher class supplied by .NET (covered in more detail in the section titled "Detecting File Changes"), the remote agent will look for files being added to this directory and all the subdirectories within it. As a result, each sales representative's configuration file will be unique. Thus, the agent assumes another characteristic listed in Table 8.1—personalization.

NOTE: In the sample application, the remote agent is only concerned with author, extension, and keyword. The code could be extended to include additional file attributes. It might also include an interface that allows users to specify which file attributes they are interested in and assign priorities to each attribute. The remote agent would then select files based on this weighted assignment.

Microsoft Agent

Microsoft Agent, version 2 (available at www.microsoft.com/msagent) is a set of software services that developers can use to add animated characters to their applications. This can be a nice feature for agent applications that do a lot of interacting with the user. The use of animated characters can add personalization and uniqueness to an agent-based application.

You can download the core components for Microsoft Agent at www.microsoft.com/msagent/downloads/developer.aspx. In addition to the core components, the download page has links to download documentation, samples, and an Agent Character Editor. It also lets you download any one of four animated characters.

The four characters available for download are:

- Genie—A blue-skinned genie that can appear and disappear in a puff of smoke.
- Merlin—A white-haired magician with a stars-and-moon cape.
- Peddy—The green parrot seen at the top of this profile box.
- Robby—A robot that looks like it came straight from an old science fiction movie.

The agents display emotions like boredom and excitement that make them seem lifelike. They will gesture and refer to certain areas of the screen to make it appear as if they live inside the user's computer.

If you wish to create your own animated character, you can do so using the Agent Character Editor. There are also third-party vendors, such as E-Clips (www.e-clips.com.au), that offer additional Microsoft Agent characters. They will even design a custom character for you. Each character can have its own unique look and personality.

Microsoft Agent utilizes the Lernout & Hauspie TruVoice text-to-speech engine to render the characters' voices. The default language is American English, but you can also download other languages at www.microsoft.com/msagent/downloads.htm##s. You can use any text-to-speech engine you wish as long as it supports the Microsoft Speech API (SAPI) version 4. Note: Windows XP users have SAPI version 5 installed by default and will need to specifically download SAPI version 4 from the Microsoft Agents downloads page.

Agents can be developed in multiple environments, including Microsoft Office, Visual FoxPro, and older versions of Microsoft Visual Studio. Since it is COM-based, it can also be referenced from a Microsoft .NET application. The Web site contains a code sample using Microsoft .NET and C# at www.microsoft.com/msagent/dev/code/dotnet.asp.

The Web site also contains information regarding Microsoft Agent licensing and distribution. You will be required to include a notice that your site "Uses Microsoft Agent technology." An additional copyright notice is required if you use any of the four characters Microsoft provides.

Using Microsoft Agent gives your interface a natural look and offers the user an alternative to the traditional point-and-click style interface. This could be nice for software agents that need to gently inform the user of certain events. The agent will be more an assistant and not just another piece of software.

Server Agent

The second agent (represented by the Windows service project named **ServerAgent**) is responsible for producing an XML file (named **FileInfo.xml**) that lists all the files and directories that have recently changed on the central server. The agent utilizes the FileSystemWatcher class to raise events every time a file or directory is added, modified, or deleted. This is covered in more detail in the section titled "Detecting File Changes."

As changes are detected, the FileInfo.xml file is updated. This file should be located on the central Web server and will be exposed to the remote agent through a Web service call. A sample version of this file is seen as follows:

```xml
<?xml version="1.0" encoding="utf-8" ?>
<agentserverpath lastupdated="7/23/2004 12:41:23 PM">
   <subdirectory1a type="dir">
      <subdirectory2a type="dir">
         <SR01.doc type="file">
          <createddate>7/20/2004 4:20 PM</createddate>
          <modifieddate>7/17/2004 5:44 PM</modifieddate>
          <extension>.doc</extension>
          <author>Sara Rea</author>
          <keywords>2003 Sales</keywords>
         </SR01.doc>
         <licensekey.txt type="file">
          <createddate>7/22/2004 3:30 PM</createddate>
          <modifieddate>7/21/2004 4:48 PM</modifieddate>
          <extension>.txt</extension>
          <author></author>
          <keywords></keywords>
         </licensekey.txt>
      </subdirectory2a>
      <postinfo.html type="file">
         <createddate>7/23/2004 12:29 PM</createddate>
         <modifieddate>6/9/2003 9:17 AM</modifieddate>
         <extension>.html</extension>
         <author></author>
         <keywords></keywords>
      </postinfo.html>
   </subdirectory1a>
   <subdirectory1b type="dir"></subdirectory1b>
</agentserverpath>
```

The FileInfo.xml file contains an attribute named lastupdated. This is used by each remote agent to determine whether changes have taken place. The remaining information is used by the remote agent to determine whether new or updated files need to be updated.

Detecting File Changes

As stated earlier, file changes are detected using the FileSystemWatcher class. This class allows you to specify a directory and watch for any changes to the files and subdirectories within it. Both the server and the remote agent will utilize this class.

For the remote agent, the class is used to monitor the local hard drive. Sales representatives can configure their agents by initially copying files they are interested in to a subdirectory within their local start path. Upon startup, the remote agent will instruct the FileSystemWatcher class to monitor the local start path and kick off code whenever a new file is added.

The code to initialize FileSystemWatcher is seen as follows:

```
Public Shared Sub SetLocalFileWatcher(ByVal StartPath As
String)
   'Create a new FileSystemWatcher object and set it's
   'properties. This watcher will be set to monitor files
   'being copied manually to the local start path or files
   'that are created new in that start path
   Dim fw As New FileSystemWatcher
   fw.Path = StartPath
   fw.IncludeSubdirectories = True 'Include subdirectories
   fw.Filter = ""                   'Watch all files
   fw.NotifyFilter = (NotifyFilters.LastWrite _
             Or NotifyFilters.FileName)

   'Add the event handlers indicating that we want to
   'be notified of file creations
   AddHandler fw.Created, _
      New FileSystemEventHandler(AddressOf LocalFileCreated)

   'Tell it to start watching
   fw.EnableRaisingEvents = True

End Sub
```

In this code, we create a new FileSystemWatcher object and set its properties to include all subdirectories and file types. We also restrict it to look only for changes to the last write time stamp and file name. Since file changes can trigger a number of different events, this prevents the event handler from being called unnecessarily.

A handler is added to indicate what method should be called when a new file is created. This handler points to a method named LocalFileCreated, which contains code to collect the file attributes and add them to the AgentSettings.xml file. The last line of code is used to initiate the monitoring process.

Chapter 8 Building an Agent

The server agent utilizes the FileSystemWatcher class to monitor the server start path and record changes to the files and directories within. Upon startup, the agent will initiate two FileSystemWatcher objects. One is used to monitor file changes, and the other monitors directory changes. In both cases, the objects will be configured to watch not only for the creation of files and directories, but also for any changes, renamings, and deletions.

Every time an event handler is executed, it will modify the FileInfo.xml file to match the change that has taken place. If someone at the central office changes a file named SalesFigures2003.doc, for example, the event handler will update the modifieddate node for that file.

Each event handler utilizes the Document Object Model (DOM) XML parser that is part of Visual Studio .NET. By using this parser, we can easily modify the contents of FileInfo.xml. In each handler the xml document is loaded and the correct node located with an XPath query. For example, the code executed when a file is renamed is as follows:

```
Private Shared Sub FileChanged(ByVal source As Object, _
        ByVal e As FileSystemEventArgs)
    'The last write time would have changed since this
    'is what we are monitoring for we will want to
    'alter the modified date entry for this file
    Dim ext As String = ""

    'Get the attributes to determine what type of file we have
    Dim fi As New FileInfo(e.FullPath)
    If fi.Exists Then
        ext = fi.Extension.ToLower
        'We will ignore temporary files
        If e.Name.IndexOf("~") < 0 And ext.ToLower <> ".tmp" Then

            'Load the XML
            Dim doc As New XmlDocument
            doc.Load(Service1._FilePath)

            'Split the path so we can parse it back for the query
            Dim arrDir As Array = e.Name.Split("\")
            Dim oldfile As String = arrDir(arrDir.GetUpperBound(0))
            'replace spaces with a dash so XML remains well formed
            oldfile = oldfile.Replace(" ", "-")

            'Loop through the array and rebuild string for XPath query
            Dim rootpath As String = ""
            Dim pos As Int16 = 0
```

```
            Do Until pos = arrDir.GetUpperBound(0) + 1
               rootpath += arrDir(pos) + "/"
               pos += 1
            Loop
            rootpath = Service1._RootDir + "/" + rootpath _
                  + "modifieddate"

            'Do an XPath query
            Dim oldnode As XmlNode = _
                  doc.SelectSingleNode("/" + rootpath.ToLower)
            oldnode.InnerText = fi.LastWriteTime.ToShortDateString + _
                  " " + fi.LastWriteTime.ToShortTimeString

            'update the lastupdated attribute of the root node
            Dim root As XmlNode = _
                  doc.SelectSingleNode("/" + Service1._RootDir.ToLower)
            Dim lastupdated As XmlAttribute = root.Attributes(0)
            lastupdated.Value = Date.Now

            'Save the file
            doc.Save(Service1._FilePath)
            doc = Nothing
         End If

      fi = Nothing
   End If
End Sub
```

Utilizing the FileInfo.xml file eliminates the need for each remote agent to scan the entire file tree every time it looks for updates. The burden of detecting file changes has been offset to the server agent. When it detects that a change has taken place, it modifies the FileInfo.xml file and updates the lastupdated attribute.

When the remote agent kicks off its processing because an Internet connection is available, it begins by using the Web service to get a copy of the FileInfo.xml file. It will examine the lastupdated date and determine whether a change has taken place since the last time it checked. Only then will it attempt to look for new files to pull.

This is one example of the potential power of multiple agents. Since each agent can assume a separate responsibility, a group of associated agents is capable of accomplishing large tasks. In our remote access solution, the server and the remote agents assume separate responsibilities that together allow them to keep each sales representative up to date.

Using the Background Intelligent Transfer Service (BITS)

Background Intelligent Transfer Service (BITS) provides the perfect way to access files remotely. Not only does BITS transfer files even after the application that initiated it exits, but it does not force a connection. Files are transferred asynchronously between an HTTP server and a remote client. BITS will adjust the transfer rate to ensure that the machine's resources are not all consumed. Most important, if an Internet connection is lost in the middle of a transfer, all is not lost. BITS will simply pick up where it left off when the connection is reestablished. Even if a file transfer takes hours or even days to complete, the system will not be compromised.

With BITS, the agent is able to function independently despite bandwidth restrictions or network interruptions. These are all-too-common problems for remote salespeople, and therefore a dependable transfer method is a must-have for remote agents.

How to Access BITS

If you have ever used the Windows Update feature, you have already used BITS. Available with Windows XP, Windows Updates automatically searches the Microsoft servers for the latest updates and patches, and then checks to see whether your machine is up to date. If it is missing any updates, BITS transfers them to your machine without interrupting or otherwise detracting from your user experience. In fact, you may have noticed the engine that allows BITS to function in the Services dialog (see Figure 8.2).

It's a great idea, and fortunately Microsoft exposes the functionality used to accomplish Automatic Updates through a set of API's. The bad part is that for now, the API's are not exposed through a Visual Studio .NET wrapper. Therefore a little work is required to get to the functionality.

TIP: BITS is utilized by one of the applications available from the Microsoft Patterns and Practices group (http://www.microsoft.com/resources/practices/default.mspx). The **Updater Application Block** can be used to quickly create self-updating applications. This feature can be invaluable for Windows Forms applications in which deployment is often a major hurdle. The application block is responsible for polling a central location for application updates. When one is available, it uses BITS to download the files and then updates the client.

For starters, you must download the latest version of the Platform SDK from MSDN. This will give you access to the BITS.idl file.

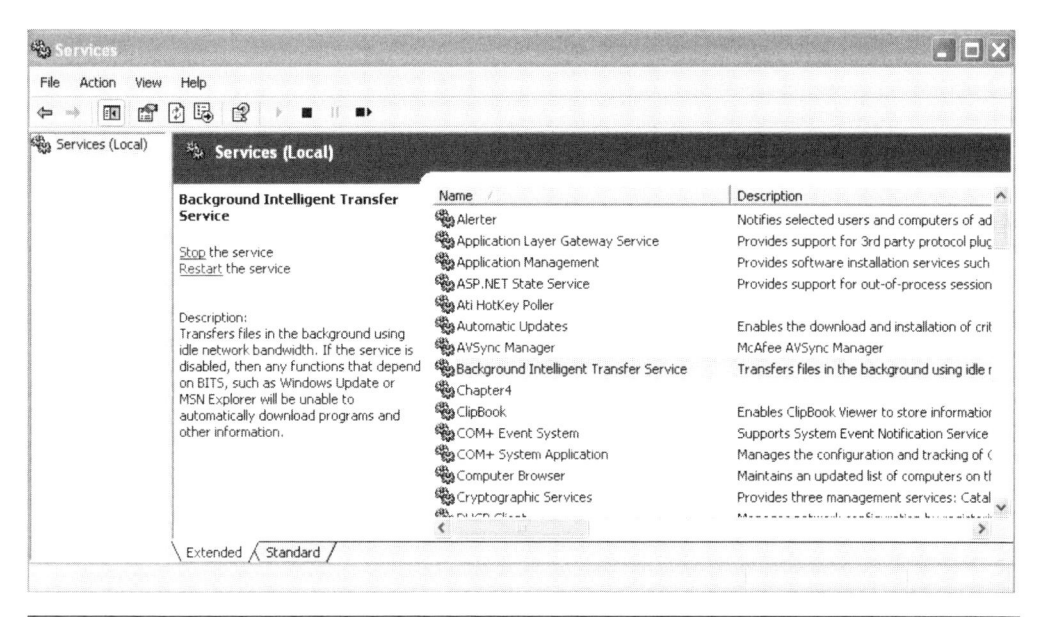

Figure 8.2 Screenshot of the Services dialog on a Windows XP machine. The Background Intelligent Transfer Service listed in Services allows Windows Update to automatically download the latest updates to your machine. It will also be used by the remote agent in this chapter to download file updates.

From there, you can use the Microsoft Intermediate Language (MIDL) compiler that is included with Visual Studio .NET to compile a type library. Next you will need to use the Type Library Importer (Tlbimp.exe) to convert the type definitions into a form useable by COM. The result of all these steps is a binary file (**BackgroundCopyManager1_5.dll**) that is available to you on the book's Web site. We can now add a reference to the binary file through References and thereby access the BITS functions.

TIP: Adding a reference to the BackgroundCopyManager1_5.dll file gives you access to the BITS functions directly but can be cumbersome to use. You may want to consider using a wrapper for BITS. This can be especially useful when you have an application that utilizes many of the complex features of BITS, such as concurrent foreground downloads or downloading ranges of files. To find out how to create your own BITS wrapper, refer to the article on MSDN titled "Using Windows XP Background Intelligent Transfer Service (BITS) with Visual Studio .NET."

Creating a Transfer Job

The transfer job is the central object in BITS. A job can consist of one or more files, and it is used to specify how files are to be transferred. The remote agent creates a transfer job using the CreateJob function, seen below:

```
Public Shared Sub CreateJob(ByVal FileList As ArrayList, _
    ByVal RemoteURL As String, ByVal LocalStartPath As String)

  Dim bcm As New BITS.BackgroundCopyManager1_5
  Dim job As BITS.IBackgroundCopyJob
  Dim jobId As BITS.GUID
  Dim bcc As New BackgroundCopyCallback
  Dim jobname As String = ""
  Dim username As String = "BITSUser"
  Dim password As String = "bitsuser"

  'The job will be named the machine name along with
  ' a date time stamp
  jobname = Environment.MachineName + "-" + _
    Date.Now.ToShortDateString + "-" + Date.Now.ToShortTimeString

  'Create the download Job that will be added to the queue
  bcm.CreateJob(jobname, BITS.BG_JOB_TYPE.BG_JOB_TYPE_DOWNLOAD, _
    jobId, job)

  'Set the job priority to normal
  job.SetPriority(BITS.BG_JOB_PRIORITY.BG_JOB_PRIORITY_NORMAL)

  'Associate all the files in the FileList with this job
  Dim strFile As [String]
  For Each strFile In FileList
    job.AddFile(RemoteURL + strFile, LocalStartPath _
      + "\" + strFile)
  Next

  'Set a reference to the BackgroundCopyCallback Interface
  'This is used to receive notification about the jobs state
  job.SetNotifyInterface(bcc)

  'Tell BITS which events we want to be notified about
  job.SetNotifyFlags(Convert.ToUInt32(Flags.IsTransferred _
    Or Flags.IsError))
```

```
    'Set Credentials by calling out BITSCredentials wrapper
    Dim wrapper As New BITSWrapper
    Dim iunknown As IntPtr = Marshal.GetIUnknownForObject(job)
    wrapper.BITSSetCredentials(iunknown, username, password)
    Marshal.Release(iunknown)

    'Activate the job in the queue
    job.Resume()
End Sub
```

Once the remote agent determines which files will be added to the transfer job, it calls the CreateJob function and passes it an array list containing all the files to be transferred. To make the job name unique, it is named as the machine name along with a date and time stamp.

The job is created as a download type, which is the default type for new jobs. The other job types are upload and upload-reply. Both of these types are used if uploading files to a server. The upload-reply type is also used to receive a reply from the server application.

For this example, we set the priority to normal, which means that all files will be marked with the same importance level. The alternative priority values are foreground, high, low, and normal. A job marked with a high priority value will transfer out of the queue before one with a low or normal value. The foreground priority is the highest value, but you should take care when using it. A job with this priority will directly compete with other applications on your machine.

BITS Authentication

Even though BITS supports secure connections over HTTPS, you will most likely want to provide additional security. You can do this by specifically setting the credentials that BITS uses to access the files on the server. BITS supports Basic, Challenge/Response, and Passport authentication schemes.

To execute the sample application, you need to create a virtual directory on your Web server from which the server files will be available. You can access directory security by executing the following steps:

1. Open **Internet Information Services** from Control Panel and Administrative Tools.
2. Right click the Default Web Site and click **New…** and **Virtual Directory**.

3. From the Virtual Directory Creation Wizard dialog, click **Next**.
4. Specify an alias name for your virtual directory and click **Next**.
5. Browse to the directory where the server files are located and click **Next.**
6. From the Access Permissions dialog, click **Next**.
7. Right-click the newly created virtual directory and click **Properties**.
8. From the Properties dialog, click the **Directory Security** tab and then click **Edit**.
9. From the Authentication Methods dialog (seen in Figure 8.3), uncheck Anonymous access and make sure **Integrated Windows Authentication** is the only item checked.

Once security is configured for the virtual directory, we will need to explicitly declare credentials using the SetCredentials method. BITS uses the Crypto API to protect credentials. The Crypto API is part of the core cryptography functionality in Windows and, like BITS, is available to developers through the Platform SDK.

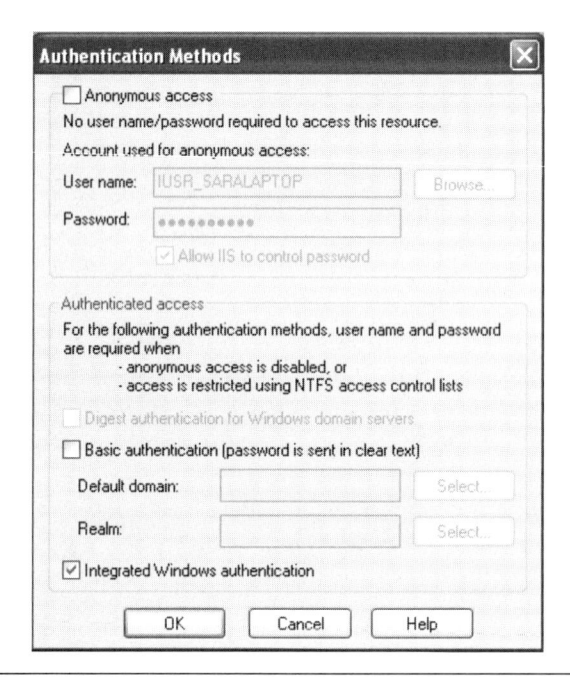

Figure 8.3 Screenshot of the Authentication Methods dialog, accessible from the Directory Security tab in Internet Information Services. When configuring the virtual directory for the sample application, make sure that Anonymous access is unchecked.

Building a Multiple Agent Solution

Unfortunately, the SetCredentials method is not included when the MIDL compiler compiles the BITS type library. To use this functionality, you have to perform an additional step. This involves writing a managed C++ wrapper to call the SetCredentials method from the native BITS library.

A C++ wrapper is included with the agent solution file on the book's Web site. It is embedded in the BITSCredentials project. The code for the BITSSetCredentials method is seen as follows:

```
void BITSWrapper::BITSSetCredentials(System::IntPtr ptr, String* _
    userName, String* password)

{

    HRESULT hr = S_OK;
    void* pv = ptr.ToPointer();
    IBackgroundCopyJob2* job;
    BG_AUTH_CREDENTIALS creds;

    const wchar_t __pin* user = PtrToStringChars(userName);
    const wchar_t __pin* passwd = PtrToStringChars(password);

    creds.Scheme = BG_AUTH_SCHEME_NTLM;
    creds.Target = BG_AUTH_TARGET_SERVER;
    creds.Credentials.Basic.UserName = (LPWSTR)user;
    creds.Credentials.Basic.Password = (LPWSTR)passwd;

    hr = ((IUnknown*)pv)->QueryInterface_
      (__uuidof(IBackgroundCopyJob2),(void**)&job);

    if (SUCCEEDED(hr))
       hr = job->SetCredentials(&creds);

    if (FAILED(hr))
      {
      BITSCredentials::BITSWrapperException* e = _
       new BITSCredentials::BITSWrapperException(hr);
      throw e;
      }
};
```

In this code, the BITSSetCredentials method accepts the user name and password as input parameters. It also accepts a pointer to the BITS transfer job. The method defaults to use the Windows challenge/response scheme (BG_AUTH_SCHEME_NTLM). Alternatively, we could have specified that it use basic authentication with the BG_AUTH _SCHEME_BASIC value. The drawback of this authentication method is that the user name and password are sent as clear text and therefore authentication is not as secure.

NOTE: When attempting to run the sample application available for download from the book's Web site, you may have to use basic authentication in order to successfully execute the code. Depending on where you execute the application and the login rights granted to the logon user, you may receive an authentication error. If this happens, change the Directory security to use basic authentication and modify the value in BITSSetCredentials.

Register for Notification

After a job has been added to the transfer queue, the next step is to determine when the files were transferred. This can be done in one of two ways. The first is to create a timer and poll for the state of the job. The job will either be in a Transferred, Disabled, Error, or Notification state. The problem with this method is that it is synchronous and requires that the job be transferred or in error before it can complete the job.

A sales representative may terminate an Internet connection at any time, even during the transfer of a job. A synchronous process would cause problems if the connection was dropped before the transfer was complete.

The remote agent instead implements the IBackgroundCopyCallback interface to maintain asynchronous processing. This allows us to register for notification whenever the job reaches a certain state. The following code from our CreateJob function is used to set a reference to the interface and tell it which events we are interested in.

```
'Set a reference to the BackgroundCopyCallback Interface
'This is used to receive notification about the jobs state
job.SetNotifyInterface(bcc)

'Tell BITS which events we want to be notified about
job.SetNotifyFlags(Convert.ToUInt32(Flags.IsTransferred _
         Or Flags.IsError))
```

Building a Multiple Agent Solution

For the sample application, we have asked to receive notification whenever a job is transferred or an error occurs. When the job has transferred, we will call the Complete method. This enables the user to see the files. Until this method is called, the files will only appear as empty temp files on the remote agent's machine.

When an error occurs, the following code is executed:

```
Sub JobError(ByVal job As BITS.IBackgroundCopyJob, _
    ByVal jobError As BITS.IBackgroundCopyError) _
   Implements BITS.IBackgroundCopyCallback.JobError
   'The job received an error, but we need to determine what type of
   'error it was
   Dim jobname As String = ""
   Dim ErrorMsg As String = ""
   Dim BITSError As String = ""
   Dim LanguageID As Integer = &H409 'Indicate language is English(US)

   If Not job Is Nothing Then
     'Get the name of the job
      job.GetDisplayName(jobname)

     'Get the error
      job.GetError(jobError)
      jobError.GetErrorDescription(Convert.ToUInt32(LanguageID), _
          BITSError)

     'Log the error using the Exception Manager application block
      ErrorMsg = "The following error was encountered trying to "
      ErrorMsg += "process the BITS job " + jobname + " : "
      ErrorMsg += BITSError
      ExceptionManager.Publish(New Exception(ErrorMsg))

     'Cancel the job
      job.Cancel()
   End If

End Sub
```

In this code we get the display name of the job, which should be the machine name and a date/time stamp (this was defined in the CreateJob function). We also get the error description and then publish the error using the Exception Management Application Block. Finally, we cancel the job so that it will no longer appear in the transfer queue. At this point, any empty temp files on the local machine should disappear.

Monitoring New Opportunities

New leads are constantly being added to the central database. The salespeople all have access to a Web application that allows them to work these new opportunities. Unfortunately, most salespeople only check the Web application once a day. In some cases it may take several hours or days for a sales opportunity to be discovered.

The remote agent contains a CheckDatabase function that is used to check for new opportunities. The function is initiated as soon as an Internet connection becomes available. CheckDatabase will make a call to the Agent Web Service and pass in the remote salesperson's e-mail address. The Web service will search the leads table for leads located in the zip code assigned to the salesperson. If the salesperson has the status of 'N' (new) and also has a notify date older than forty-eight hours, the contact information is returned.

NOTE: The Web Service featured in the sample solution is not considered secure. At a bare minimum, a production application would want to consider enabling point-to-point security using SSL (Secure Sockets Layer). To enable SSL, readers would need to request a certificate from a certification authority utility on the Web server.

Readers can obtain a certificate from a recognized authority like Verisign (http://www.verisign.com), or they can generate their own using the secure certificate wizard in Internet Information Services Manager.

Once a certificate is downloaded, a pending certificate request can be installed on a Web server using the IIS Manager. At this point, requests made to the Web service would have to include the HTTPS header instead of HTTP. This will ensure that any traffic between the Web service and the client is encrypted.

Every time the CheckDatabase function finds new leads, it displays a message box to the user (see Figure 8.4). Thus, the remote agent exhibits one more agent characteristic—the ability to communicate with the user.

Figure 8.4 Screenshot of the dialog box used to notify the remote salesperson of new sales opportunities. A notification will be sent to the salesperson every forty-eight hours until the lead is worked or no longer has the status of new.

Summary

- Software is an agent that acts in the best interest of its user and possesses at least three of the following characteristics:
  - Functions independently
  - Reacts to its environment
  - Able to communicate
  - Personalized
  - Able to learn
- The sample solution is an example of multiple agents working together to reach a common goal: updating the user. In this case, the agent solution assumes the top four items in the list of characteristics. It consists of a windows service located on a remote sales representative's laptop—a windows service located on a central Web server—and a Web service that is used by the remote agent to retrieve data from the central server.
- Remote and server agents both utilize Microsoft's FileSystemWatcher class to automatically monitor the file system for updates. Remote agents monitor new files to update the user's configuration file. Server agents monitor the results in the update of an xml file that lists all the available files and their attributes.
- Using Microsoft's Background Intelligent Transfer Service (BITS) to transfer files allows the remote agent to not only function independently, but also to efficiently communicate with an outside data source. The impact on the sales representative is minimized because BITS automatically adjusts the transfer rate. Most important, the files will be transferred to the user despite network interruptions.

- BITS allows you to receive notifications when a job is transferred or encounters an error. This enables the remote agent to process the transfer job asynchronously. Whenever an error is encountered, the error is logged and the job canceled. When the job is transferred, it is marked complete so that the user can see the transferred files.
- Remote agents have the ability to monitor new leads added to the central database. When a new record is discovered, the contact information for that opportunity is displayed to the salesperson through a popup dialog.

CHAPTER 9

The Future of Enhanced Computing

Enhanced computing seeks to blur the lines between human and computer interaction. Technologies typically reserved for AI applications can be used to enhance traditional applications and make them more useable. The goal is to make the user's experience as natural and intuitive as possible. Another goal is to extend the capabilities of current applications in order to help the user do more with less effort. For the purposes of this book, enhanced computing involved the use of mobile devices, speech recognition, data-mining, and other Microsoft technologies and products. It may soon involve the use of many more technologies emerging from Microsoft Research or other third-party vendors, such as natural-language understanding and facial recognition.

The discussion in this book focuses primarily on Microsoft technologies. This is mainly because of the great acceptance and proliferation of Microsoft products. Microsoft spends almost as much on research and development as on sales and marketing. Just remember that the overall goal of this book is to show you how to use AI technologies to enhance and extend the user's experience with more natural computing.

The present chapter features some upcoming products and technologies that Microsoft has to offer. The first section, titled "The Next Development Platform," focuses on development tools and server-based products expected to be released within the next few years. These products are in either the alpha or the beta stage, and more than likely you have already heard about them. They are listed in Table 9.1.

> **NOTE:** The information in this chapter is based on preliminary documentation for software not yet released and on documentation available from Microsoft Research. Therefore, the information is subject to change and may be different at the time a product is released.

The next section, titled "Microsoft Research," features a few of the projects currently under development or near completion at Microsoft Research (MSR). MSR supports several research areas (listed in Table 9.2) that consist of multiple research groups. The projects these groups are working on show potential in the area of enhanced computing and should form the basis for new products from Microsoft.

The end of the chapter will briefly discuss how AI factors into the future of enhanced computing. The section titled "Other Areas of AI" highlights a few additional branches of AI that may be of further interest to readers, along with Web sites you can visit for more information. Also included is a profile box that features a newly formed company named Sonum Technologies. Sonum produces a natural-language processor that may dramatically change the way humans interact with their computers.

The Next Development Platform

The .NET platform was a huge initiative for Microsoft, and the company plans to continue in that direction with a whole line of products focused around the .NET framework. Microsoft hopes to make development easier for us developers. At the same time, it plans to expand on what can be done with the same applications. Table 9.1 lists the main components of what Microsoft calls the "Next Development Platform."

The plan is to release the next generation of Visual Studio.NET (code name Whidbey) by 2005. This version will offer many productivity advantages for developers and will tightly integrate with the next version of SQL Server, SQL Server 2005. This new version of SQL Server represents a major upgrade of the product and includes an overhauled version of Analysis Services.

Analysis Services 2005

On the near horizon, **SQL Server 2005** (code name Yukon) offers some wonderful upgrades in the area of Analysis Services. The biggest improve-

Table 9.1 Microsoft developer tools scheduled for release sometime in the near future. These products represent the next generation of development tools Microsoft is offering. They should enable developers to create some powerful and intelligent-based applications.

Product	Description
SQL Server 2005 (code name Yukon)	The next release of SQL Server will include an updated version of Analysis Services. Analysis Services 2005 will offer a new interface and five new data-mining algorithms.
Visual Studio.NET, 2005 (code name Whidbey)	This release should correspond with the release of SQL Server 2005 and will provide support for it.
Longhorn	This is the next big Windows operating system. Focusing on security and stability, it uses a new application model and markup language to create Longhorn-based applications.
Orcas	This is the release of Visual Studio.NET that will correspond with the release of Longhorn. It will allow you to access the new features of Longhorn.

ments in **Analysis Services 2005** are changes to the interface, the inclusion of five new mining algorithms, and the ability to mine data in "real time."

The basic concepts of data mining remain. You still create an Analysis Services database from either an OLAP cube or a relational database. Mining models are initially built using a wizard and then refined with an editor. Mining models are trained against test data, and developers still need to make sure they are working with clean data. You can utilize Analysis Services 2000 and create some very useable applications even if your company is not ready to move immediately to SQL Server 2005. You can then migrate the application to Analysis Services 2005 when it becomes available.

What has changed is that working with Analysis Services should be quicker and easier. Also, you now have the ability to take advantage of some significant upgrades. Instead of abandoning or neglecting data mining, Microsoft has invested some serious time and effort in improving its capabilities. It has added additional algorithms that expand the types of data-mining solutions developers can create.

This section will present some of the new data-mining features expected with the release of SQL Server 2005. It will also discuss migrating an existing 2000 mining model to the new version.

NOTE: The information in this section is based on the SQL Server 2005 Beta 2 release version. Some things may change with the final release.

A New Interface

Perhaps the most noticeable difference between Analysis Services 2000 and 2005 is the interface. Database administrators and developers no longer need separate tools to manage SQL Server databases and Analysis Services databases. You can now view both from one tool known as the **SQL Server Management Studio**.

For developers creating data-mining solutions, projects exist inside a Visual Studio Solution file just like any other project. Referred to as the **Business Intelligence (BI) studio**, this is quite nice: everything is in one place, and you get access to a familiar and consistent interface.

Like the 2000 version, Analysis Services 2005 includes wizards that allow you to create a data source and a mining model. However, you now have the ability to define a **Data Source View** (DSV). This is a virtual view of the actual data and can be used to specify computed columns. In Chapter 5, we had to reference a view inside SQL Server 2000 named vw_shipments. With Analysis Services 2005, you can create a virtual column known as a named calculation. This is good for keeping the code used in your data-mining solution separate from the actual database. Instead of having to store special tables or views inside the relational database, you can utilize the data source views.

A DSV is also useful when you have a database that contains hundreds or thousands of tables. The DSV only needs to include the tables you are interested in mining. You can also use it to select data from multiple data sources, such as databases on other servers or even text files.

Analysis Services 2005 comes with twelve views that can be embedded into your Visual Studio .NET application as Windows Forms controls. The views allow you to create and edit mining models and give the developer a different way of visualizing the results.

The new version includes a query editor that resembles SQL Servers Query Analyzer. It also includes another query builder that has a Microsoft Access style interface. Queries are performed using the **Multidi-**

mensional Extensions (MDX) language, which has been enhanced in Analysis Services 2005. This will enable you to build a mining model and then use the query tools to extract meaningful information from the results. It could be quite useful if you are starting from scratch with a database and do not know what you are trying to predict.

New Mining-Model Algorithms

Analysis Services 2005 features seven data-mining algorithms—five more than in the 2000 version. In addition, the original two algorithms, decision trees and clustering, have been updated.

The new algorithms are listed below:

1. Association rules—Used to create a set of rules used in predictions. Most useful in making predictions against large amounts of transactional sales data.
2. Time series—Used to predict trends; can be useful when working with financial data, such as stock prices.
3. Naive Bayes—Used only against noncontinuous variables (for example, a product name) and therefore performs very quickly.
4. Sequence clustering—In addition to grouping similar data into clusters, it uses sequence analysis to determine the order in which events occur.
5. Neural nets—Based on an AI technique, this is useful for determining things like whether a customer is good or bad. It is the most thorough algorithm and therefore the most time consuming.

Mining Data in Real Time

Analysis Services 2005 will continue to support the method of processing data used in the 2000 version. This method is a "pull" method in which data used to process the model is pulled from the data source at the time it is processed. In Chapter 6, data was refreshed on a daily basis. For most situations this is all right, since data mining is generally used to extract meaning from historical data that does not change all that much. Also, mining involves looking for trends in the data and not querying for specific values.

With the new version, you can now use a push method to retrieve data from a Data Transformation Services (DTS) package or a custom application. Another option, in between the two, is to use a proactive cache when you are working with data from an OLAP data source. In this scenario, data is refreshed based on predefined parameters, such as the amount of time between data pulls.

Migrating a Mining Model Created with SQL Server 2000

A migration wizard is included with Analysis Services 2005 that allows you to migrate a mining database created with Analysis Services 2000. You still have to preprocess the mining models once they are migrated, but at least you do not have to recreate them from scratch. The limitations on migrating cubes as of the beta 2 version include not being able to migrate remote partitions and linked cubes. Linked cubes have been replaced with linked measure groups.

Individual mining models can also be copied to Analysis Services 2005 by using a PMML (Predictive Model Markup Language) query. You can then create a mining model in Analysis Services 2005 by using the Create Mining Model statement and referencing the PMML retrieved. This method does not copy the bindings, though, so you will only be able to view the content in Analysis Services 2005 and not be able to reprocess the model. This could be useful, however, if you want a quick way to view the results of an old mining model using the new tools in Analysis Services 2005.

Longhorn

Longhorn is the code name for the next big Microsoft operating system. The final client version of this operating system is not expected to arrive before 2006, but when it does arrive, it should offer computing advances that can be utilized by many intelligent-based applications (the server version is expected to be released sometime in 2007).

The client version will include two pillars known as Avalon and Indigo. Avalon is the presentation layer, and Indigo is the communications layer. The initial release should be followed by the release of a new storage system known as WinFS as a beta version. WinFS represents a significant change in the way data is organized and accessed by applications.

NOTE: The information in this section is based on the Longhorn alpha release version. Some things will undoubtedly change with the final release.

Avalon

Longhorn will use a new markup language known as Extensible Application Markup Language (XAML). XAML is similar to HTML in that you can control the layout of text and controls on a page. But it also allows you to add procedural code using languages like C#, Visual Basic.NET, and JScript.Net. The procedural code mixed with XAML will function similarly to the current code-behind files used in .NET. You can have a simple application that consists only of XAML or one that consists of both (this is the type that most developers will create).

A significant change for developers is the introduction of the application model. The new model provides a single programming model for creating different types of applications. Developers will be able to create applications that take advantage of the best features of Web- and Windows-based applications. Thus you will be able to create applications that can be deployed easily like current Web applications, but can also run offline like current Windows applications. Both Web and desktop applications will look and function essentially the same. The biggest difference will pertain to where the code resides.

Blurring the lines between application-development methods will eliminate the need for certain tradeoffs, such as having a rich user interface versus an easy deployment scenario. This should create more opportunities for developers to implement enhanced computing techniques.

Indigo

Indigo provides for secure communication among applications and is a key piece of the seamless computing vision. It incorporates Web services and allows you to communicate in one of two ways:

- Stateless—The less reliable method, representing the way Web services are utilized currently.
- Stateful—A session exists between the sender and the receiver so that the communication is stable and secure. With sessions you can specify exactly how a message should be received. This is especially important when you have Web services sending information over unreliable networks. For example, even if a connection is interrupted, a stateful session can pick up the communication later when it is available.

Secure and reliable communication is critical for most businesses. It is also important for agent-based applications in which data is available remotely or there is a need to communicate with other agents. Therefore, the ability to improve the way Web services are implemented is an important next step for enhanced computing.

WinFS

Computer storage space is increasing by leaps and bounds every day. A typical user's hard drive is well over 100 GB. Modern-day applications are quickly filling the unused space as more and more files and file types are added to the mix. WinFS, which stands for Windows Future Storage, is a key component that represents the new storage subsystem. It will depart from the typical way of storing data as files inside folders. WinFS will not be included in the initial client release of Longhorn, but it will be incorporated later and represents an important piece of the puzzle.

WinFS will use a query language known as OPath to locate information. It also allows you to relate items and therefore make them more meaningful. Preliminary documentation gives an example in which a sales proposal is related to the salesperson and the fiscal sales quarter it was created in. This relationship could then be used when searching for proposals from a certain quarter.

WinFS Rules

The platform known as WinFS Rules is one of the most interesting parts of WinFS for enhanced computing. With WinFS Rules, you can create rules that enable users to personalize their experience. This platform will enable developers to create their own rule-based or expert-based applications. In this case, the expert will be the user who knows which documents are most important and how the information should be presented to them. Admittedly, the rules will apply only to data stored in the WinFS and not to other areas. But in many cases this may be enough. After all, managing the growing number of files and messages we have is quite a task.

WinFS rules follow a structure similar to the one governing the rules presented in Chapter 7. The rule itself is made up of a condition and a result. The condition is based on a Boolean function that evaluates to either true or false and can contain multiple conditions. Multiple rules can be grouped together into what is known as a rule set. Decision points are used to limit the number of options exposed to the user when defining rules. Otherwise, the user would be completely overwhelmed by the number of potential conditions and results that would make up a rule.

Most Microsoft Outlook users are familiar with the rules used in filtering out junk mail. The interface for WinFS rules is expected to follow a style that resembles the way Outlook creates rules.

WinFS Notification Service

The WinFS Notification service is similar to the FileWatcher class utilized in Chapter 8. It is used to notify you of specific changes to the file system. What is new is that you can set up what are known as long-term subscriptions. These allow you to receive notifications even after an application has been restarted.

Mobility

Mobility is a critical consideration for most businesses today. Workforces are expanding their size and are widely dispersed. Laptops and handhelds are slowly replacing desktops. The business world needs devices that are easy to use and easy to connect with. But devices must still offer complex functionality and be able to deliver critical data as close to real-time as possible. Microsoft recognizes the growing demand for smarter devices and addresses these needs in the next version of Longhorn.

Network awareness is one important need for mobile applications. No longer can applications assume that the user has access to a stable network connection. Longhorn will provide a single API named Network Location API or NLA. Developers can access all network parameters from this location and intelligently determine whether the network is available. If it is not, then this needs to be accounted for with as little user intervention as possible.

Using the NLA, the developer can determine not only whether the network is available but can also whether the user has a high or low bandwidth connection. The application can then make adjustments accordingly. This would be especially important for applications that automatically initiate file transfers.

Microsoft Research (MSR)

If Microsoft has anything to say about it, we will eventually live in homes straight out of an episode of *The Jetsons*. The research group envisions a home where the kitchen counter displays a menu that helps you prepare dinner and the refrigerator adds items to your shopping list as you remove them. It may sound like science fiction, but it is not as far away as you think.

Table 9.2 Main research areas at Microsoft Research. Each of these areas includes several groups working on multiple projects. Members of each research group generally work on more than one project and often work across groups and research areas.

Project	Description
Algorithms and Theory	This mathematically based group is working on several projects that range from game theory to quantum computing. The Intelligent Systems group is working specifically on new algorithms for data-mining and improving handwriting recognition for handheld devices.
Hardware Development	This group aims to develop devices that interface with the user more naturally. It has built a bone-conductive microphone named Who Is Talking to You (WITTY) that should reduce background noise and increase successful speech recognition.
Human-Computer Interaction	This area is the basis for many different groups and a broad range of projects at MSR. It involves interacting with the user in better ways and also includes research in the reasons people use their computers and how that experience can be improved overall.
Machine Learning, Adaptation and Intelligence	This area focuses on creating software that can learn and includes projects involved in data and text mining, document processing, facial recognition, and audio fingerprinting. It also includes groups dedicated to natural-language processing and understanding, which is critical to understanding spoken text from a user.
Multimedia and Graphics	This area seeks to enhance the user's experience by taking advantage of the increasing amounts of memory and hardware capabilities. Projects in this area include collaborative video viewing, image editing, and a project that aims to digitize every piece of information a person can collect.
Search, Retrieval, and Knowledge Management	Information retrieval is becoming more critical as the amount of digitized information grows at an accelerated pace. This area aims to make the process of searching and retrieving information more efficient and easier for the user. It includes a project called Approximate Query Processing which looks for new ways to query and browse data.

Project	Description
Security and Cryptography	This involves research in creating secure systems on both open and private networks. Members in this area consult on security for Microsoft products and are working on a biometric authentication method.
Social Computing	Also involved heavily in human to computer interaction, this area includes projects designed to enhance the user's experience. It involves speech-based projects like the multi-modal conversational user interface, which is based on continuous speech recognition and language understanding.
Software Development	This area's primary goal is to make developers more productive. It involves research into new languages, and work from this area has been used to enhance Microsoft developer tools.
Systems, Architectures, Mobility and Networking	Addressing the needs of a mobile society, this area includes projects in networking, databases, and distributed systems.

In fact Microsoft hopes to release many products known as smart personal objects. These are everyday items customized for the individual user and able to deliver specific information. Wristwatches, alarm clocks, and key chains are all examples.

The first of these products, a smart watch, is already available for purchase from MSN Direct. The watch currently allows you to access sports, weather, news, and stock quotes. Of course, if the trend catches on (as seemly quite likely), it may soon be possible to deliver even more customized functionality via a user's wrist.

The smart watch is just one example of how the world is becoming more mobile and of the need for better software to interface with this new world. Another is Xnav, a Prototype device that allows the user to navigate an application using one-handed touch access. This would be useful not just for busy people, but for the blind and the handicapped.

This section features projects at Microsoft Research (research.microsoft.com) that if not yet ready are expected to make their way into products within the near future. The MSR motto is "Turning ideas into reality." The group comprises dozens of subgroups, with each working on multiple projects (see Table 9.2). Many of the technical advances seen in current Microsoft products originated from this group.

Speech-Related Technologies

Speech is a major initiative for Microsoft. It is part of a larger concept referred to as the Natural User Interface, or Natural UI, which involves creating natural and expressive interactions with the user. This is primarily accomplished using speech-processing capabilities but can also involve natural language and machine learning. The Natural UI is intended to ease interaction with smart devices—not merely devices like PDA's and Tablet PC's, but devices loaded in your car, Internet television, and screen phones.

Kai-Fu Lee is the corporate vice president of the Natural Interactive Services Division of Microsoft. He recently gave a presentation in which he stated:

> Natural UI will arrive as an evolution. . . . But, in 10 years, Natural UI will be viewed as the largest revolution since Graphical UI.

The Speech group hopes to improve human-to-computer interaction by giving computers the ability to recognize spoken words and even to understand their meaning. Of course, this is the tricky part. The group's researcher are hard at work trying to improve speech recognition, grammar understanding, and text to speech using several different methods.

One way speech recognition can be improved is through the ability to detect emotion in speech. This is a technique that could be very useful for speech applications that interface with customers. The software will be able to respond appropriately if it can recognize the speaker's emotion.

The work from this group was the basis for the Speech Application Programming Interface (SAPI) and also for the newly released Microsoft Speech Server. In fact, some of the researchers from this group are now working in the Speech Platforms Group, which is responsible for the Microsoft Speech Server product.

Recently, I had the opportunity to speak with James Mastan, director of marketing for the Speech Platforms Group. The profile box titled "The Future of Speech at Microsoft" contains excerpts from that conversation.

One of the group's first prototypes was the MiPad, which stands for multimodal interactive notepad. This device, which was first demonstrated in 2000, combines speech-recognition technology with pen input. The user can choose to use either method when accessing e-mail, schedules, or contact information. Work in this area was the basis for multimodal application development with Speech Server.

The Future of Speech at Microsoft

In late August 2004, I spoke with James Mastan, director of marketing for the Speech Platform Group at Microsoft. I was able to ask him about some of the technologies we can expect to see coming from the group.

I began by asking about work being done in the area of personalization. For instance, what can be done to improve the recognition of speech for each individual user?

I told him that as a user of the Speech SDK, I would like to see it move away from the need to rely on the grammar. The process of creating a grammar can be quite cumbersome for applications that should anticipate a broad range of responses.

He suggested that more consideration should be given to application design in the immediate time frame. There are many well-documented techniques on this subject available on the Microsoft Speech Server Web site at www.microsoft.com/speech.

He also had the following to say:

> The goal is exactly as you say, instead of having [as] in today's case, the user adapts to the system—the reverse is the goal— to have the system adapt to the user. So, we have technologies already in research that are pretty far along that enable self-learning.

In a follow-up to his response, I asked when we might anticipate these self-learning techniques to be implemented in the Speech Server product. His response was:

> Absolutely in the next five years, potentially within the next three years.

He also informed me of a project named YODA that is currently under development. In describing the project, he said:

> It is a dictation program that interacts with e-mail and makes inferences. For example, if you want to send e-mail to Joe, Tom, Fred, and Harry. If it knows for example that my e-mails in the last four weeks have gone to Joe Thomas and Mary Henry, etc., then it can infer those are the people I want to send e-mail to and populate these names in the To line. . . . It learns from your usage pattern. . . . The goal is to enable self-tuning systems.

He told me that the Speech Platforms Group has plotted out what it anticipates will be the error recognition rate over the next few years. He said that humans currently have a 2 percent error recognition rate. He expects that the error rate for speech-recognition systems will probably approach human levels by the year 2011.

(continued)

I asked Mr. Mastan what new advances were expected to be implemented in the Speech Server product within the next year. He told me of the following:

- International language coverage
- VOIP (Voice over IP)
- Improved noise filtration
- Enhanced grammar authoring and debugging tools
- Fine-tuned controls for authoring prompts
- Enhanced dialog authoring tools

He also told me that the trend is to go to packaged speech-based applications, such as the ones being produced by Solar Software (www.solarsoftware.com). This company is featured in a profile box in Chapter 3 and currently produces a software package known as Vocal Help Desk. The software allows Windows network administrators to initiate administrative functions using speech. He added:

> So, you do not have to create custom applications every time you want to develop something. So, lets make this more like the computer software market where you buy a box of speech enabled something and install it on your backend and it works.

In closing, I asked Mr. Mastan how near the Speech Platform group was to creating a fully speech-enabled computer that could be operated by a user using continuous speech. He responded:

> That is a goal that Microsoft has and the odds are that the best way to do that is to speech enable Windows. You can assume that is a direction we are headed to within the next five years.

There are many exciting things coming out of Microsoft that will support enhanced computing. Speech processing is probably the most key technology in this area. It will be vital in the acceptance of other technologies that strive to improve human-to-computer interaction.

Notification Platform

Created by the Adaptive Systems and Interaction team at Microsoft Research, the Notification Platform project is based around the idea of an intelligent agent. The technology is already the basis for some of the .NET platform and should be part of other upcoming products. Someday the intelligent capabilities of this platform may even be made available to developers through an API.

One of the reasons the field of AI has had such a slow start is that there are so many things humans do that seem to be innate and do not follow the standard rules of logic. On the opposite side, there are many things that computers can do that humans find difficult. For instance, computers are sometimes better than humans at calculating large figures and at remembering things accurately. Computers, moreover, do not suffer from the same limitations as humans. For instance, computers do not have to eat or sleep.

The Notification Platform takes advantage of the things that computers can do better than humans. It consists of programs that assist users in their daily activities. For instance, one program, named Priorities, is used to assign priorities to e-mails and determine which ones the user wants to see. It uses a neural network to help it learn from the user and know which priorities to assign.

Machine Translation

The MindNet project involves building semantic networks in order to extract meaning from large amounts of data. This knowledgebase project has been utilized as a data repository by the Machine Translation project.

This project is based on machine learning and is used internally at Microsoft to process the company's huge quantities of technical documents. Documents that would take a human months to process can be processed by the Machine Translation project in a single night. The data-driven project parses sentences and assigns them to categories that are later associated. The technology has already been used in the Microsoft Word 97 grammar checker and the natural-language query function of the Microsoft Encarta 98 Encyclopedia.

What About AI?

I predict that artificial intelligence will enter the mainstream so slowly that one day we will ask, "When did this get here?" There will not be one product or one robot that represents everything AI has to offer. Although a truly conscious machine may someday be developed— and this is debatable—it will certainly not be any time soon.

I am optimistic that many of the limitations that have hindered the field of AI and computing will continue to fall. Limitations will be removed through advances in both hardware and software. The average desktop today can outperform the largest supercomputer of ten years ago. The trend toward improvement will continue. Hardware limitations will become less of a problem as more and more computers are networked together. Every computer in a network can absorb a little bit of the processing needs so that all the computers together function as a supercomputer.

Software will advance in the same way that competition among businesses escalates. To meet global and local business needs, software developers will need to be creative in the ways they approach solutions.

American Association for Artificial Intelligence

The American Association for Artificial Intelligence (AAAI) is a nonprofit organization dedicated to increasing awareness of the technologies surrounding artificial intelligence. Its Web site (www.aaai.org) contains links to AI-related topics and is a good resource for anyone who wants to know more about the field.

The association has more than six thousand members and publishes a quarterly named *AI Magazine*. This publication contains information on some of the latest research efforts in the field.

The AAAI hosts annual conferences that bring together leading researchers in the field. The National Conference of Artificial Intelligence and the Innovative Applications of AI Conference cover a wide variety of topics, ranging from knowledge-based reasoning to robot exhibitions. The association also hosts fall and spring symposiums that offer a workshop-like setting for smaller groups of invited participants.

The Web site contains an "AI in the News" Web page (www.aaai.org/AITopics/html/current.html) that features links to current AI-based articles. The headlines are sorted and grouped by date and cover virtually every area of AI from beginning to expert level.

The Web site also features a resources page which provides general information about AI along with a calendar of AI-related events and links to AI-related organizations (www.aaai.org/Resources/resources.html). This is a good resource for readers who want to get up to speed on AI-related technologies.

Other Areas of AI

This book has touched on only a few AI-based technologies (speech recognition, data mining, rule-based systems, agents). There are many other branches (see Table 9.3) that you may want to explore. This section discusses a few of them.

Fuzzy Logic

Fuzzy logic is a branch of AI that takes account of various "real-world" factors. It was created because not all algorithms are able to deal exclusively with 1's and 0's. Fuzzy logic is able to interpret a broader range of variables and their associated values, a very useful capability when the inputs are contradictory and might cause traditional algorithms to respond incorrectly. It was first introduced in the 1960s as a result of dealing with natural-language understanding.

Fuzzy logic is especially effective when dealing with input from digital sensors such as cameras and electrical sensors. As a result, the manufacturing industry has been one of the primary users of this technology so far. It is especially important for controlling machine temperatures and speed.

Robots receive their input from a variety of mechanical devices, and fuzzy logic can be helpful in controlling some of them. It has contributed to breakthroughs in handwriting and voice recognition where even humans have trouble.

Fuzzy logic comprises several different algorithms, and there are many theories about how exactly to approach this subject. Readers interested in learning more may want to check out www.fuzzy-logic.com. The Web site references an online book that presents fuzzy logic in a very understandable way.

Game AI

The first AI games were variations of board games like checkers or chess. Now that so many hardware advances have been made and memory is cheap, the games industry has exploded. Games that claim to have "AI inside" are often the most sought after. They usually involve some sort of simulation. "Age of Empires" (see Figure 9.1), "Mindrover," and "Mission: Impossible" are all games of this kind. The games industry is hugely competitive, and games these days are as graphics-intensive as a Hollywood movie.

Chapter 9 The Future of Enhanced Computing

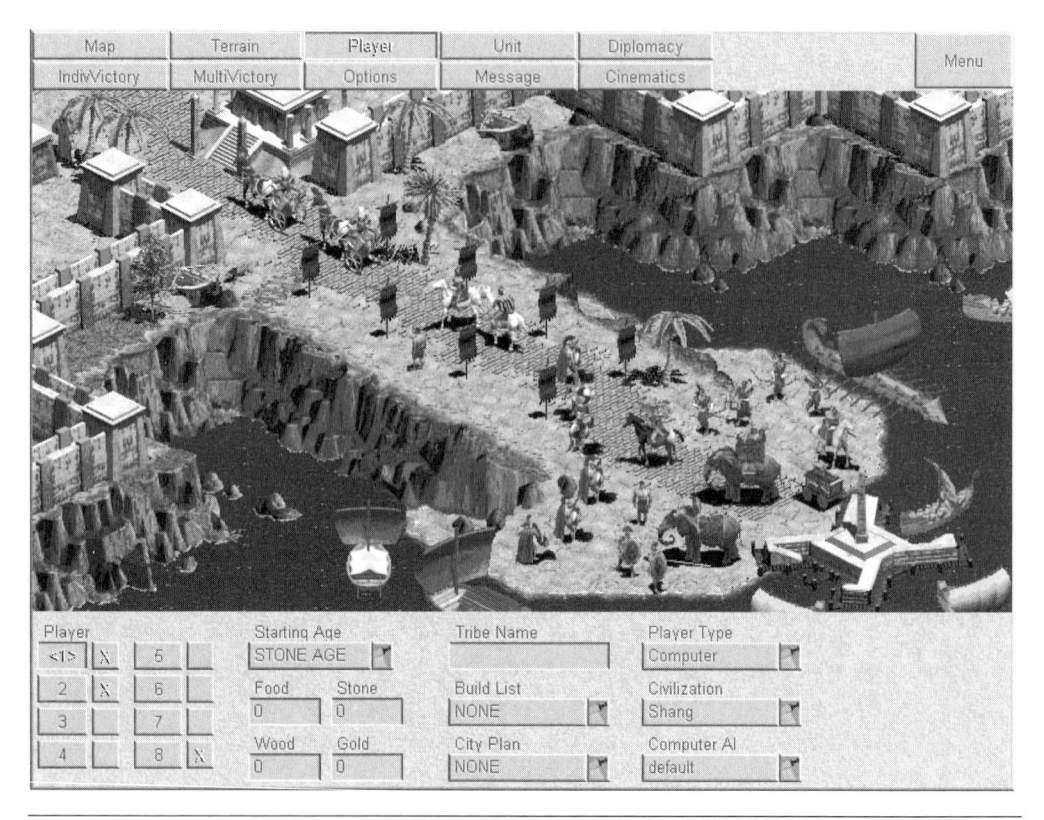

Figure 9.1 Screenshot of the scenario editor used in Microsoft's "Age of Empires," a strategy game that spans 10,000 years. This is just one of many games that AI technologies have made more life-like and appealing.

There are many commercially available SDK's that allow developers to quickly add AI functionality to their games. For instance, DirectIA (Direct Intelligent Adaptation) is a behavior simulation program designed by the MASA group (www.animaths.com). This company is based in Paris, and although its products are good, they are too expensive for game hobbyists. Another product that may be used to create games written in C++ is Spark (www.louderthanabomb.com). It is a fuzzy logic editor that features real-time graphical debugging. Although you may not consider games to be a business-oriented topic, game development is a huge industry. If you are interested in learning more about this AI branch, you can visit www.gameai.com.

Genetic Programming

Genetic programming, also known as evolutionary programming, seeks to utilize some of the same biological factors that drive human evolution. It uses variables that represent chromosomes, genes, and traits. This is not as scary as it first may seem to those who hated biology. Genetic programming can be very effective in systems that need to determine an optimal path. It is being used more frequently in industries that must solve complex scheduling issues.

In most cases, genetic programs involve the creation of several potential solutions that are evaluated to determine whether they are "fit." Programs deemed fit, according to some predefined function, will be used to "breed" a new group of potential solutions. The others will be eliminated. The evaluation process is continued until it is determined that no improvements can be made and only one optimal solution remains.

A growing number of researchers are becoming interested in genetic programming. This area can involve computer programs that create themselves. For more information, refer to www.genetic-programming.com.

Microsoft.NET is fully capable of producing an application based on genetic programming. *MSDN Magazine* published an article about genetic programming in August 2004. In the article, titled "Survival of the Fittest: Natural Selection with Windows Forms," Brian Connolly presents a program written with Microsoft C#.

Table 9.3 Areas of AI not directly addressed in earlier chapters. These areas should offer value to traditional business applications, and the reader may want to explore them further.

Area	Description
Fuzzy Logic	The programmatic interpretation of inputs that cannot always be expressed in Boolean values. Instead of the logic always being true or false, it could be something in-between.
Game AI	The enhancement of traditional games with AI-based technologies in an effort to make the games more realistic.

(continued)

Area	Description
Genetic Programming	Genetic programming can be used to solve general problems with a process that resembles natural selection.
Natural Language Processing	Natural language processing allows people to communicate with their computers in the same way they communicate with one another—through "natural" language.
Neural Networks	An attempt to simulate the way the human brain thinks. They are most useful at detecting patterns and in learning from their experiences.
Machine Learning	A software program that is able to learn based on its inputs. This usually involves training by a user and can be one of the most complex branches of AI.
Robotics	Most people associate artificial intelligence specifically with this branch. Robotics represents a wide range of machines, ranging from those that simply clean your carpet to ones that can intelligently dismantle a bomb.

Natural Language Processing

Natural language processing involves more than just recognizing what the user is saying; it involves understanding as well. Language understanding has long been a major hurdle for the AI industry. For years, products have featured speech-processing abilities that can interpret spoken text into commands or queries. The problem with most of these products is that they do not handle language variability very well.

The overall goal of natural language processing for users to communicate with their computers using "natural" language. Users should be able to speak to their computers much the same way we speak to one another and have the computer understand them.

This chapter features a recent startup company named Sonum Technologies that has developed a patent-pending natural language processor. The product holds much promise in the area of natural language processing.

Sonum Technologies

Headquartered in Baltimore, Sonum Technologies (http://www.sonumtech.com) has created a patent-pending technology known as the Natural Language Processor (NLP). The NLP is different from other speech-based products in that it can handle language variability efficiently. It can handle things like poor grammar, incomplete sentences, and ambiguous information. The goal is to communicate with the user using the smallest amount of effort.

Sonum's NLP is a pattern-recognition algorithm that simplifies the process of language understanding by breaking spoken text down into stages. It uses a knowledge base which consists of three tables. The first stage uses a table to match recognized words with semantic symbols. The next stage groups words into phrases ,and the last stage identifies concepts.

In September 2004, Sonum introduced NLP at the annual SpeechTek Exposition and Conference (http://www.speechtek.com). It demonstrated the NLP integrated with Microsoft Excel and a custom-built Personal Information Manager (PIM). Videos of both demonstrations are available on the company's Web site. Both applications were written in C# under the .NET Framework 1.1. Speech recognition was accomplished using ScanSoft's newly released speech engine, Dragon NaturallySpeaking 8 (http://www.scansoft.com/naturallyspeaking/).

In the Excel demonstration, a user relying only on spoken commands entered and manipulated data in a spreadsheet. The PIM demo shows a woman creating and editing contact information and then adjusting her schedule for the upcoming week. The following dialogue is an excerpt from the demonstration:

> **Woman:** "Hello There"
> **Computer:** "Hello to you"
> **Woman:** "Would you make a new contact for Ralph Johnston?"
> **Computer:** *Opens the new contact form.*
> **Woman:** "He lives at 873 Brown Circle Road, Baltimore, Maryland, 21208. And can you put (410) 874–5156 as his cell phone number?"
> **Computer:** Information is populated into the associated fields on the new contact form.
> **Woman:** "Looks fine. Save it."
> **Computer:** *Saves the record and responds with,* "The contact is saved."

(continued)

> **Woman:** "When is my earliest appointment this coming Monday?"
> **Computer:** "Your earliest appointment on September 20, 2004 is a group meeting with your supervisor which begins at 1:00 PM and ends at 3:30 PM."
> **Woman:** "Change the date to this Monday. Schedule this from 8 to 9 in the morning.
> **Computer:** *Changes appropriate fields on the Schedule form.*
> **Woman:** "Save this for me."
> **Computer:** *Saves record and responds with,* "I am saving it now."
>
> In the PIM demonstration, the woman is able to speak to the computer as she would to a human personal assistant. She is able to initiate new commands without being guided through the application or restricted in what she can say.
>
> In December 2004, I had an opportunity to communicate with Sonum's co-founder and chief technical officer, Dr. Randy Ford. The technology behind the NLP was based on a thesis written by Dr. Ford. I was able to ask him specifics about the NLP. In response to my question concerning the availability of the product, he responded:
>
>> We are currently integrating the NLP into several business solutions. The first of which will be to market by the end of first quarter 2005. Shortly thereafter an NLP product toolkit will be available for use by the developer community.
>
> Sonum's NLP is an AI-based technology that has tremendous potential to change the way humans communicate with their computers. It is just another step toward making a reality of the type of interactions now seen only in science fiction movies.

Neural Nets

Neural nets are designed to emulate the thing that all AI applications are trying to be like—the brain. Borrowing from many years of cognitive research, neural nets attempt to simulate the activity of neurons, the basic building block of the brain. The human brain is known to contain hundreds of billions of these brain cells, and researchers suspect that the interaction between them is what forms thoughts.

At one time neural networks were seen as the solution to the question of AI. They soon fell out of favor, and many projects based on neural-network techniques were abandoned. In the last few years neural networks have begun to regain popularity. They are now seen as very useful in solving certain kinds of problems, such as pattern recognition. In fact, the next version of Analysis Services features a new algorithm based on neural-network processing.

Machine Learning

Machine learning is the branch of AI that aims to enable software programs to learn from data or even from the results of previously executing on a dataset or set of conditions. This technology has been used in a wide range of applications and has enormous potential for enhanced applications.

Machine learning can be useful in areas like data mining and information retrieval. In fact, many machine-learning techniques were utilized in the making of the Microsoft Analysis Services software. Machine-learning techniques have been used, and will continue to be, in other Microsoft products including Speech Server.

Machine learning has also been used to enhance games by enabling them to learn from the users. A game that learns in this way is better able to recommend appropriate strategies to the user.

Generally, machine learning involves some sort of training process in which the program is notified when it makes a bad decision. It then must have the ability to adjust the way it makes decisions based on this input. Readers interested in learning more about the fundamentals of machine learning are encouraged to read "Data-mining: Practical Machine Learning Tools and Techniques with Java Implementations" by Ian H. Witten and Eibe Frank (http://www.cs.waikato.ac.nz/~ml/weka/book.html).

Robotics

The field of robotics is perhaps the most visible and entertaining aspect of AI. Most people think of robotics when they hear the term AI, because it is hard for them to envision intelligence coming from something that is not humanlike. Honda recently began an intense marketing campaign to announce its advanced humanoid robot named ASIMO (see Figure 9.2).

The field of robotics is not concerned simply with the construction of these machines. It also involves the creation of software to guide their movements. This is the trickiest part, because so many skills are needed to navigate physical spaces. Most robots have great difficulty just moving through a room. There have been great advances in this area, and some of the most significant have come from MIT's research laboratory (see www.ai.mit.edu/projects/humanoid-robotics-group/cog/cog.html). It is there that the Cog project seeks to bring all areas of AI into one functional whole.

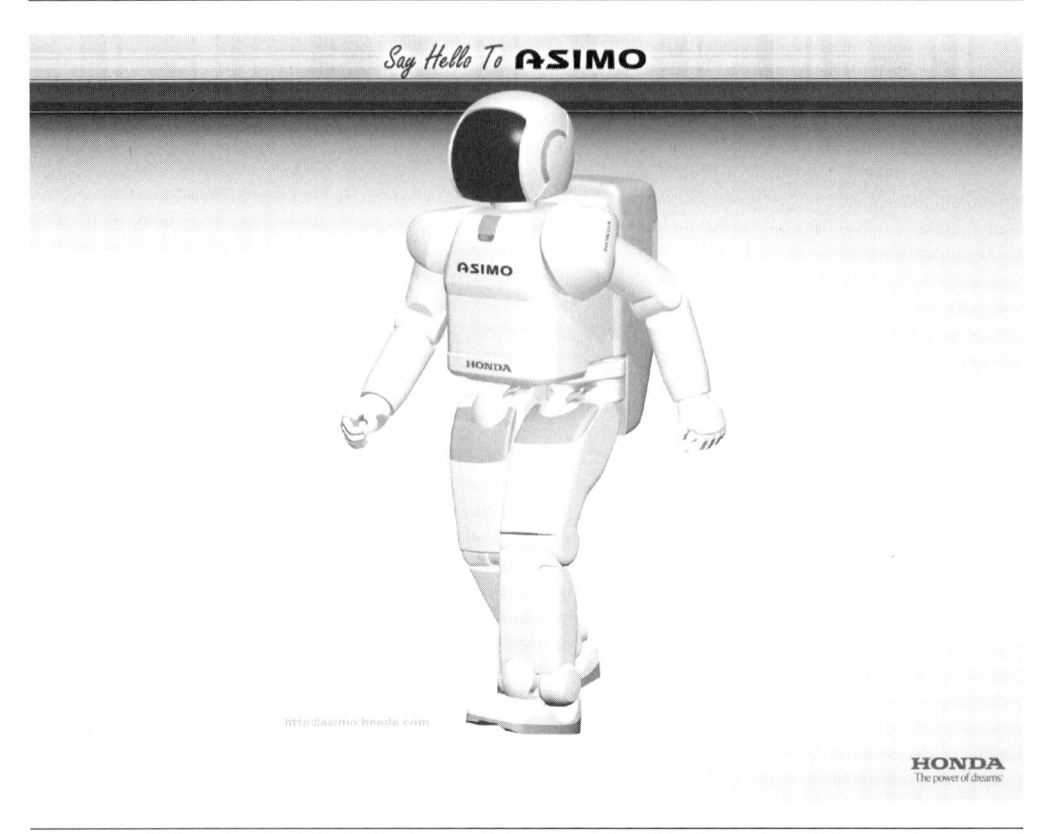

Figure 9.2 ASIMO is an advanced humanoid robot that was sixteen years in the making. Developed by engineers at Honda Motors Corporation, ASIMO will become the basis for robots designed to assist the elderly or to replace humans in performing dangerous work.

Opportunities for Developers

This is an exciting time to be a developer. Significant feats can be accomplished with relatively little effort. Many advances have been made over the years that contribute to the accelerated environment. So, in a sense, you can stand on the shoulders of giants and wave your hands in the air saying, "Hey, look at me." Now, isn't that exciting?

Visual Studio.NET is a wonderful tool for creating powerful distributed applications. The upcoming versions will be even more powerful. They will be based on some exciting technologies coming out of Microsoft Research. Table 9.4 lists resources for developers looking for additional opportunities.

Go to the Microsoft Research Web site (research.microsoft.com) and sign up for the newsletter. Stay on top of what technologies are emerging

Table 9.4 Free online resources that can keep you informed of the latest research at Microsoft and some prestigious universities. Each of these sites allows you to sign up to receive e-mail notifications of new events or information.

Resource	Description
Microsoft Developer Network (MSDN)	Visit the online MSDN Web site at msdn.microsoft.com. It contains documentation for all Microsoft products along with news about upcoming products and tools. You can sign up to receive a biweekly newsletter or receive RSS feeds.
Microsoft Research	Visit the Microsoft Research Web site at research.microsoft.com. It includes information about all projects and research areas. It also contains easy-to-read feature articles that can quickly get you up to speed on the latest research. You can sign up to receive a newsletter or RSS feeds.
Multi-University Research Laboratory (MURL) Seminar Series	Visit the MURL Web site at murl.microsoft.com which hosts a variety of lectures from some of the largest scientific universities, as well as private companies like Microsoft. This site contains information that was once only available to students and visitors to the participating universities and companies. You can sign up to receive email notifications of new lectures.

from this group. You may also want to visit the Multi-University Research Laboratory at murl.microsoft.com. This site makes available lectures from major universities like Carnegie-Mellon, Massachusetts Institute of Technology, Stanford University, and the University of Washington. This is an incredible source of knowledge that was previously only available to students at those universities.

I challenge each and every developer reading this book to go out and find some product or technology that will make your application better. Don't just settle for the traditional way of computing or the standard database-driven application. Find ways to give your users more natural interfaces and more customized computing experiences. Push the envelope, and don't be afraid to break new boundaries in your organization.

Glossary

A

ADOMD—Active Data Objects Multidimensional Library .NET Object model available as a free download from MSDN. Version 8 can be used by applications to access an XML for Analysis 1.1 compliant data provider. This library is used to communicate with SQL Servers Analysis Services

Agent Software agent used to perform tasks on behalf of its user. As defined by the author, agents possess one or more of the following characteristics: function independently, able to communicate, reactive to their environment, personalized, able to learn.

AI—Artificial Intelligence Term used to describe machines that can think and reason like an intelligent human. The many different branches of AI include, but are not limited to, artificial life, data mining, genetic programming, machine learning, natural language processing, neural networks, robotics, speech processing, and software agents.

Alignment In Microsoft's Speech Server SDK, the process by which words in the transcription element are matched to the words in the wave file. Alignments are formed automatically when a wave file is imported or recorded using the prompt editor.

Analysis Services Product available with Microsoft SQL Server that can be used to create multidimensional databases and perform data-mining functions.

API—Application Programming Interface Set of functions exposed so that other developers can access the functionality within an application. API's are commonly supplied for operating systems and other system-level programs.

ASP—Active Server Pages Web pages compiled on-the-fly by the Web server that hosts them. In addition to HTML, they can contain embedded JavaScript, VBScript, or PerlScript code used to generate HTML dynamically.

Avalon   Code name for the presentation subsystem that is part of the next Microsoft operating system (code name Longhorn).

B

BI—Business Intelligence   The ability to increase the competitive advantage of a business by more efficient processing of information. Generally involves such areas as decision support, data mining, and risk analysis.

BI Development Studio   Bundled with SQL Server 2005, a development tool used to connect directly with an Analysis Services database. Has a similar interface to Visual Studio and allows you to create a data-mining solution.

BITS—Background Intelligent Transfer Service   Microsoft tool used by applications to transfer files asynchronously across a network using limited bandwidth.

C

Case   For data mining, the data and relationships that identify a single object you wish to analyze. For example, a product and all its attributes, such as product name and unit price.

Case Set   For data mining, a collection of related cases. Typically involves the way the data is viewed and not necessarily the data itself.

Closed Loop Processing   System designed to feed information back into itself. Can be used in data mining to make predictions more accurate.

Clustering Algorithm   One of two popular algorithms used by Analysis Services to mine data. Classifies data into distinct groups. As opposed to the decision trees algorithm, does not require an outcome variable.

Confidence Score   For Microsoft Speech Server SDK, a percentage value that represents the confidence that the Speech Recognizer is correctly interpreting the user's speech.

Continuous Variable   An input for a data-mining model built with Analysis Services. Usually is a numeric-based value that has an infinite range of possibilities.

D

Data Cubes (see also OLAP Cubes)   Multidimensional data structures built from one or more tables in a relational database. Usually resides in a Online Analytical Processing (OLAP) database.

Data Mining   Process of extracting meaningful data and predictive results from large amounts of data. Often tied to machine learning because to form predictions, a program must adjust its behavior based on the data it receives.

Data-Mining Algorithm Mathematical formula that is the basis for analyzing large amounts of data with a mining model. Microsoft Analysis Services 2000 utilizes two algorithms, decision trees and clustering.

Data Warehouse The ability to collect and store large amounts of data in a structure in which the data can easily be browsed. Generally a multidimensional structure so that data can be drilled down into.

DDL—Data Definition Language Set of definitions used to describe a database schema. For Microsoft SQL Server, specific commands that can be used to do such things as create and alter a database.

Decision Trees Algorithm One of two popular algorithms used by Analysis Services to mine data. Creates a tree that allows the user to map a path to a successful outcome.

Discretized For Microsoft Analysis Services, a set of discrete values. Discretized is a value used to identify the content type of a input variable for a mining model.

DMO—Distributed Management Objects Set of objects used to programmatically manage Microsoft SQL Server. Also known as SQL-DMO.

DOM—Document Object Model Part of Microsoft XML Core Services (MSXML) used to standardize the way applications access XML documents.

DSO—Decision Support Objects In Microsoft SQL Server, the set of functions used to programmatically administer SQL Server. Can be used, for example, to manage servers, databases, and mining models.

DTMF—Dual Tone Multi-frequency Tones High and low tones assigned to each button on a telephone. The summation of the wave amplitudes associated with these tones indicates which button has been pressed.

Dynamic Grammar Grammar file created on-the-fly using code and Microsoft Speech Server SDK. Generally used to create a grammar in which data values may change often and are loaded from a database.

E

Enhanced Computing Term used in this book to designate applications that utilize AI-based technologies to enhance the user's experience or increase the efficiency of the application.

EQ—English Query Microsoft tool used to create applications that accept natural language queries against data from any OLE DB data source.

Expert Systems The knowledge collected from specific experts. Typically utilize a knowledge-base to store rules that experts follow when solving problems.

Extractions In Microsoft Speech Application SDK, words or phrases that can be combined to form whole phrases.

F

FileSystemWatcher In the Microsoft .NET Framework, a class that allows you to watch for changes to files and subdirectories in a specified directory.

Fuzzy Logic Problem-solving methodology used in systems that must interpret vague or imprecise information. Can be used to make decisions in cases where the input is not always clear and therefore traditional logic would fail.

G

Game AI Games enhanced by incorporating an AI-based technology. Can include a wide range of AI branches, such as machine learning, genetic algorithms, and fuzzy logic.

Genetic Programming Branch of AI that attempts to solve problems with techniques known as evolutionary algorithms because they are based on concepts related to natural selection and are used to "breed" computer programs.

Grammar File In Microsoft Speech Application SDK, a grammar file holds definitions of every possible word or phrase spoken by the user.

H

HTML—Hypertext Markup Language Standard markup language used by most Web pages to represent text, images, hyperlinks, etc.

I

Indigo Code name for the set of communication technologies included with Microsoft's next operating system (code name Longhorn). Indigo is a communications subsystem built around the Web Services architecture.

IVR—Interactive Voice Response Systems Telephony-based automated system that allows customers to retrieve or enter information while using a telephone. Most IVR systems are installed to automate help-desk functions.

J

JavaScript Scripting language used to programmatically control Web pages. Based on the Java programming language; can be used on either the client side or the server side, and is available as a scripting language for ASP and ASP.NET pages.

L

Longhorn Code name of the next Microsoft operating system, expected to be released sometime in 2006. Will contain pillars known as Avalon (for presentation), Indigo (for communication), and WinFX (API).

M

Machine Learning   Tied closely to data mining, a computer program able to modify its behavior over time based on the inputs it receives.

Manifest File   For applications built with Microsoft Speech Server SDK, an XML-based file (mainfest.xml) used to identify the application start page and to specify resource files that can be preloaded to improve performance.

MDX—Multidimensional Expressions   Syntax used to query multidimensional data sources in Microsoft SQL Server OLAP services. Similar to Structured Query Language (SQL).

MindNet   Knowledge representation project currently under development at Microsoft Research. Can be used to acquire knowledge by building semantic networks.

Mining Model   Method used by Microsoft SQL Server to analyze a dataset. Stores the predicted values that result from processing the model and not the actual data processed.

MSDN—Microsoft Developer Network   Free resource for Microsoft developers available at http://msdn.microsoft.com. The Web site offers access to documentation, white papers, code examples, newsgroups, and other helpful media.

MSSContextExtract   Log analysis tool, available with Microsoft Speech Server SDK, used to reconstruct wave files associated with particular user conversations. The command-line tool is executed from the Speech Application SDK command prompt.

MSSLogToText   Log analysis tool, available with Microsoft Speech Server SDK, used to convert an .etl (event trace log) file into a text file. The command-line tool is executed from the Speech Application SDK command prompt.

MSSUsageReport   Log analysis tool, available with Microsoft Speech Server SDK, used to provide a summary of the events raised during a trace session. The command-line tool is executed from the Speech Application SDK command prompt.

Multimodal Applications   Application that allows users to choose the input mechanism best for their needs. Input can be entered using speech, handwriting, or traditional point-and-click method.

MURL—Multi-University Research Laboratory   Web site that hosts scientific lectures and seminars from several prestigious universities and research facilities. Available at http://murl.microsoft.com.

N

Naive Bayes Algorithm   New data-mining algorithm expected to be included in the Analysis Services 2005 release. Can be used to quickly mine data against noncontinuous variables.

Neural Network Software that closely resembles the way a human brain thinks by simulating neurons that communicate with one other. Simulated neurons are assigned weights which the program adopts through a process of training or learning.

NLU—Natural Language Understanding Process whereby a computer parses and interprets human language in the same way a human would. Extracts meaning not only by identifying words but by interpreting the sentence structure.

O

OCR—Optical Character Recognition Technology for scanning printed or handwritten documents and storing the results on a computer.

Office XP Interop Assembly that allows unmanaged code providing access to Office XP functionality to be called from managed .NET code. Acts as a wrapper to some of the core Office XP products, such as Microsoft Word and Excel.

OLAP—Online Analytical Processing Technology whereby raw data is stored in a multidimensional format so that it can be analyzed easily by decision-makers. An OLAP server, such as Microsoft's Analysis Server, is able to store and process large quantities of OLAP data.

OLE DB for Data Mining Microsoft specification extending the OLE DB standard that comprises the set of COM-based interfaces exposing data from various sources. Contains detailed information about things like query syntax, mining models to utilize, prediction functions, and the XML format to store mining-model results.

Orcas Code name for an upcoming release of Visual Studio that should coincide with the release of Longhorn. Part of Microsoft's Roadmap to the future for development tools and expected to follow the release of Whidbey.

P

PBX—Private Branch Exchange Enterprise telephone system responsible for managing a limited number of external phone lines. Originally used analog technology, but recently there has been a switch to digital technology.

Postamble For grammars built with Microsoft Speech Server SDK, words and phrases that appear at the end of a user's spoken text.

Preamble For grammars built with Microsoft Speech Server SDK, words and phrases that appear at the beginning of a user's spoken text.

PSTN—Public Switched Telephone Network Collection of public telephone networks owned by governments and private companies.

R

Reflection In this book, designates the Microsoft .NET namespace (System .Reflection) used to access assembly components, such as modules, methods, fields, and events.

Rule-based Systems Software that utilizes a set of IF…THEN rules to process program inputs and produce a decision.

S

SALT—Speech Application Language Tags Extensions to HTML that enable telephony and multimodal applications to communicate with external devices and Web services. Governed by the online SALT Forum at http://www.saltforum.org. Microsoft Speech Server is SALT compliant.

Sequence Clustering New data-mining algorithm expected to be included in the Analysis Services 2005 release. Builds data-mining applications that group similar data into clusters and use sequence analysis to determine the order in which events occur.

SES—Speech Engine Services Key component of Microsoft Speech Server responsible for providing text-to-speech and speech-recognition functionality to multimodal and telephony applications.

Smartphones Mobile device that integrates voice and data and can function much like a Personal Digital Assistant (PDA).

SML—Semantic Markup Language XML and many other formats used to represent knowledge available on the World Wide Web are semantic markup languages. For Microsoft Speech Server SDK, output generated by the speech recognizer is stored as SML output and appears as a valid XML document with the top-level element named "SML."

Speech Recognition Process whereby a computer is able to map a digital speech signal into text. The speech-recognition engine in Microsoft Speech Server converts digital signals into phonemes and then into words before it sends them to the speech application.

Speech Synthesis (see also Text-to-Speech) Process whereby text typed into a computer is read aloud using a computer-generated voice. For Microsoft Speech Server, this is handled by the prompt and TTS engines. The prompt engine puts together prerecorded words from the prompt database. The TTS engine produces the synthesized output heard by the user.

SQL—Structured Query Language Query language used to access data from a relational database, such as Microsoft SQL Server and other OLE DB compliant databases. The syntax includes high-level commands such as SELECT, INSERT, DELETE, and UPDATE.

SQL Server Management Studio For the next release of SQL Server (2005), SQL Server Management Studio combines the functionality of Enterprise Manager, Query Analyzer, and Analysis Manager into one tool for the Administrator.

T

TAS—Telephony Application Services Key component of Microsoft Speech Server responsible for providing a SALT runtime environment for telephony applications.

Telephony Applications For Microsoft Speech Server SDK, speech-based applications in which the user interacts with the application using voice commands over a standard telephone or a cellular phone.

Testing Dataset A set of historical data processed by a trained data-mining algorithm. The results of processing the testing dataset can be used to determine whether the mining model was defined accurately.

Threshold A value that once met or exceeded will indicate whether a certain condition has been met. A threshold value is used in Chapter 7 to determine when a question entered by the user matches an existing question in the database.

TIM—Telephony Interface Manager A third-party component available from Microsoft partners such as Intel and Intervoice. Used by Microsoft Speech Server to interpret signals from a telephone to a telephony card..

Time Series Data-analysis technique useful in measuring sequential and nonrandom data sequences. A time series algorithm is expected to be released in the next version of Microsoft SQL Server.

Training Dataset In Microsoft Analysis Services, a set of data used to initially process a data-mining algorithm. It should contain historical data that has been cleaned to remove outliers or incomplete data.

Transcriptions In Microsoft Speech Server SDK, the word and phrases spoken by prompts. Can be associated with a recorded wave file imported or recorded by the SDK.

True AI Software applications that perform most like an intelligent human being. Also commonly referred to as "Strong AI" or "Real AI."

TTS—Text-to-Speech Also known as speech synthesis. Process whereby text typed into a computer is read aloud using a computer-generated voice. For Microsoft Speech Server, this is handled by both the prompt engine and the TTS engine. The prompt engine puts together prerecorded words from the prompt database. The TTS engine produces the synthesized output heard by the user.

W

Wave File File used to store digital audio in a waveform format. Wave files are associated with a .wav file extension.

Whidbey Code name for the next release of the .NET Framework and Visual Studio .NET development tools.

Windows Service Microsoft application designed with Visual Studio.NET and executed on a server or workstation as a service. Allows the application to be controlled by the operating system and thus can function independently of user control.

WinFS Code name for the new file storage subsystem originally expected to be bundled with Longhorn. Now expected to be in beta testing when the Longhorn client becomes available.

WinFX Code name for the programming model used to access the next Microsoft Operating System (code named Longhorn) through managed classes.

WinInet Set of Microsoft classes used by developers to easily access Internet protocols such as HTTP, FTP, and Gopher.

X

XML—Extensible Markup Language Flexible format for representing data that creates a series of hierarchical tags to store information. Ideal for sending formatted data across the Web because it has a small footprint and utilizes accepted standards.

Y

Yukon Code name for the next release of Microsoft SQL Server 2005, expected to be released in the first half of 2005.

Bibliography

Acosta, Michael. August 13, 2003. "The Business Value of Business Intelligence Through Microsoft SQL Server 2000 Analysis Services." MSDN Webcast. [Online]. Available from World Wide Web (http://www.microsoft.com/usa/webcasts/ondemand/2170.asp).

Acronymics, Inc. 2004. "Why, When, and Where to Use Software Agents." [Online]. Available from World Wide Web (http://www.agentbuilder.com/Documentation/whyAgents.html).

Barnes, Robert. June 29, 2003. "Announcing the Microsoft Speech Server V1 Beta 1." MSDN Webcast. [Online]. Available from World Wide Web (http://ems.interwise.com/msfm/live/viewevent.asp?id=2127).

Biglin, Brian. September 23, 2003. "How to Broaden Your Business Intelligence Offering with Microsoft SQL Server 2000 Reporting Services." MSDN Webcast. [Online]. Available from World Wide Web (http://www.microsoft.com/usa/webcasts/ondemand/2175.asp).

Bigus, Joseph, and Bigus, Jennifer. 2001. *Constructing Intelligent Agents Using Java*, 2nd ed. New York: John Wiley.

Bishop, Todd. November 17, 2003. "Gates Outlines 'Seamless Computing' at Comdex." *Seattle Post-Intelligencer Reporter*.

Charan, Eric. 2004. "Introduction to Data Mining with SQL Server. SQL-Server-Performance.com." [Online]. Available from World Wide Web (http://www.sql-server-performance.com/ec_data_mining.asp).

Clark, Jason. 2003. "BITS: Write Auto-Updating Apps with .NET and the Background Intelligent Transfer Service API." *MSDN Magazine*. Vol. 18, No. 2.

Connolly, Brian. 2004. "Survival of the Fittest: Natural Selection with Windows Forms." *MSDN Magazine*. Vol. 19, No. 8.

de Ville, Barry. January 2001. "Data Mining in SQL Server 2000." *SQL Server Magazine*.

Economist.com. June 10, 2004. "A Golden Vein. Science Technology Quarterly." [Online]. Available from World Wide Web (http://www.economist.com/science/tq/PrimterFriendly.cfm?Story_ID=2724407).

Esposito, Dino. 2004. "A First Look at Writing and Deploying Apps in the Next Generation of Windows." *MSDN Magazine*. Vol. 19, No. 1.

Foley, Mary Jo. January 8, 2004. "Gates Salutes the Seamless Computing Experience. Microsoft Watch."

Ford, Randy. 2004. "Re: Contact." E-mail to the author. December 6.

Franklin, Stan and Graser, Art. 1996. "Is It an Agent, or Just a Program? A Taxonomy for Autonomous Agents." *Proceedings of the Third International Workshop on Agent Theories, Architectures, and Languages*. [Online]. Available from World Wide Web (http://www.sage-estcompanies.com/whitepapers/Agent-or-Program.pdf).

Gavalakis, Peter. June 7, 2003. ".NET Telephony Server Platform. MSDN Webcast." [Online]. Available from World Wide Web (http://www.microsoft.com/usa/webcasts/ondemand/2016.asp).

Gurzick, David. December 5, 2004. "Re: Answers to Your Sonum NLP Questions." E-mail to the author.

Hogan, James P. 1997. *Mind Matters*, New York: Ballantine Publishing Group.

Horvitz, Eric. August 26, 2004. "Re: Notification Platform." E-mail to the author.

Hura, Susan L. August 20, 2003. "The Truth about Multimodal Interaction. MSDN Webcast." [Online]. Available from World Wide Web (http://www.microsoft.com/usa/webcasts/ondemand/2196.asp).

Irving, Richard. June 30, 2003. "Introducing the Microsoft Speech Application SDK V1 Beta 3. MSDN Webcast." [Online]. Available from World Wide Web (http://ems.interwise.com/msfm/live/viewevent.asp?id=2130).

Jones, M. Tim. 2003. "AI Application Programming." Charles River Media.

Kahn, Jennifer. 2002. "It's Alive." *Wired*. Vol. 10, No. 3.

Kaprielian, Steve. September 24, 2003. "Speech Recognition in Practice. MSDN Webcast." [Online]. Available from World Wide Web (http://www.microsoft.com/usa/webcasts/ondemand/2366.asp).

Keyes, Jessica. 1990. *The New Intelligence*. New York: HarperCollins Publishers.

Kurzweil, Ray. 1999. *The Age of Spiritual Machines*. New York: Penguin Books.

Kuyatt, Steve. 2004. "Re: Feedback on the Text." E-mail to the author. December 6.

Lee, Kai-Fu. 2003. "User Interface in the Digital Decade. Next Generation Technology Day PowerPoint Presentation." [Online]. Available from World Wide Web (http://research.microsoft.com/asia/news_events/news/2003/students_Kai_Fu_lee.ppt).

MacKenzie, Duncan. February 28, 2003. "Background Copying. Microsoft Developer Network." [Online]. Available from World Wide Web (http://msdn.microsoft.com/library/default.asp?url=/library/en-us/dncodefun/html/code4fun02292003.asp).

MacLennan, Jamie. 2004. "Unearth the New Data Mining Features of Analysis Services 2005." *MSDN Magazine*. Vol. 19, No. 9.

Masters, Timothy. 1993. Practical Neural Network Recipes in C++. San Diego, CA: Academic Press.

Michetti, Greg B. April 13, 2004. "Microsoft Research: The Company in 10 Years." *CNEWS TechNews*.

Microsoft Case Studies. August 18, 2003. "ComputerFleet: Data-mining Solution Promotes Efficiency and Lowers Cost." [Online]. Available from World Wide Web (http://www.microsoft.com/resources/casestudies/casestudy.asp?CaseStudyID=14375).

Microsoft Case Studies. June 16, 2004. "GMAC Commercial Mortgage: Executives Gain Access to Their E-mail, Calendar, and Contacts from Their Phones with Microsoft Speech Technologies." [Online]. Available from World Wide Web (http://www.microsoft.com/resources/casestudies/casestudy.asp?CaseStudyID=15505).

Microsoft Case Studies. June 16, 2004. "Landstar System: Transportation Company Uses New Speech Server Solution to Drive Costs Down, Customer Satisfaction Up." [Online]. Available from World Wide Web (http://www.microsoft.com/resources/casestudies/casestudy.asp?CaseStudyID=15510).

Microsoft. 2004. "Microsoft Speech Application SDK." [Online]. Available from World Wide Web (http://msdn.microsoft.com/library/default.asp?url=/library/en-us/sasdk_usermanual/html/um_gets_tips.asp).

Microsoft. 2004. "Speech Server Product Datasheet." [Online]. Available from World Wide Web (http://download.microsoft.com/download/f/1/8/f188e828-abcc-4cdf-9860-c7b161149387/9559_SpeechBro_Web%20v1.pdf).

Microsoft. August 11, 2004. "Description of Programming with Outlook Rules." [Online]. Available from World Wide Web (http://support.microsoft.com/default.aspx?scid=kb;en-us;324568).

Microsoft. August 14, 2003. "HOWTO: Determine the Connection State of Your Local System and Initiate or End an Internet Connection by Using Microsoft Visual Basic .NET." [Online]. Available from World Wide Web (http://support.microsoft.com/default.aspx?scid=kb;en-us;821770).

Microsoft. August 9, 2004. "Dsofile.exe Lets You Edit Office Document Properties from Visual Basic and ASP." [Online]. Available from World Wide Web (http://support.microsoft.com/default.aspx?scid=kb;en-us;224351).

Microsoft. "Data Mining Enhancements." MSDN Library. [Online]. Available from World Wide Web (http://msdn.microsoft.com/library/default.asp?url=/library/en-us/olapdmad/aggettingstart_80xj.asp).

Microsoft. "Data Mining Models. MSDN Library." [Online]. Available from World Wide Web (http://msdn.microsoft.com/library/default.asp?url=/library/en-us/olapdmad/agminingmodels_9ugj.asp).

Microsoft. July 2002. "Best Practices for Business Intelligence Using Microsoft Data Warehousing Framework." MSDN Library. [Online]. Available from World Wide Web (http://msdn.microsoft.com/SQL/sqlwarehouse/AnalysisServices/default.aspx?pull=/library/en-us/dnsql2k/html/sql_analservbp.asp).

Microsoft. July 2004. "Overview of the Analysis Services Development and Management Environments." [Online]. Available from World Wide Web (http://msdn.microsoft.com/library/default.asp?url=/library/en-us/dnsql90/html/OvASDMEnvr.asp).

Microsoft. "Performance Study of Data Mining Algorithms. MSDN Library." [Online]. Available from World Wide Web (www.msdn.microsoft.com/library/default.asp?url=/lbrary/en-us/dnsql2k/html/sql2k_analysisdm.asp).

Microsoft. September 2001. "Microsoft Research: A Computing Research Center Dedicated to Pioneering the Future of Technology." [Online]. Available from World Wide Web (http://research.microsoft.com/news/presskit/msresearchbg.htm).

O'Kelly, Peter. 2004. "Microsoft's Platform Strategies for 2006 and Beyond." *Windows Server System Magazine*. Vol. 4, No. 8

Paul, Seth, Gautam, Nitin and Balint, Raymond. September 15, 2002. "Preparing and Mining Data with Microsoft SQL Server 2000 and Analysis Services." MSDN Library. [Online]. Available from World Wide Web (http://msdn.microsoft.com/library/default.asp?url=/servers/books/sqlserver/mining.asp).

Petrie, Charles J. December 1996. "Agent-Based Engineering, the Web, and Intelligence." [Online]. Available from World Wide Web (http://www.cdr.stanford.edu/NextLink/Expert.html).

Potter, Stephen, and Larson, Jim. June 2002. "VoiceXML and SALT." *Speech Technology Magazine*. [Online]. Available from World Wide Web (http://www.speechtechmag.com/issues/7_3/cover/742-1.html).

Rector, Brent. 2003. "Introducing Longhorn for Developers. MSDN." [Online]. Available from World Wide Web (http://msdn.microsoft.com/longhorn/understanding/books/rector/default.aspx).

Riciputi, Joel. 2004. "The Latest Trends in Speech Applications. Nuance Webcast." [Online]. Available from World Wide Web (http://www.nuance.com/learn/webcast/index.html).

Rieger, Robert. June 8, 2003. "Text-to-Speech and the .NET Speech Platform." MSDN Webcast. [Online]. Available from World Wide Web (http://www.microsoft.com/usa/webcasts/ondemand/2059.asp).

Ross, Suzanne. 2004 "Computers That Talk to You. MSDN Research News & Highlights." [Online]. Available from World Wide Web (http://research.microsoft.com/displayArticle.aspx?id=670).

Ross, Suzanne. 2004 "Flavors of Innovation. MSDN Research News & Highlights." [Online]. Available from World Wide Web (http://research.microsoft.com/displayArticle.aspx?id=613).

Ross, Suzanne. 2004 "The Digital Butler. MSDN Research News & Highlights." [Online]. Available from World Wide Web (http://research.microsoft.com/displayArticle.aspx?id=148).

Soni, Sanjay, Tang, Zhaohui and Yang, Jim. August 2001. "Performance Study of Microsoft Data Mining Algorithms." Microsoft SQL 2000 Technical Articles. [Online]. Available from World Wide Web (ms-help://MS.MSDNQTR.2004APR.1033/dnsql2k/html/sql2k_analysisdm.htm).

Sonum Technologies. 2004. "Sonum Technologies Multi-Stage Pattern Reduction Algorithms for Natural Language Processing" [Online]. Available from World Wide Web (http://sonumtech.com/assets/nlpwhitepaper.doc).

Susac, Denis. September 14, 2004. "Re: Web Usage Mining." E-mail to the author.

Susac, Denis. September 23, 2002. "Web Usage Mining with SQL Server 2000." *ASP Today*.

Witten, Ian and Frank, Eibe. 2000. Data-Mining: Practical Machine Learning Tools and Techniques with Java Implementations. San Diego, CA: Academic Press.

White, Scott. October 2003. "Set Credentials" Online Posting. Microsoft.Public.Windows.BackgroundTransfer. (http://communities.microsoft.com/newsgroups/default.asp?icp=mscom&slcid=US).

Whitney, Russ. September 2002. "Using ADO MD with .NET." *SQL Server Magazine*.

Wright, Jason. January 28, 2004. "A New Voice on NOAA Weather Radio." [Online]. Available from World Wide Web (http://www.srh.noaa.gov/bmx/aware/noaawxr.html).

Index

A

AAAI (American Association for Artificial Intelligence), 244
AboutAI Web site (Web usage) case study, 156
Access
   BITS (Background Intelligent Transfer Service), 218
   hands-free, 19
   Microsoft Data Application block, 117
   multimodal applications, 18
   PocketPCs, 103
   remote, 206
   telephony applications, 16
Active Data Objects Multidimensional (ADOMD) library, 142
Add to my schedule button, 102
Add to waiting list button, 102
Adjustment phase (rule-based systems), 173, 196–197
ADOMD (Active Data Objects Multidimensional) library, 142
ADOMD.NET SDK, 142
Advantages of Visual Studio.NET, 8
Adware, 204
Agents, 4
   characteristics of, 202–203
   commercially available, 203–204
   Microsoft Agent, 212
   multiple, 205–214, 216–226
   servers, 213–214
AI (artificial intelligence), 1–2, 243
   EC (Enhanced Computing), 4–5, 7
   effect of, 3–4

   fuzzy logic, 245
   games, 245
   genetic programming, 247
   machine learning, 251
   neural nets, 250
   NLP (natural language processing), 248
   robotics, 251
   seamless computing, 6–7
   Visual Studio.NET, 8
Algorithms
   Analysis Services 2005, 233
   data-mining, 111–113
American Association for Artificial Intelligence (AAAI), *See* AAAI
Analysis, 41
   data-mining results, 154–156
   mining model results, 134, 138
Analysis Manager, 128
Analysis Services, 110, 230–233
   data-mining
      algorithms, 111–113
      analyzing results, 154–156
      applying, 141–143
      building models, 128–131
      building prediction queries, 153
      closed-loop processing, 166–169
      generating schedules, 145
      loading databases, 114–122, 124–127
      measuring success, 157–162
      modifying databases, 145–146
      querying, 151–152
      refreshing, 147–149

271

Analysis Services (*cont.*)
  results, 134, 138
  training models, 133
  tuning, 163–166
Microsoft SQL Servers, 7, 110
APIs (application programming interfaces)
  SAPI (Speech Application Programming Interface), 16
  TAPI (Telephony API), 16
  WinInt (Windows Internet) API, 210
Application of Results phase (rule-based systems), 173
Application programming interfaces. *See* APIs
Applications
  EC (Enhanced Computing), 4–7
  loading, 53–54
  LoadSampleData, 117
  multimodal
    building, 81
    creating, 78–79
    executing sample applications, 83–84
    loading databases, 80–81
    preloading Manifest.xml files, 102
    retrieving queries, 95–101
    running on PocketPCs, 103
    tuning, 103–106
    viewing Web pages, 85–93
  multiple agents, 207–214, 216–226
  rule-based (databases), 176–188, 190–197
  SALT (Speech Application Language Tags), 15
  SASDK (Speech Application SDK), 14, 48
    creating applications, 22–31, 33–38
    debugging applications, 38–40
    installation of, 21
    multimodal applications, 18
    telephony applications, 16
  seamless computing, 6–7
  Speech Debugging Console
    applying, 95–96
    multimodal applications, 103–105
  telephony
    building, 51–57, 59–68
    creating speech applications, 46–47
    loading databases, 48–49
    navigating, 70–71
    tuning user prompts, 71–73

Applying
  data-mining predictions, 141–143
    analyzing results, 154–156
    building prediction queries, 153
    closed-loop processing, 166–169
    generating schedules, 145
    measuring success, 157–162
    modifying databases, 145–146
    querying, 151–152
    refreshing, 147–149
    tuning, 163–166
  multiple agents, 205–214, 216–226
  prompt functions, 57–59
  speech controls, 34–38
  Speech Debugging Console, 95–96
  threshold values, 183–188
  Version 2 database files, 163–166
ApplyThreshold function, 185
Artificial intelligence. *See* AI
Attach Database dialog box, 49
Attaching SQL databases to telephony applications, 48–49
Attributes, 214
Attributes box, 136
Authentication, 221
Authentication Methods dialog box, 222
Avalon, 234–235

B

Background Intelligent Transfer Service (BITS), 205, 210–221, 224–226
Base rules for multimodal applications, 93
Bell Labs, 13
Benefits of business speech, 19
BI (Business Intelligence) studio, 232
BITS (Background Intelligent Transfer Service), 205, 210–221, 224–226
BizTalk Server 2004, 173
Brooks, Rodney, 3
Building
  agents
    applying multiple agents, 205–214, 216–226
    characteristics of, 202–203
    commercially available, 203–204
  applications, 176–188, 190–197
  dynamic grammars, 60–61

Index 273

mining models, 128–131
multimodal applications, 81
    executing sample applications, 83–84
    preloading Manifest.xml files, 102
    retrieving queries, 95–101
    running on PocketPCs, 103
    tuning, 103–106
    viewing Web pages, 85–93
prediction queries, 153
telephony applications, 51–57, 59–68
Business Intelligence (BI) studio, 232

C

Call Viewer Utility, 106
Case studies
    AboutAI Web site (Web usage), 156
    ComputerFleet, 124
    GMAC Commercial Mortgage, 47
    Landstar Systems, 83
Characteristics of agents, 202–203
CheckSynonyms function, 187
Classes, FileSystemWatcher, 214–217
Cleaning databases, 125
Closed-loop processing, 166–169
Clustering, 113
Code, executing, 53–54
Commands (File menu)
    Add Project, 25
    New Project, 22
    Open URL, 40
Commercially available agents, 203–204
Components
    of MSS (Microsoft Speech Server), 13
    of SASDK (Speech Application SDK), 14–21
ComputerFleet case study, 124
Condition Matching phase (rule-based systems), 173
ConditionMatchPhase function, 190–191
Configuration
    login, 56–65
    Telephony Servers, 41–42
    user navigation paths, 51–53
    values for semantic items, 96–98
Connecting telephony applications, 45. *See also* telephony applications
Content Detail Editor, 137–138
Content Navigator box, 136

Controls
    customization, 38
    DataTableNavigator, 68
    Listen, 88–90
    page, 62–65
    PasscodeQA, 63
    Query page, 87
    RuleRef, 63
    Semantic Map, 62
    speech
        applying, 34–38
        ordering, 66
    Speech Application, 37
Copernic Agent Professional, 203
CreateJob function, 220–221
Customization of controls, 38. *See also* configuration

D

Data Definition Language (DDL), 133
Data Link Properties dialog box, 129
Data Source View (DSV), 232
Data Transformation Services (DTS), 106
Data-mining
    Analysis Services 2005
        algorithms, 233
        migrating, 234
        real time, 233
    applying, 141–143
    closed-loop processing, 166–169
    databases
        analyzing results, 154–156
        building prediction queries, 153
        generating schedules, 145
        measuring success, 157–162
        modifying, 145–146
        querying, 151–152
        refreshing, 147–149
    definition, 4
    SQL servers, 110
        algorithms, 111–113
        building models, 128–131
        loading databases, 114–122, 124–127
        results, 134, 138
        training models, 133
    tuning, 163–166

Database administrator (DBA), 172
Databases
 cleaning, 125
 loading
  applying multiple agents, 206
  data-mining, 114–122, 124–127
 modifying, 145–146
 multimodal applications, 80–81
 populating, 116
 prompt editor, 25
 rule-based systems, 172
  building applications, 176–188, 190–197
  phases of, 173
 telephony applications, 48–49
 Version 2 files, 163–166
 Zoom Lending, 175–176
DataTableNavigator control, 68
DBA (database administrator), 172
DDL (Data Definition Language), 133
Debugging
 applications, 38–40
 Speech Debugging Console
  applying, 95–96
  mulitmodal applications, 103, 105
Decision Support Objects (DSO), 128
Decision trees, 111
Defining rulestypes, 179
Design
 login, 56–65
 Telephony Servers, 41–42
 user navigation paths, 51–53
 values for semantic items, 96–98
Detection of file changes, 214–217
Dialog boxes
 Attach Database, 49
 Authentication Methods, 222
 Data Link Properties, 129
 Installation Guide, 21
 New Project, 22
 Prerequisites, 21
 Process, 133
 Speech Controls Outline, 67
Dialog speech controls, 35, 38
DirectIA (Direct Intelligent Adaptation), 246
Dragon's NaturallySpeaking, 28, 249
DSO (Decision Support Objects), 128
DSV (Data Source View), 232
DTMF (Dual Tone Multi-frequency), 17

DTS (Data Transformation Services), 106
Dual Tone Multi-frequency. See DTMF
Dynamic grammars, building, 60–61

E
E-mail rules, 192–193
EC (Enhanced Computing), 4–7
 AI, 243–248, 250–251
 MSR (Microsoft Research), 237, 240–242
 opportunities for developers, 252
Editors
 Content Detail Editor, 137–138
 grammar, 30–33
 Mining Model Editor, 128
 prompt, 23
  databases, 25
  extractions, 26
  recording tool, 28–30
  transcriptions, 26
 Relational Mining Model Editor, 132, 147
 Semantic Script, 33
Effect of AI (artificial intelligence), 3–4
Enhanced Computing. See EC
Executing
 code, 53–54
 multimodal applications on PocketPCs, 103
 Search routine, 98–99
Extensible Application Markup Language (XAML), 234
Extractions, prompt editor, 26

F
File menu commands
 Add Project, 25
 New Project, 22
 Open URL, 40
File System Watcher functionality, 205
FileInfo.xml file, 214
Files
 detecting changes, 214–217
 log, 105
 Manifest.xml, 102
 Version 2 database, 163–166
FileSystemWatcher class, 214–217
Folders, Grammars, 23

Formatting. *See also* configuration
  multimodal applications, 78–79
    building, 81
    executing sample applications, 83–84
    loading databases, 80–81
    preloading Manifest.xml files, 102
    retrieving queries, 95–101
    running on PocketPCs, 103
    tuning, 103–106
    viewing Web pages, 85–93
  queries, 86
  results, 100–101
  SASDK (Speech Application SDK), 22–31, 33–38, 48
  startup Web pages, 56–65
  telephony applications
    building, 51–57, 59–68
    creating speech applications, 46–47
    loading databases, 48–49
    navigating, 70–71
    tuning user prompts, 71–73
  transfer jobs, 220–221
  user navigation paths, 51–53
  views, 126–127
Functions. *See also* commands
  ApplyThreshold, 185
  CheckSynonyms, 187
  ConditionMatchPhase, 190–191
  CreateJob, 220–221
  Get Product Info, 66
    ordering speech controls, 66
    retrieving product information, 67–68
  GetOpportunitiesList, 68
  PriorityEvaluationPhase, 193, 196
  prompt, 57–59
  VerifyPasscode, 56–65
Future of enhanced computing
  AI (artificial intelligence), 243–251
  Analysis Services 2005, 231–233
  Avalon, 234–235
  Indigo, 235
  Longhorn, 234
  mobility, 237
  MSR (Microsoft Research), 237, 240–242
  .NET, 230
  opportunities for developers, 252
  WinFS, 236
Fuzzy logic (AI), 245

G
Games (AI), 245
Gates, Bill, 6
GeneratePurchases routine, 122, 157–162
Generating schedules, 145
Genetic programming (AI), 247
Get Product Info function, 66
  ordering speech controls, 66
  retrieving product information, 67–68
GetOpportunities.aspx page, 68
GetOpportunitiesList function, 68
GMAC Commercial Mortgage case study, 47
Grammars, 23
  dynamic, 60–61
  editors, 30–33
  multimodal applications, 88–93
  preambles/postambles, 91–93

H
Hands-free access, 19. *See also* access
History of AI, 2–3

I
IE (Microsoft Internet Explorer), 18
IIS (Internet Information Services), 81
Indigo, 235
InsertPurchaseDetailNew stored procedure, 162
Installation
  Guide dialog box, 21
  SASDK (Speech Application SDK), 21
Interactive Voice Response systems. *See* IVR
Interfaces
  Analysis Services 2005, 232
  SASDK (Speech Application SDK), 14
  TAPI (Telephony API), 16
  TIM (Telephony Interface Manager), 17
  WinInt (Windows Internet) APIs, 210
Internet Information Services. See IIS, 81
Internet telephony applications, 45. *See also* telephony applications
Items, setting values for, 96–98
IVR (Interactive Voice Response) systems, 13

J
Jobs, creating transfer, 220–221

K

Keywords, PREDICTION JOIN, 153
Knowledge base, 172. *See also* rules
Kyoto Prize in Advanced Technology, 9

L

Landstar Systems case study, 83
Languages
    DDL (Data Definition Language), 133
    MDX (Multidimensional Extensions)
        language), 233
    PMML (Predictive Model Markup
        Language), 234
    SALT (Speech Application Language
        Tags), 15
    SML (Semantic Markup Language),
        33
    VoiceXML, 2.x, 16
    XAML (Extensible Application Markup
        Language), 234
Lastupdated attribute, 214
Libraries, 142
Listen control, 88–90
Load Data button, 117
LoadGrammarFile method, 60
Loading
    applications, 53–54
    databases, 175–176
        applying multiple agents, 206
        building rule-based applications, 176
        data-mining, 114–122, 124–127
        multimodal applications, 80–81
        telephony applications, 48–49
    sample applications, 83–84
LoadSampleData application, 117
Logging
    MSS (Microsoft Speech Server), 105
    Speech Debugging Console, 103–105
Logins, configuring, 56–65
Longhorn, 234. *See also* Microsoft; operating
        systems
Loops, closed-loop processing, 166–169

M

Machine learning (AI), 251
Machine Translation project, 243
Main query page (Review.aspx), 86
MainMenu.aspx page, 66

Maintenance for rule-based applications,
    179–188
Manifest.xml files, 102
McCarthy, John, 2
MDX (Multidimensional Extensions)
    language, 233
MeaningCount property, 188
Measuring success of data-mining, 157–162
Methods, LoadGrammarFile, 60
Microsoft
    Agent, 212
    Data Application block, 117
    Internet Explorer. *See* IE
    Research. *See* MSR
    seamless computing, 6
    Speech Application SDK, 7
    Speech Server. *See* MSS
    SQL Servers Analysis Services, 7
    XML Parser (MSXML), 143
Migration, data-mining, 234
Mining Model Editor, 128
Mobility, 237
Models
    data-mining
        analyzing results, 154–156
        building prediction queries, 153
        closed-loop processing, 166–169
        generating schedules, 145
        measuring success, 157–162
        querying, 151–152
        refreshing, 147–149
        tuning, 163–166
    mining
        building, 128–131
        training, 133
Modifying databases, 145–146
Monitoring new opportunities, 226
MSR (Microsoft Research), 9, 237, 240–242
MSS (Microsoft Speech Server)
    analysis and reporting, 41
    components of, 13–21
    databases, 48–49
    log files, 105
    SASDK (Speech Application SDK), 48
MSSContentExtract, 105
MSSLogToText tool, 105
MSSUsageReport tool, 105
MSXML (Microsoft XML Parser), 143

Index

Multidimensional Extensions (MDX) language, 233
Multimodal applications, 18
  building, 81
    executing sample applications, 83–84
    preloading Manifest.xml files, 102
    retrieving queries, 95–101
    running on PocketPCs, 103
    tuning, 103, 105–106
    viewing Web pages, 85–93
  creating, 78–79
  loading databases, 80–81
Multiple agents, applying, 205–214, 216–226
Myhrvold, Nathan, 9

N

National Weather Service (NOAA), 13
Natural language processing (NLP), 173, 248
Navigation
  telephony applications, 70–71
  user paths, 51–53
.NET, enhanced computing, 230
Neural nets (AI), 250
New opportunities, monitoring, 226
New Project dialog box, 22
Next Development Platform, 230
  Analysis Services 2005, 230–233
  Avalon, 234–235
  Indigo, 235
  Longhorn, 234
  mobility, 237
  .NET, 230
  WinFS, 236
NLP (natural language processing), 173, 248
NOAA (National Weather Service), 13
Notification
  registration for, 224–226
  WinFS, 236
Notification Platform, 242

O

Objects, 128
OCR (Optical Character Recognition), 3
OLE DB for Data Mining, 113
OpenSpeech Recognizer (OSR), 30
OpenURL command (File menu), 40
Operating systems, 6
Opportunities
  for developers, 252
  monitoring new, 226
Optical Character Recognition (OCR), 3
Optimization. *See also* configuration
  data-mining models, 163–166
  user prompts, 71–73
Ordering speech controls, 66
OSR (OpenSpeech Recognizer), 30
Outlook rules wizard, 193

P

Page controls, 62–65
Parameters, tuning data-mining, 166
PasscodeQA control, 63
Paths, 51–53
PDA (Personal Digital Assistant), 45
Phases of rule-based systems (databases), 173
Platforms
  Next Development, 230
  Notification Platform, 242
PMML (Predictive Model Markup Language), 234
PocketPCs, 103
Populating databases, 116
Postambles, 91–93
Postbacks, 64
PreambleRule, 92
Preambles, 91–93
Predicting data-mining
  algorithms, 111–113
  analyzing results, 154–156
  applying, 141–143
  building models, 128–131
  building prediction queries, 153
  closed-loop processing, 166–169
  generating schedules, 145
  loading databases, 114–122, 124–127
  measuring success, 157–162
  modifying databases, 145–146
  querying, 151–152
  refreshing, 147–149
  results, 134–138
  with SQL servers, 110
  training models, 133
  tuning, 163–166
PREDICTION JOIN keyword, 153

Predictive Model Markup Language
    (PMML), 234
Preloading Manifest.xml files, 102
Prerequisites dialog box, 21
Priority Evaluation phase (rule-based
    systems), 173
PriorityEvaluationPhase function, 193, 196
Process dialog box, 133
Processing closed-loop processing, 166–169
ProcessMiningModel procedure, 149
ProductList.aspx page, 67
Products, 66
    ordering speech controls, 66
    retrieving product information, 67–68
ProductThresholds table, 115
Programming code, 53–54
Prompts
    editors, 23
        databases, 25
        extractions, 26
        Recording tool, 28–30
        transcriptions, 26
    functions, 57–59
    tuning users, 71–73
Properties
    MeaningCount, 188
    SynonymList, 188
PSTN (Public Switched Telephone
    Network), 16

Q

Queries
    data-mining models, 151–152
        analyzing results, 154–156
        building prediction queries, 153
        measuring success, 157–162
    preambles/postambles, 91–93
    retrieving, 95–101
    scripts, 86
Query Analyzer, 126, 145–146
Query page
    controls, 87
    Review.aspx, 86

R

Real time data-mining (Analysis Services
    2005), 233
Recording tool, 28–30

Records, 122. *See also* databases
Refreshing data-mining models, 147–149
Registration for notification, 224–226
Relational Mining Model Editor, 132, 147
Remote access for multiple agents, 206.
    See also agents
Reporting, 41
ResponseAutos table, 189
Results
    analyzing, 154–156
    data-mining, 134–138
    formatting queries, 100–101
Retrieving
    product information, 67–68
    queries, 95–101
Robotics (AI), 251
Rule-based systems, 5, 172
    building applications, 176–188, 190–197
    phases of, 173
RuleRef control, 63
Rules
    base, 93
    e-mails, 192–193
    PreambleRule, 92
    TitleQuery, 94
    TopLevel, 95

S

SalesScheduling database, loading, 48–49
SALT (Speech Application Language
    Tags), 15
Sample applications, executing code, 53–54
Samuel, Arthur, 2
SAPI (Speech Application Programming
    Interface), 16
SASDK (Speech Application SDK), 14
    applications
        creating, 22–31, 33–38
        debugging, 38–40
        installation of, 21
        multimodal applications, 18
        telephony applications, 16, 48
ScanSoft, Inc., 28
Schedules
    generating, 145
    loading, 48–49
Scripts, creating queries, 86
Seamless computing, 6–7

Index 279

Search routine, executing, 98–99
Semantic items, 96–98
Semantic Map control, 62
Semantic Markup Language (SML), 33
Semantic Script Editor, 33
Servers
   agents, 213–214
   MSS (Microsoft Speech Server)
      components of, 13
      SASDK (Speech Application SDK), 14–21
   postbacks, 64
   SQL (Structured Query Language), 110
   Telephony Server, 41–42
Services, Analysis Services, 110. *See also* Analysis Services
SES (Speech Engine Services), 14, 102
ShortInitialTimeout property, 101
SML (Semantic Markup Language), 33
Solution Explorer, 26
Sonum Technologies, 249
Speak Query button, 95
Speech
   applications
      creating, 22–33
      debugging, 38–40
   business benefits of, 19
   controls
      applying, 34–38
      ordering, 66
   MSS (Microsoft Speech Server)
      components of , 13
      SASDK (Speech Application SDK), 14–21
   multimodal applications
      building, 81
      creating, 78–79
      executing sample applications, 83–84
      loading databases, 80–81
      preloading Manifest.xml files, 102
      retrieving queries, 95–101
      running on PocketPCs, 103
      tuning, 103–106
      viewing Web pages, 85–93
   SASDK (Speech Application SDK). *See* SASDK
   telephony applications
      building, 51–59, 63–68
      creating, 46–47
      loading databases, 48–49

      navigating, 70–71
      SASDK (Speech Application SDK), 48
      tuning user prompts, 71–73
Speech Application Controls, 37
Speech Application Language Tags. *See* SALT
Speech Application Programming Interface. *See* SAPI
Speech Application SDK (Microsoft), 7
Speech Application SDK. *See* SASDK
Speech Controls Outline dialog box, 67
Speech Debugging Console, 38
   applying, 95–96
   multimodal applications, 103–105
Speech Engine Services. *See* SES
Speech recognition (processing), 5
Speech-related technologies (MSR), 240
Spyware, 204
SQL Servers Analysis Services (Microsoft), 7
SQL (Structured Query Language)
   data mining models, 234
   databases, 48–49
   servers, 110
Startup Web pages, formatting, 56–65
SynonymList property, 188

T
Tables
   ProductThresholds, 115
   ResponseAutos, 189
Tags, SALT (Speech Application Language Tags), 15
TAPI (Telephony API), 16
TAS (Telephony Application Services), 14
TASim (Telephony Application Simulator), 40
Telephony applications, 16
   building, 51–57, 59–68
   navigating, 70–71
   speech applications
      creating, 46–47
      loading databases, 48–49
      SASDK (Speech Application SDK), 48
      tuning user prompts, 71–73
Telephony Interface Manager. *See* TIM
Telephony Server, configuration of, 41–42
Templates
   creating applications, 22–31, 33–38
   debugging applications, 38–40

Text
    grammar editors, 30–33
    multimodal applications
        building, 81
        creating, 78–79
        executing sample applications, 83–84
        loading databases, 80–81
        preloading Manifest.xml files, 102
        retrieving queries, 95–96, 98–101
        running on PocketPCs, 103
        tuning, 103, 105–106
        viewing Web pages, 85–93
Text-to-speech. *See* TTS
The Enable HTTP Unsecure checkbox, 144
Thresholds, applying values, 183–188
TIM (Telephony Interface Manager), 17
TitleQuery rule, 94
Tools
    BizTalk Server 2004, 173
    Call Viewer Utility, 106
    debugging, 40. *See also* debugging
    MSSContentExtract, 105
    MSSLogToText, 105
    MSSUsageReport, 105
    Recording, 28, 30
    Speech Debugging Console, 38
TopLevel rule, 95
Tracing log files, 105
Training mining models, 133
Transcriptions, 26
Transfer jobs, creating, 220–221
Trees, decision, 111
Troubleshooting. *See* debugging
TTS (text-to-speech), 26
Tuning. *See also* optimization
    data-mining models, 163–166
    multimodal applications, 103–106
    parameters, 166
    speech applications, 38–40
    user prompts, 71–73
Turing Award of the Association for Computing Machinery, 9
Turing, Alan, 2
Types of rules, defining, 179

U
Use Audio button, 96
User navigation paths, designing, 51–53
User prompts, tuning, 71–73
Utilities. *See* tools

V
Values
    semantic items, 96–98
    thresholds, 183–188
VerifyPasscode function, 56–65
Version 2 database files, applying, 163–166
Viewing
    log files, 105
    Web pages, 85–93
Views, creating, 126–127
Visual Studio.NET, advantages of, 8
Vocal Help Desk, 65–66
Voder, 13
Voice Manager Exchange, 70
VoiceXML, 2.x, 16

W
Web pages
    multimodal applications, 85–93
    startup, 56–65
Web-based applications, 14
    creating applications, 22–31, 33–38
    debugging applications, 38–40
    installation of, 21
    multimodal applications, 16–18
WinInet (Windows Internet) API, 210
Wizards
    Outlook rules, 193
    Speech SDK, 25

X
XAML (Extensible Application Markup Language), 234

Y
Yukon. *See* Analysis Services

Z
Zoom Lending (databases), 175–176

Register Your Book

at www.awprofessional.com/register

You may be eligible to receive:
- Advance notice of forthcoming editions of the book
- Related book recommendations
- Chapter excerpts and supplements of forthcoming titles
- Information about special contests and promotions throughout the year
- Notices and reminders about author appearances, tradeshows, and online chats with special guests

Contact us

If you are interested in writing a book or reviewing manuscripts prior to publication, please write to us at:

Editorial Department
Addison-Wesley Professional
75 Arlington Street, Suite 300
Boston, MA 02116 USA
Email: AWPro@aw.com

Visit us on the Web: http://www.awprofessional.com

Wouldn't it be great

if the world's leading technical publishers joined forces to deliver their best tech books in a common digital reference platform?

They have. Introducing
InformIT Online Books
powered by Safari.

- **Specific answers to specific questions.**
InformIT Online Books' powerful search engine gives you relevance-ranked results in a matter of seconds.

- **Immediate results.**
With InformIT Online Books, you can select the book you want and view the chapter or section you need immediately.

- **Cut, paste and annotate.**
Paste code to save time and eliminate typographical errors. Make notes on the material you find useful and choose whether or not to share them with your work group.

- **Customized for your enterprise.**
Customize a library for you, your department or your entire organization. You only pay for what you need.

Get your first 14 days FREE!

For a limited time, InformIT Online Books is offering its members a 10 book subscription risk-free for 14 days. Visit **http://www.informit.com/onlinebooks** for details.

Safari TECH BOOKS ONLINE

informit.com/onlinebooks

InformIT Online Books

informIT

www.informit.com

YOUR GUIDE TO IT REFERENCE

Articles

Keep your edge with thousands of free articles, in-depth features, interviews, and IT reference recommendations – all written by experts you know and trust.

Online Books

Answers in an instant from **InformIT Online Book's** 600+ fully searchable on line books. For a limited time, you can get your first 14 days **free**.

Safari
POWERED BY
TECH BOOKS ONLINE

Catalog

Review online sample chapters, author biographies and customer rankings and choose exactly the right book from a selection of over 5,000 titles.